Chicken Soup for the Soul®

Grandmothers

Chicken Soup for the Soul: Grandmothers
101 Stories of Love, Laughs, and Lessons from Grandmothers and Grandchildren
Jack Canfield, Mark Victor Hansen, Amy Newmark

The publisher gratefully acknowledges the many publishers and individuals who granted Chicken Soup for the Soul permission to reprint the cited material.

Front cover photo courtesy of Getty Images/©Purestock. Back cover photo courtesy of iStockphoto. com/LattaPictures (© Derek Latta). Interior photos courtesy of iStockphoto.com/manley099 and /BlackJack3D (© Evgeny Terentev).

Cover and Interior Design & Layout by Pneuma Books, LLC
For more info on Pneuma Books, visit www.pneumabooks.com

Distributed to the booktrade by Simon & Schuster. SAN: 200-2442

Publisher's Cataloging-in-Publication Data
(Prepared by The Donohue Group)

Chicken soup for the soul : grandmothers : 101 stories of love, laughs, and
   lessons from grandmothers and grandchildren / [compiled by] Jack Canfield,
   Mark Victor Hansen, [and] Amy Newmark.

   p. ; cm.

   Summary: A collection of 101 true stories by grandmothers and grandchildren
about their mutual love for each other and the experience of becoming and being a
grandmother.
   ISBN: 978-1-935096-64-1

   1. Grandmothers--Literary collections. 2. Grandchildren--Literary collections.
3. Grandparent and child--Literary collections. 4. Grandmothers--Anecdotes. 5.
Grandchildren--Anecdotes. 6. Grandparent and child--Anecdotes. I. Canfield, Jack,
1944- II. Hansen, Mark Victor. III. Newmark, Amy. IV. Title: Grandmothers V. Title:
101 stories of love, laughs, and lessons from grandmothers and grandchildren

PN6071.G7 C54 2011
810.8/02/035253   2010938811

PRINTED IN THE UNITED STATES OF AMERICA
on acid∞free paper
20 19 18 17 16 15 14 13 12 11   03 04 05 06 07 08 09 10

Chicken Soup for the Soul®

Grandmothers

101 Stories of Love, Laughs,
and Lessons from Grandmothers
and Grandchildren

Jack Canfield
Mark Victor Hansen
Amy Newmark

Chicken Soup for the Soul Publishing, LLC
Cos Cob, CT

Contents

❸

~Making a Difference~

❹

~Grand Friends~

❺
~The Name Game~

❻
~Through the Generations~

❼
~Grand Fun~

❽

~From the Mouths of Babes~

❾

~Oh My Aching...~

⑩
~Grand Adventures~

Introduction

I have been a Chicken Soup for the Soul editor for thirteen years, and this may be my favorite book! I was the lucky person who got to read all of the stories submitted for *Chicken Soup for the Soul: Grandmothers*. Thousands of you submitted stories for this book over the last few years. I read each and every one, and had the difficult task of narrowing those thousands of stories down to a couple of hundred finalists.

When I started reading the stories for this book, my three sons didn't seem to be in any hurry to make me a grandmother. Many of my friends were grandmothers and, without exception, they said, "Until you become a grandmother, you can't understand how it feels."

And then, just when I was least expecting it, I got the news. My son Mike and my daughter-in-law Crescent were pregnant! Suddenly I was to become that person I was reading about. I couldn't believe it.

When Crescent was just a few months pregnant, we went along for the gender determination ultrasound. Even at that early stage of development, it was an amazing experience to see our grandson. At seven months we went along for another ultrasound. This time our baby was fully formed; we could see his facial features, his arms, hands and tiny fingers, his legs, feet and ten tiny toes. And he was moving so much! I gasped and had tears in my eyes when I realized I had seen that face on the monitor before. It was Mike's face—looking just as he had when he was born.

Finally Elijah was born—while we were proofreading this

manuscript! And he is, of course, the most beautiful baby in the whole world. Seeing MY son hold HIS son was the most incredible experience!

My husband and I had kept a beautiful white wicker bassinet for our future grandchildren. All three of our sons had been placed in it when they came home from the hospital. And now Eli is sleeping peacefully in it. My heart is overflowing with the most amazing feelings. My friends were right.

When I started reading stories for this book I didn't have any idea that I would become a grandmother. While still reading submissions I got that exciting news; and right before the book was finished and sent to our printer, I actually became... a grandmother.

The wonderful staff at Chicken Soup for the Soul has been sharing my experiences with me. Of all the women in our company, I am the first to become a grandmother. It has been so much fun to share the process with them and they have been so supportive and excited right along with me. We are truly a team. I do apologize for sending them all of those pictures but they seem to like them!

So what did I learn by reading thousands of stories? What is a grandmother? Is she that little old lady with white hair and orthopedic shoes who sits in her rocking chair? Not by a long shot! She can be younger or older, but she is a loving, caring, hard working, fun-loving, adventure seeking, vibrant, intelligent woman. She can do anything. She is me!

Our publisher, Amy Newmark, will probably be the next grandmother in our group, so she and I had a wonderful time working on these stories together. This book is a gift to all grandmothers—both new grandmothers and experienced grandmothers—from the heart of the Chicken Soup for the Soul editorial staff. We hope you enjoy reading it as much as we enjoyed creating it for you.

~Barbara LoMonaco

Chapter
1

Grandmothers

Grand Wisdom

Grandmother's Gift

*Books are the quietest and most constant of friends; they are the
most accessible and wisest of counselors, and the most patient of teachers.*
~Charles W. Eliot

My grandmother has been gone for many years now and
while she was alive, we were not particularly close.
We saw each other infrequently and each conversation was strained. How is it possible that a woman whose life only
briefly intersected with mine would influence me in such a profound
way? This is a story of a grandmother who loved a little girl and
bestowed upon her a gift. She did not know if she would ever receive
a thank you. This grandmother knew that what she had to give was
one of the greatest gifts a child could receive.

My grandmother lived alone, far away in an apartment in a big
imposing building my brother, sister and I called "the castle." She
was well educated, spoke several languages, traveled through Europe
alone, collected antiques, and listened to opera. Her apartment was
decorated with antiques and filled with hundreds of books she read
and spoke of often.

I lived in suburban Long Island and only saw her once each
year or so. My father would call her on Sunday nights and ask me
to speak on the phone with her. I would wail at the thought. My
father would always make eyes at me, which told me I didn't have
a choice. He would always insist that she missed me and loved me
but I didn't really ever believe him. I knew she would ask me about

school, about what I was reading and what I was learning about. I was a horrible student who could never pay attention and squirmed in my classroom seat. I wanted to be outside playing and talking with my friends.

I would begrudgingly take the phone and speak to her for a few long moments. "I wish this lady would get a clue to what life is really about," I would think as I hung up the phone. Her inability to know what was important was never more evident than at gift-giving time.

Each year, on Christmas morning, my brother, sister and I would run down the stairs and see a beautiful tree surrounded by brightly wrapped packages. We would dive into the pile with great delight, ripping the paper and revealing all the latest toys. Eventually, I would see an odd-looking package deep under the tree that I knew could only be from Grandmother. She never used traditional Christmas paper and her presents always had brightly colored ribbons in yellows, oranges or lavender. Each year I would take that package, feel the weight of it in my hand, knock on it with my fist and hear a sharp tap. "Another book, just like every year!" I would think and then promptly toss it aside without even opening it. I would gleefully play with my toys on Christmas morning and for days and even weeks after. Eventually, I would open Grandmother's gift and glance through the pages of the book she had chosen. My grandmother, in her distinctive, beautiful handwriting, would inscribe each book: "To Elizabeth Rose, with love, from Grandmother." I would read the book and sometimes memorize the text. I still didn't count this as playing, or having fun. I certainly knew in my heart that reading a book or talking about school was no fun for a child.

As the years passed, my interest in school remained minimal. It was all too boring and formal for me. I was more resistant than ever to speaking to Grandmother on Sunday evenings. School, books and what "interesting things I had learned lately" were boring topics for old people to discuss. Didn't Grandmother know that all I cared about was friends, clothes and boys? Each Christmas, more books were under the tree, reinforcing my belief that she really didn't care.

Although I was not interested in school, I had enormous patience with younger children. Our neighbor across the street asked me to help her daughter with her homework after school. I was able to teach her in the way I wish I were able to learn. I made up songs and stories to help her memorize facts and we played games to test what she had learned. Her mom remarked, "You should become a teacher when you grow up Liz; you are so good at helping children." At first, the idea seemed ridiculous to me. I was a terrible student. How could it ever happen?

Slowly the idea took root and I decided to give college a try. Having a goal made things easier for me and I began to apply myself. Selecting courses and having different teachers suited me as well. My second semester, I sat in my first required education class — Children's Literature. The professor spoke about making children's books come alive, filling children's worlds with rich vocabulary, and the characteristics of a classic children's book. It was my favorite class and I was always eager to get there and participate in each discussion. About midway into the class our teacher discussed the differences between a children's book that is here for the moment and those that are enduring classics. She flashed a list of books on her overhead projector that included titles that had been awarded a Newbery Medal or were Caldecott winners. It was then a lump began to form in my throat.

Armed with a handwritten copy of my teacher's list of classics, I raced home, dropped my schoolbooks and ran to the basement. There in the corner on a dusty shelf sat the most amazing collection of children's books any teacher could hope to have. As I ran my fingers across the bindings of *Frederick*, *Tales from the Ballet*, *The Trumpet of the Swan* and *Stuart Little* memories came flooding back. Memories of receiving these books, staring at those pages late at night curled up in my bed and gazing at beautiful pictures. I remembered my grandmother reading Leo Lionni's *Frederick* to me when she came to visit one spring. I was so sure I had figured out the ending, and finding out I was wrong delighted me.

It was then I realized I didn't remember most of the toys I had gotten all those Christmases and with the exception of one old doll, all of the mounds of presents did not make it to my adulthood. Most, in fact, were discarded soon after they were played with or were broken or sold at garage sales. Now I stood before a treasure that I would not trade for anything. As I bent back the cover of *Make Way for Ducklings*, I saw my grandmother's familiar and stylish handwriting that read, "To Elizabeth Rose, with love, from Grandmother." Love was exactly what my grandmother had been giving me all of my years. She resisted the happiness of a beaming child opening an expensive toy and replaced it with a gift that was a part of her. She didn't give me what I wanted in my little girl mind, but what she knew I needed—a gift for the soul that would last a lifetime. Now I saw how wise she had been and how each book was so carefully selected at different times of my life.

I sat down that day and wrote my grandmother a letter. I expressed as well as I could how much I was enjoying school and how my collection of children's books was a treasure. I wrote about my happy memories reading them and about how much I knew I was loved. I placed my letter in a box with a pillow that had a mallard duck on the front. It looks like the duck in the book, *Make Way for Ducklings*, I wrote. This letter was as much for me as it was for her and I planned on telling her more about school and hearing more about her favorite books each time we spoke. Sometimes, what we plan never happens. Shortly after she received my letter, my grandmother died. My aunt who lives nearby told me how much my words had meant to her in her final days.

I continued to water the seed she planted so long ago. I graduated college with honors and received my master's degree in remedial reading. I became a teacher and I try my best to plant those tiny seeds in all my students. Sometimes I can see the world of words opening up right before their eyes. Some students squirm and do not pay attention, but I do not lose faith or feel as if all my efforts won't someday change their lives and that seed won't take root. I know now that I don't have to see the finished product to believe that a work I have started may take many years to reach completion.

I find that I am most happy now only when I am stealing moments in my busy day to read a good book. Although my own children can now read independently, I still take delight in reading aloud to them. This summer I read them *Island of the Blue Dolphins* and they would groan when I called them over to listen. Undaunted, I would read, and by the close of each session they would always ask for more. Now, I consider my time reading peaceful, a world of possibilities, second only to church. As I open the cover to a new book, I feel the shadow of my grandmother beside me and it is almost as if the inside cover of every book reads, "To Elizabeth Rose, with love, from Grandmother."

~Elizabeth Rose Reardon Farella

Queen of Hearts

They might not need me; but they might. I'll let my head be just in sight;
a smile as small as mine might be precisely their necessity.
~Emily Dickinson

After the great American poet, Emily Dickinson, died, her home in Amherst, Massachusetts was sold to my grandparents, Hervey and Ethel Parke. There in the heart of New England, they raised their five children. My father was born in the home, which is now owned by Amherst College and is open to the public as the Emily Dickinson Museum.

The house at 280 Main Street was officially called a mansion, we were informed, because it had four chimneys, not because the property included formal gardens and a grass tennis court. It also offered a wonderful cupola high above the roof where children could peek out and spy on the entire town. Doors and stairs creaked with mystery. Walls were said to harbor old poems stuffed behind the plaster by the famous former resident. Grand, sprawling, full of nooks and crannies, it became the perfect playground for sixteen lively grandchildren.

We called our grandparents Nai Nai and Yeh Yeh, the Chinese terms for revered grandmother and grandfather, not because we had a wonton noodle in our heritage, but because my aunt and uncle served as missionaries in China in the early 1940s, and they were the first of the clan to supply grandchildren. Once their children used these terms of endearment, the pattern was established and the rest of us adopted the same honorifics.

Nai Nai, by the time I arrived on the scene, was already an older woman. During the day, her snow-white hair was pulled back in a neat bun, but at night I remember sitting on the black leather chaise at the end of her bed and watching her brush out the long strands. To me she looked like the woodcut illustration of the first wife of Mr. Rochester in my child's copy of the Brontë novel, *Jane Eyre*. "Like the woman who was raving mad?" she laughed when I told her so.

My grandmother delighted in having fresh flowers from the garden appear in vases all about the house. She would walk in the gardens and point to the ones she wanted us to cut and indicate where they might look best. "Those would look nice on the mantel in the library. The others can go in the parlor."

Her heart always wanted the house to look its best because from time to time, random visitors knocked at the door and asked to see the place where Emily once wrote her poems. Without fail, Nai Nai would welcome these complete strangers and offer them a tour. Before they left, she would invite them to enjoy a hot cup of tea and read some of their favorite poems aloud. She knew the lines herself by heart. Her head would nod as she listened to her guest recite, "I'm Nobody! Who are you? Are you—Nobody—Too? Then there's a pair of us!"

Early in the evening, like a shepherd rounding up his flock, she would announce bedtime and shoo all of us grandchildren up the oval staircase to the Austin Room, the Emily Room or the Lavinia Room. As we grew older, we were still sent upstairs by 8:00, the hour she herself retired to her bed. Even as teens, we obediently continued to follow her lead, only to sneak downstairs half an hour later for a raucous round of games in the library.

Parlor games were an important part of our life in Amherst. Most of us learned to manipulate the cards in a playing deck well before we learned to read. We began with simple games of matching hearts, diamonds, spades and clubs. Then we spread the cards out on the floor and played Memory. Later we worked up to games with more and more complicated rules—Canasta, Cribbage, Canfield. Each game had its own rules, and no Parke ever relaxed the rules just because the opponent was a child. My cousins and brothers and I all knew Nai Nai's favorite phrases. If she was losing, she'd quote the dime novels she grew up with: "I'll get you yet, Nod Nixon, he cried, as he shook his fist in the villain's eye!" Or she would promise ominously, "The worm will turn!"

Nai Nai had no fears about her grandchildren becoming card sharks. Her theory was that learning to play cards was character-building. Card games taught a person to win and lose graciously. No one ever wins all the time, so the loser might as well learn to be pleasant even when he is "skunked" and then congratulate the other player. Just as importantly, when you were lucky enough to win, you were not to flaunt that victory at the expense of your cousin's humiliation. Nai Nai's personal attitude was that she never lost: Either she got the highest score or she won bragging rights about having "such smart grandchildren."

If our hearts are as warm and welcoming as my grandmother's, then we too will all be winners.

~Emily Parke Chase

3

Are You Sure You Have Alzheimer's?

*Her grandmother, as she gets older, is not fading
but rather becoming more concentrated.*
~Paulette Bates Alden

"Cynthia, I just thought I should tell you that I think I have Alzheimer's." Grandma's e-mail held a confidential tone and I knew that if I'd been talking to her in person she would have whispered her concern to me in an undertone usually reserved for talking about people who have passed on. My grandfather, her husband, had Alzheimer's disease for a few years before he died, but that was more than twenty years ago and now Grandma was ninety-seven and in a nursing home. She had lived on her own, balanced her checkbook and paid her own bills until she was ninety-six, but ever since Grandpa died she had self-diagnosed herself with Alzheimer's on many occasions.

I read on. "I almost forgot to take my medicine this morning and I never do that. And..." I could tell the big news was coming now, "I was writing an e-mail to my sister's daughter and I couldn't think of her grandchildren's names." An almost audible gasp was coming through at the end of that statement.

I wondered for a brief moment if I should tell her that I had found my box of aluminum foil in the refrigerator that morning. But I knew better than to mention it to her. In a previous similar situation she hadn't taken comfort that her forty-something-year-old grand-daughter also had memory lapses, but had sent me a return e-mail with the concern that both of us might have Alzheimer's.

The e-mail continued. "I am getting good exercise here though. The rooms are arranged on outside walls so that there is a circle around the whole floor. The nurse's station is in the center. So I've been walking around that circle several times a day.

"And I had the maintenance man measure the tiles on the floor," she went on. "They are 13 inches square. I walked around the circle and figured out that there are 167 tiles. If you multiply 167 by 13 inches, you get 2,171 inches." Grandma went on to say that she had figured out how many inches there are in a mile and divided that by the number of inches on the floor, and had done the necessary math to figure out that if she walked around the circle a certain number of times, she would have walked a mile.

My head was spinning by the time I read all her calculations but I realized that she had done them all correctly. I hit REPLY on my computer and began to type.

"Are you SURE you have Alzheimer's?"

~Cynthia Morningstar

Granny's Bible

A single conversation with a wise man is better than ten years of study.
~Chinese Proverb

I will never forget the first time I heard my granny quote the Bible. No, not the King James version. You know which one I'm talking about. The one that you actually live by every day of your life.

I was about eight years old at the time and a real brat. I had been fighting with the little girl next door and she was almost as mean as I was. We were pretty deep into battle when she threw a rock and hit me square between the eyes. Clutching my head and sobbing, I ran straight into the house to tattle. Granny met me at the door after seeing me come running across the lawn and hearing my screams.

"What's wrong?" she asked in her usual gruff way.

"That little girl threw a rock and hit me in the head," I managed through the tears.

"Well," said Granny smugly, "you just go pick up the biggest rock you can find and hit her back!"

I stopped crying immediately. "But Granny," I stammered. "I don't think..."

"Listen," she interrupted. "The Bible says feed them out of the same spoon." I happily obeyed. I never realized it then, but that was only the beginning of a lifetime of "Bible quotes" that would help me through life's biggest obstacles.

Several years later, and before I had enough sense to realize it,

I was engaged to be married. My fiancé left it up to me to pick our wedding date. I unknowingly picked the date on which his mother had died many years ago. Instead of telling me that he didn't want to get married on this particular day, he told me he didn't want to marry me at all! I was simply heartbroken. I wandered through the house until I found Granny sewing in the den. I fell on my knees, laid my head in her lap, and started to cry.

"Granny, my fiancé doesn't love me. He doesn't want to marry me," I said.

"Well, that no good punk," she said angrily. "You just go tell him that the Bible says what goes around comes around. Someday he'll want to marry a girl and she'll do him the way he's doing you."

"But Granny," I said, "I don't think that the..."

"Listen," she interrupted. "You just go tell him what I said. You'll get your feller back." I married him in two months.

After our first three months of marriage bliss, we had our first fight. Oh, how that broke my heart. Packing my bags, I decided to go back home. When Granny saw me coming up the walk, she met me at the door.

"Well, what's wrong?" she asked. I was already clenching my jaw to keep from crying.

"We had a huge fight and he called me a spoiled brat," I told her.

"Come here," she said wearily. Putting her arm around my shoulder, she guided me into the kitchen where she put water on for tea. "So he called you a spoiled brat," she said over the whistle of the kettle. She looked very thoughtful as she poured water into waiting cups. "Okay," she said. "You just go right back home and tell him that the Bible says it takes one to know one."

"But Granny," I started to say, "I don't think..."

"Listen," she interrupted, "I was reading the Bible before you were even a twinkle in your daddy's eye." I did as she said and that was our last fight for a long time.

Before long I was expecting my first baby. Granny put me right to work crocheting a baby blanket. I could crochet fairly well, but let's just say Martha Stewart would never hire me to make anything for her. I became extremely flustered and did a double loop when I should have done a single.

"Oh gosh," I wailed. "I'll never learn this." I showed her what I had done. "Granny, I'm just going to do another double and no one will ever know the difference." That was the wrong thing to say.

"Yes it will make a difference," she said sternly. "Besides, the Bible says that two wrongs don't make a right."

My mouth dropped to the floor. "But Granny," I said. "I don't think the Bible…"

"Listen," she interrupted, "do you want your baby bundled in a blanket that wasn't made properly?" I unraveled the whole thing and started over.

I took my son to see Granny a while ago. She was sitting on her front porch crocheting and drinking tea. She was getting old but her usual spunk was still there. I sat down in the chair beside her and poured myself some tea. My son toddled off into the house to find the treat that Granny always had for him. After a while, we got to talking and forgot all about him. "Oh no," I gasped at the realization. "I forgot all about that kid."

As I started to get up, Granny reached for my arm and gently pushed me back down into my chair.

"You think he's going to keep meddling when he hears you coming? No, he's smarter than that," she added, with pride in her eyes. "Besides, the Bible says that you have to lay over to catch a meddler."

"But Granny," I said, "I don't think," and then I stopped. All through my years Granny had been quoting me the Bible. Her Bible, and it had always solved whatever problems had been thrown in my path. Smiling and shaking my head, I went into the house to get my son. Carrying him out on the porch, I placed him in the chair beside Granny. "Well Granny," I said, "I think I'm going to run to the store and get us all some ice cream." Pointing to my son, I asked, "Do you mind if he stays here? I'll only be a minute."

"Sure," she nodded. As I turned the car around and headed down the drive, I stopped and looked in my rear view mirror. There they were, two of the most precious people in my life. She, leaning over and quoting her Bible and he, hanging on to every precious word. I knew how he felt. He'll question it someday, but when he grows up he'll realize everything he holds dear is because of the Bible — Granny's Unforgettable Bible.

~Robin Rylee Harderson

"My grandma hasn't missed a Sunday in 40 years, but she still mixes things up. I'm pretty sure 'Thou shalt call thy grandmother daily' is NOT in the Bible."

Grandma Knows

Patience is the companion of wisdom.
~St. Augustine

It's tough getting a date when you're 6' 1". And a girl. When I started my never-ending growth spurt in the seventh grade, my mother constantly told me to stand up straight. "Be proud of your height!"

But I wasn't proud. I longed to be petite like my friends. Instead, my endless arms and legs seemed to have lives of their own, and not once during my middle or high school years was I ever asked to a school dance. It was almost a relief. My long limbs would only have looked ridiculous on the dance floor, I consoled myself.

I always had friends, but I loved books more than anything. Going to the library every Saturday afternoon to check out new books made me feel rich and satisfied. If I didn't get asked to Prom, at least I could lose myself in a book and forget about high school dances for a while.

In college, I dated a few boys. One was even taller than I was. But by the time I started teaching at a small Catholic high school in the middle of Nebraska, there was nobody special.

"Don't you worry," my grandmother encouraged me. "There's somebody out there for you."

My grandmother and I were especially close, and she was always certain a tall prince was waiting in the wings for me.

I rolled my eyes. "And who do you think is out there for me, Grandma?"

She looked at me with knowing love. "Somebody tall. Somebody who loves books," she said. "Somebody like John Boy Walton."

"John Boy Walton!" I snorted.

"What's the matter with John Boy?" she said. "He's perfect for you."

It was probably just as well John Boy Walton didn't show up just then because in 1979, my mother died of breast cancer. As the oldest of ten, I moved back home for a while to help care for my younger siblings. And then, three years later, my grandmother, who was grieving the loss of my mother, her only daughter, became ill, too. We spent more and more time together during those final months of her life. One evening, a few weeks before she died, she eyed me thoughtfully.

"He's out there, you know," she said.

"Who?"

She looked at me. "You know who. John Boy."

"Grandma," I sighed.

"Be patient," she said. "One day you'll meet your John Boy and have tall beautiful children." Her eyes filled. "And you'll look back and think, 'It all worked out the way it was supposed to.'"

After Grandma died, I was lonelier than I'd ever been in my life. I was twenty-eight years old, Mom and Grandma were gone, three of my younger siblings had recently married, and even my dad was dating again. I felt like a middle-aged mother whose children have left the nest.

But that summer of 1983, our school principal called me into his office.

"I thought you'd be interested to know I hired a history teacher today," his eyes twinkled. "He's 6' 8" and his name's John Howard."

John, I thought. John Boy?

John Howard rolled up Central Catholic High School's circular drive that autumn in his tiny 1976 Volkswagen Rabbit. One long arm hung lazily out the window with knuckles that nearly grazed the street.

"Wow," one of my students said. "He looks like a gorilla in that little car."

John Howard was not John Boy Walton. He was a basketball player and coach, and he bordered on the bizarre. I observed him warily those first few months. He pulled rubber chickens out of his file cabinet. He donned a pair of glasses with a fake nose and mustache when he taught the Industrial Revolution. And one day, running down the hall late for class, he decided to surprise his students by leaping through the door of his classroom like Superman. But when you're 6' 8" you shouldn't leap through anything. Slamming his head against the door jam, he nearly knocked himself out.

All things considered, I wasn't sure about Mr. Howard's stability.

Four nights before Christmas in 1983, Nebraska endured one of its worst snowstorms ever. School had already been canceled for the following day, and I sat in my small living room bundled up in an old comforter listening to the wind howl.

Suddenly, the doorbell rang, and I was astonished to see John Howard towering over my front door.

"What are you doing?" I gasped, as I pulled him inside.

"I thought you might like to see a movie," he said casually.

I stared at the blowing snow. "In this?"

He shrugged. "Why not?"

Against my better judgment, I slid into my coat, and the two of us hunched low against the wind and fought our way to his little car.

"Are you sure you can drive in this?" I was concerned about the fading visibility.

"I can drive in anything," he said cockily, as he backed out of my driveway and promptly slid into the big Buick parked across the street.

Fortunately, the Buick was unharmed, but the rear end of John's Rabbit sported a deep half moon dent.

We went to see *Terms of Endearment*, and, I'm ashamed to say, talked and laughed through the entire movie. Thankfully, we were the only ones in attendance. It turned out John Howard loved books! We talked about our favorite books right through the death scene.

Afterwards, we went to a nearly empty bar and grill for a sandwich. But no sooner had we shed our heavy coats than John leapt up.

"We have to go," he said. "I forgot I don't have enough money."

"I have money," I protested.

But he wouldn't hear of it. So out into the blizzard we went once again to drive to a nearby ATM. ATMs were relatively new in 1983, and I asked him if he'd ever used one.

"I use them all the time," he assured me with that same cocksure attitude. But obviously he'd never used this particular ATM. As I sat and watched him from the warmth of the car, he stood in the small cubicle of the bank scratching his head in bewilderment.

I laughed as I observed him do battle with that ATM, and suddenly, in a moment of crystal clear awareness, I thought, "I'm going to marry that guy."

And a year later I did. Every student in the school came to our wedding.

That was twenty-five years ago. John and I are still teaching at Grand Island Central Catholic High School, only now we're teaching the children of that first generation of students. And we have two sons of our own—very tall sons. Our younger son Tommy is eighteen years old and 6' 6" and plays football for the University of Nebraska at Omaha, and our older son Kenny is twenty-two and stands 6' 11". He played basketball for the University of Denver and Regis University. Their height and athletic accomplishments have provided our family with many adventures.

Six years ago when he was sixteen, Kenny won a trip for our entire family to Los Angeles where he played one on one with the mighty Shaquille O'Neal. I remember sitting there between my husband and my handsome younger son in Los Angeles, watching our older son play the bigger-than-life Shaq. And it suddenly occurred to me, "It's all worked out so great."

I shivered suddenly and thought of my long-gone beloved grandma. She had foretold this moment, and I hadn't believed her. I wished so much that she could have been there to meet her two great-grandsons and know how happy I was with my "John Boy."

But something told me she knew. All those years ago, I had doubted her unwavering belief. But she knew.

She always knew.

~Cathy Howard

6

Chicken Soup for the Soul

Go Finger

Some people, no matter how old they get, never lose their beauty —
they merely move it from their faces into their hearts.
~Martin Buxbaum

My friend Bonnie is petite, blond, and a grandmother of three. When she's standing up straight in stiletto heels (which she'd never ever in a million years, actually wear), she's about 5 feet 4 inches tall. She weighs slightly more than a hefty Golden Retriever, even when she's soaking wet and claims she feels bloated.

She's a typical working mother and grandmother. She dresses conservatively, loves her children and grandchildren to pieces, attends church, pays her bills on time, recycles old newspapers, eats five helpings of fruits and vegetables every day and flosses frequently. She writes thank you notes. She knocks before entering.

Bonnie recently demonstrated some ways of behaving that we all want to believe are important — some behaviors that our parents harped on for most of our formative years:

Size doesn't matter.

And attitude is everything.

Bonnie didn't carry anybody out of a burning building. She didn't single-handedly hoist a wrecked school bus off a child's crushed shoulder and hold the vehicle aloft while rescuers pulled the victim to safety. She didn't foil a carjacker or cripple a mugger in a dark alley, then tie him up with her pantyhose. She didn't give anybody the Heimlich or CPR or even first aid.

She showed a burly young whippersnapper that he should mind his manners and manage his nasty temper. I'll bet this guy's mother, if she had been there, would have slapped Bonnie on the back and thanked her profusely.

Here's what happened. Bonnie was getting off the expressway at an unfamiliar exit. One of the lanes on the surface drive was closed and she was afraid she'd miss her chance to make a right turn. She eased into the far right lane a little bit too soon and much too quickly.

She ticked off the driver behind her. He and his passenger, both big men in their thirties or forties, were angry. The hulking driver did what many drivers do. Locked and snug in his steel-and-chrome-and-glass bullet, with his windows rolled up, his radio blaring and his ego inflated to XXL, this young man made eye contact with Bonnie and flashed her an overused, well-known digital hand signal.

His mistake. Now Bonnie was ticked, too.

But unlike Mr. Important, Bonnie was raised right. She didn't speed up and return the visual favor, nor did she honk or shake her delicately gloved fist.

She pulled up beside the young man and rolled down her window. She indicated that he should roll down his window too.

Amazingly, he did.

"I'm so sorry," she said. "I'm not familiar with this exit. The lane was blocked. I wanted to turn right and I pulled over much too soon. Sorry."

Mr. Aggressive blushed and stammered. "He looked like he wanted to slide under the dashboard and disappear," Bonnie said.

He apologized. He said he usually didn't make such gestures. His passenger looked embarrassed and flustered. The driver said he was sorry and that he'd never do it again.

Bonnie rolled up her window and drove on.

Grandmothers: 1

Whippersnappers: 0

~Margie Reins Smith

Gramma's Advice

There are two lasting bequests we can give our children.
One is roots. The other is wings.
~Hodding Carter, Jr.

My son, Christopher had completed his Marine Corps training, his Officer Candidates School in Quantico, Virginia and had just accepted a position with the Sacramento Police Department.

But no matter how old or well trained a grandchild becomes, he is still a little boy to his grandmother. After a sixteen-week course to prepare him for patrol duty, he became a rookie assigned to a seasoned officer. After a period of time, he was assigned his own patrol car, a permanent assignment in the worst part of town and was on his own. He would be riding alone.

Chris excitedly called my mother to tell her the exciting news.

"Guess what, Gramma. I got my own patrol car!"

"Oh well. That's nice. Where will you be patrolling?"

"Gramma, I'm out on Del Paso Boulevard. There's lots of excitement out there."

"Oh. That's a pretty rough area of town. Will you have a partner?"

"No Gramma. I've got a car and I'm all by myself now. I even have a permanent assignment."

"Well, what will your hours be?"

"I'm working graveyard from eleven at night to eight in the morning."

"In the dark? You're going to be driving around in that area of town all night in the dark?"

"Yep."

"Well, you keep your doors locked, the windows rolled up and don't talk to strangers."

~Linda Burks Lohman

"I was packing heat long before you were, grandson."

8

Best Friend

Grandchildren are the dots that connect the lines
from generation to generation.
~Lois Wyse

y daughter and son-in-law are... let's say... overpro-
tective parents. So much so that thoughts of leaving
my grandson for an entire weekend were unthink-
able. They took him everywhere and hadn't left him for longer than
a few hours since birth.

By the time he was three, I took the situation into my own
hands. After all, I was his grandmother, and Travis should have been
developing some memories with me. They lived more than 150 miles
away, so it wasn't as though I could drop in now and then. Travis
knew me only as a guest who came and went. I longed to be able to
put him to bed, get up with him in the morning and spend the day
playing. I wanted to know his personality. Why, I didn't even know
what activities he liked.

After his third birthday, I talked up the offer of a weekend with
Nana. Knowing the responsibility that went with the offer, I must
admit it was pretty scary for this grandmother. It had been thirty-five
years since I had children, and I worried. Would something happen
to this precious child on my watch? Would I be able to make a proper
decision if something went wrong? To add to my anxieties, Travis's
feelings were a concern. This was a child who had never spent time

with a babysitter. His entire security was deep-rooted in Mom and Dad.

I also knew it would be as traumatic for the parents to be away from their son as it would be for my grandchild to have someone else care for him. My daughter was more than particular about her son's care, and given the fact that she was unsure if I could measure up, created anxiety in Travis. Goodness, you'd have thought I'd never had children of my own.

Still, I felt it was time.

At first, my daughter and son-in-law thought the idea shocking, but after thinking about it, they admitted a weekend alone sounded therapeutic. They finally agreed, and we settled on a weekend in September.

The day was crisp, with the hint of autumn in the air, and I could hardly wait to get to their farm. I arrived with bundles of toys, homemade cookies, lots of love, and excitement.

I was left with detailed written instructions. I loved the part where my daughter wrote, "Don't leave the bathroom while he's in the tub." An entire paragraph was devoted to bedtime. Basic rituals like, "Be sure he goes to the bathroom before you put him in bed," were noted.

As we stood in the driveway, waving goodbye, I whispered a silent prayer for wisdom, and told them not to worry.

Travis and I started our day with games. This went well. However, every now and then, Travis would look up and say, "Mommy and Daddy will be home soon, okay Nana?"

I smiled and gave him a hug reassuring him. "Yes they'll be back in two days."

We laughed, played tag, and hide-and-seek. He was trying, but the whole time he kept a vigil out the window with signs of worry written on his face.

Dinnertime arrived. Travis refused to eat. "I want to wait for Mommy and Daddy. I'll eat with them."

The words from his high-pitched voice weren't harsh, only factual. I hesitated, then gave him a wink and poured a glass of milk. I wanted so much to show my daughter that leaving Travis on occasion was a good thing. Perhaps more to the point, it was important for Travis to trust me. We needed to have a relationship.

I set the milk in front of him. "Honey, they won't be back until Sunday. I'm sure Mommy wouldn't want you to go hungry. She likes your tummy to be full and happy."

My psychology didn't work.

"No." His face scrunched into a scowl, his eyes shut tight, and I sensed tears were coming. Feelings of failure began to cloud my mind.

Finally, I sat down and in a firm but gentle tone said, "Travis, I am in charge until your parents get back. So far, I think we're having quite a good time, don't you?"

He looked skeptical, but nodded yes.

"So, let's eat." I looked at my plate and forked a bite of macaroni and cheese. I didn't look up—just ate.

I could feel his eyes watching me. Soon, without a whimper, he started eating. It was a turning point.

Later after playtime and his bath, I suggested a bedtime story. His face lit up and he ran to pick out his favorite books. I sat in the old rocker that had once been mine, and cradled him in my arms. I read to him. By the second book, I felt him relax. Was he actually feeling secure? He snuggled and reached for my hand, holding it tight. His eyes became heavy, almost closing. I kissed his forehead and put the book down.

I tucked him into bed, pulled a blanket up around his shoulders, and whispered, "I love you, sweetheart. I sure had a good time today."

Travis opened sleepy eyes and smiled. "Nana, you're my best friend, aren't you?"

"You bet I am," I replied, "and I can't wait until tomorrow when we'll have more fun."

We've had many weekends since, once even an entire five days, but I'll never forget that first time when we became best friends.

~Arlene Rains Graber

The Courage to Dream

Grandmother — a wonderful mother with lots of practice.
~Author Unknown

Every summer growing up, my brothers and I would visit my dad. Because he and his wife worked, he'd ask my grandmother to come stay with him to act as our babysitter. To me, Grandma was more than a babysitter. She taught me about life and opened my eyes to dreams I never imagined were possible.

Because my dad's house was so small, Grandma and I shared a double bed in the upstairs bedroom. With no air conditioning, those hot, humid nights would have been unbearable had I not had my grandma. Her habit was to read every night before going to bed. On the really hot nights, we'd stay up almost all night reading because it was too hot to sleep.

Those summers, I discovered so many new worlds in that stuffy room in Bound Brook. When I'd read all the Nancy Drews I could find, Grandma handed me her Harlequins. Paris, Rome, tropical islands, and even the refreshing cold of Alaska became the places of my dreams. I remember being in awe of the magical lives these authors must lead.

Even in the most miserable heat, those nights were the most precious of my life. Passing books back and forth with Grandma, and feeling so loved and cherished because she was one of the few people who didn't complain that I always had my nose in a book. Grandma encouraged my love of books, giving me the acceptance I craved.

It was Grandma who first taught me how to dream. "Wouldn't it be nice to write a book someday?" I said those words as a half-wish, wondering if she'd think all the stories I'd penned in my notebook a silly waste of my time.

"Well, why not? You could write a book." Her answer encouraged me to show her some of the things I'd written. She liked my stories, and told me how good they were. I never doubted her when she held up whatever book she was reading and said, "Someday, I'll read one of yours." My grandma never doubted. "If anyone can do it, you can."

I grew up, went to college, and was promptly told by a professor that not only would I never make it as a writer, but that whoever told me I was a good writer knew nothing about good writing. As I studied, I quickly learned that I could never make a living as a writer or have a writing career. I set aside my writing dreams, telling myself that someday, when I retired, I'd try my hand at finally writing a book.

But I couldn't stop writing for long. Grandma had put the love of a good story so deep in my heart that I couldn't let it go. At first I wrote in secret, but then I started to pursue my dream more seriously. Unfortunately, my grandma's health had gotten to the point where she was no longer able to travel to see me, and with my young family, we had no money to go see her. I didn't have her encouragement to tell me how wonderful my writing was, but I surrounded myself with others who could help me. I decided that when I sold my first book, I'd use the money to take my family to visit her.

In my naiveté, I believed it would be an easy task. My grandma had never met my husband or children, but I was sure she'd meet them soon. I wanted my children to know the woman who'd been such an encouragement to me. I'd passed on my love of stories to them, and so it only seemed fitting that they meet the woman who'd inspired me.

However, years passed. I collected a stack of rejection letters. Our finances were too tight for us to even think of making a trip to visit my grandma. Each time I heard that her health had another setback, I panicked, wondering how I was going to ever let her know that her faith in me had not been misplaced. And each time she pulled through, I breathed a sigh of relief and strengthened my resolve to publish a book and dedicate it to her.

Ten years later, I still did not have a book contract. I'd managed to get some devotionals published, but nothing that allowed me to dedicate an entire book to her. Grandma's health had deteriorated to the point that we weren't sure how much longer she'd remain with us. I grieved the potential loss of a beloved grandmother, and I despaired at not being able to make her proud. My husband insisted that I make the trip to visit her so that if she died, I wouldn't have to live with the regret of not being able to tell her one last time how much I loved her.

Though the woman in the hospital bed had all kinds of tubes sticking out of her, I immediately recognized her as my grandma. She could barely speak, but as I showed her the devotional book and the story with my name on it, she rasped the words I'd longed to hear. "I'm proud of you."

Over the next several days, I sat by her bed, talking, holding her hand, and catching up on the years we've missed. I realized that as much as I'd considered the past ten years of writing completely unsuccessful, she looked at my life as being a success. Though I'd wanted to be able to give her a book dedication so she knew how much her influence meant to me, she already knew. It didn't matter how many years or miles separated us, she still knew me, and she still knew my heart.

Unfortunately, our visit ended much too soon, but fortunately, Grandma pulled through her health crisis. I'm still working toward the coveted book contract. But instead of having the pressure to prove to my grandmother that her faith in me was not misplaced, I work in the freedom of knowing I don't need a contract to make her proud.

Thanks to Grandma, I had the courage to write my first book. And my second, and every one thereafter. Grandma gave me the courage to send my first book to a publisher, and even though they told me no, I had the courage to send the next one. And every one thereafter. Because my grandma told me I could do it.

So many people say they dream of doing a thing, but many times, they lack the courage to even try. Grandma provided that courage for me. And even though I haven't reached my goal yet, I know I will. And someday, I pray that some other little girl will lie in bed with her grandma, reading my books, and dare to dream all the possibilities for her life. Because with her grandma's help, she's sure to achieve them.

~Danica Favorite

The Locket

A house needs a grandma in it.
~Louisa May Alcott

had always been close to Grandma. Yet, the summer she moved in with our family it seemed as if my life had turned upside down. I was sixteen years old and suddenly all the house rules had changed, and with them, my relationship with my beloved grandmother.

In years past, Grandma had always been the industrious sort. A visit to her house always meant a fresh batch of cookies and an eager ear. Since my mom worked, it was Grandma who introduced me to many of my childhood pleasures. We grew snapdragons and sunflowers. She taught me how to make a beaded purse, coat candy apples, cross stitch a pillow. Then Grandma had a heart attack, and the robust woman of my youth was suddenly frail and old. When my father brought her to our house with her belongings, she reminded me of a pale, wilted flower.

It had already been a tough summer. My boyfriend of six months, Jared, had recently broken up with me. I'd like to say it was mutual, but in reality I felt dumped. Jared was the first boy I really loved, and even though I was only sixteen I felt a deep connection with him that, now broken, left me feeling less than whole. It's not as if I didn't have other opportunities either. Several guys had asked me out, and at least a few times I had accepted my girlfriends' invitations for a double date. But my heart wasn't in it, and it's no wonder they rarely asked me out a second time. Since I was spending more time at home these days, Grandma's intrusion into my life seemed especially difficult.

I groaned inwardly when my mom rapped on my bedroom door, calling me to dinner. "Can't I just grab some food later?" I asked.

"Donna. Your grandma's here. We're going to eat as a family."

Eat as a family. Since when was that a big priority? I couldn't even blame my grandmother, because it was my mom who suddenly seemed to get all kinds of ideas in her head. Turn off the TV, Grandma's napping. No friends over this afternoon, Grandma's tired. The list went on and on.

Ordinarily, I wouldn't have minded so much, maybe even welcomed the opportunity to spend time with Grandma. But that was before Jared. Now I just wanted to crawl into my room, listen to music, and not be disturbed.

I was downstairs buttering my toast, my iPod blaring, and I didn't hear Grandma enter the kitchen. I could tell she was just glad to see me, which made me feel instantly guilty.

"Hi Grandma," I said. "You look good this morning." She did. The pale cornflower blouse she wore complemented her complexion, and today she reminded me of her old self. "What can I get you for breakfast?"

"Is there any of that pumpernickel bread left? I'll have a slice of that with my morning coffee."

I brought Grandma her toast with her favorite marmalade that I knew she'd want. I joined her at the table, and it dawned on me that this was the first time I'd sat down with her since she'd arrived, without prodding from my mother. I sighed.

"I'm sorry I've been a bit distant lately," I said.

Grandma bit her toast. "You're sixteen. I was sixteen, too, once."

That was all she said, but I could see the reflection in her expression. Some people you can't possible imagine they were ever sixteen, but not my grandma. I can't explain why, but somehow I could truly picture her at sixteen, her skin smooth and the same bright blue eyes. On a date, perhaps. Maybe with a boy like Jared.

"I would like to show you something," she offered.

Grandma returned and first she showed me a music box carved from delicate rosewood. It was exquisite. When she opened the heavy lid, I could see a large spindle, the components of the music box, through a clear glass window. The spindle turned and the tune "Somewhere My Love" from *Dr. Zhivago* filled the dining room.

"It's beautiful, Grandma. What's in the other box?"

It was a heart-shaped blue velvet box, and Grandma opened it to reveal a small, etched silver locket. "Go ahead," she said. "Open it."

"It's Grandpa! You were so young."

"Yes. Very. Your grandpa gave this locket to me on our wedding day."

"It's pretty, but I especially love the music box. When did Grandpa give you that?" I asked.

"He didn't," she said. "It was a gift from my fiancé. My first fiancé, before your grandpa. We were engaged to be married when he was killed in a training accident on the army base." Grandma's face grew wistful. "It wasn't even war time. I wasn't prepared for the tragedy. Or the grief."

I whispered quietly, "I'm sorry. I didn't know."

"Of course you didn't, dear. I met your grandpa at church and he was always trying to cheer me up with a funny joke or just some kind words. I was grieving, and I'm afraid I wasn't very nice to him."

"But he didn't give up."

Grandma smiled. "No. He didn't give up. It took a while, but eventually I began to break out of my sorrow. There was so much to love about the world. And I grew to love your grandpa much more than I ever loved Stan. You see, Grandpa—Tom—we shared a life. We had children together. Grew old together. We shaped who each other became."

Unexpectedly I felt my lashes grow wet. Jared wasn't my fiancé, only a boyfriend. Why couldn't I let go? "How did you know?" I asked.

"I can see it in your face."

"I guess you think I'm being pretty silly about Jared. It's not like he's dead or anything."

Grandma folded her worn hand over mine. "I don't think you're being silly at all. You loved him and you no longer have him, and now you're hurting."

Suddenly I found myself telling Grandma everything. How I'd met Jared. All the fun times we had. And the painful break-up. We were still talking when the phone rang. It was my friend Melanie inviting me to go to the movies with her and Michael and Sean. I said yes.

When I returned home that night Grandma was in bed. I almost didn't see the object on my pillow in the darkness. It was the blue velvet box, the locket that Grandpa had given Grandma on their wedding day. There was a note with it as well. I turned on the light at my bedside and read Grandma's grand, scrawling penmanship: "To my dear Donna, wishing you a lifetime of love." Grandma had chosen to give me the locket instead of the music box I had so admired, the locket that was a gift from the man who gave her a second chance at love. It was a gift that represented the future and not the past. I couldn't wait to tell Grandma about my date the next morning.

~Donna Brothers

Grandmothers

Becoming a Grandmother

11

Bewitched by Baby T

It is as grandmothers that our mothers come into the fullness of their grace.
~Christopher Morley

By the time my siblings and I were forty-seven, thirty-eight, and thirty-two, my poor mother had given up on becoming a grandmother. I never kept a boyfriend long enough to get serious, my brother had a girlfriend who wasn't interested in children, and the youngest, my sister, who had been married for ten years, had always claimed she didn't want kids. While my mom's friends became grandparents one by one, she lost hope.

The worst were the baby showers. "I just hate them," my mother complained. "They're so boring!" She would go to the showers begrudgingly, always looking for an excuse to leave as soon as she'd presented the obligatory gift.

Then my sister's biological clock kicked in. At sixty-nine, my mother finally became a grandmother! For months beforehand she worried about all the millions of things that could go wrong, but finally the baby arrived, and my mother had something to brag about to her friends.

I didn't have a chance to fly home to see Tia until she was three months old. It was a frigid February night when my mom rescued me from the airport in Springfield, Illinois.

"Baby T is so cute! Your sister will bring her over tomorrow so you can meet her right away!"

"That's great," I said, unsure. As far as I had noticed, all grandparents said their grandchildren were cute, and half the time it wasn't close to true.

"How's Grandma?" I asked.

"I wish I'd had it as good as my mother did! She became a grandmother when she was only fifty!"

I'd often thought about that fact. My maternal grandparents were both fifty when I was born, so they had plenty of energy to take care of me. At nearly the same age, I was becoming an aunt myself. I didn't know what to expect; I'd been such a self-centered teen when my sister was born that I only paid attention to her when she got in my way.

During the ride home from the airport, I tried to tell my mother about my life back in Arizona, but I couldn't get a word in edgewise. She was all Baby T this and Baby T that and Baby T smiled and Baby T turned over and... and... and!

When we reached the house, I was surprised to find that my parents' normally neat living room was a disaster zone. A baby blanket hugged the floor, and a stack of disposable diapers prevented anyone from sitting on the couch. Toys dominated the study and the living room, and Baby T was only three months old!

I slept uneasily, dreaming of the smelly diaper pail I remembered from my brother's childhood.

My mother called my sister early the next morning. "How's my baby?" she asked enthusiastically.

"I'm fine," my sister shouted through the phone. The baby who for thirty-two years had been my sister now found her special position usurped by her own daughter. Elise wasn't taking it calmly. (Secretly, I thought it was good for her to know how my brother and I had felt when she came along.)

An hour later Mom and I were peacefully having coffee when she detected a noise at the front end of the house.

"She's here!" my mother screamed. She set down her cup and ran to the front door.

This was strange. While my mother had always been an avid water skier, I had rarely seen her run. Also, though I'd always known her to be precise with language (she'd taught middle school English most of her career), she'd exclaimed "She's here!" and I was pretty sure my mother was referring to the baby, and I was equally sure the baby hadn't driven herself over for a visit.

Despite the bitter cold that my mother normally avoided, she raced outside without stopping to put on a coat and sped to the car.

"There she is!" my mother cried out as she opened the car door.

"It's nice to see you too, Mom," my sister said, but my mother didn't hear her. She was wrestling with the straps of the car seat.

"Look, she's sleeping!" my mother whispered.

"She's been doing that a lot lately," my sister said wryly.

"Baby T needs a blanket! It's cold outside!" my mom cried. Before my sister could do anything to stop her, my mom had bundled up the baby and gotten her inside the house. She set Baby T on the baby blanket on the living room floor as if she were porcelain and sat beside her.

"She's so sweet!" my mom said softly.

"You don't have to whisper," my sister said. "She's out cold."

We left Mom staring at Tia, and Elise and I went into the kitchen for snacks.

"See what I mean?" my sister said. "Mom's not the same person. I hardly recognize her."

"It's kind of weird." My sister had warned me on the phone, but I hadn't internalized it. I was too busy remembering when we had been young, and what I remembered was Mom hurrying around the house, getting home from school and throwing dinner together. She was always in motion because she had five thousand things to do. Weekends were worse because she had to do even more, and now she was sitting in the living room doing nothing more than watching a sleeping baby.

"I tried to tell you," my sister said, "but I knew you would have to see if for yourself. She's a whole different person."

"Mom hasn't let me say a word since I got here. She only talks about the baby."

"Guess what?" Elise frowned. "We don't count anymore."

Elise and I launched into a long, uninterrupted conversation.

"Why, you had a little nap!" From the living room boomed a voice reminiscent of an actor on a kiddie show.

My sister rolled her eyes.

"You got tired of sleeping! You wanted to know what was going on!"

Elise rolled her eyes again.

I started to get up, but she held out her hand. "Just wait. It'll get worse."

And indeed it did.

"What were you dreaming? Were you a big girl already? And now do you want to meet your auntie?"

For the next ten minutes, we heard this and other examples of high-pitched baby talk.

"Pat a cake, pat a cake," my mother chanted.

"This I've got to see," I said, hurrying into the other room.

An adorable wide-eyed baby, dressed in white flannel, straddled my mother's leg.

"Make me a BIIIIIIG cake!" When Mom got to the word "big," she spread my niece's hands out wide.

I was stunned. This bewitched woman was unrecognizable! I had never seen my mother happier. She'd become a new youthful self, discovering the miracle of birth for the first time.

"And we'll roll it up and stick it in a pan. And then we'll eat it ALLLLLLLLL up!"

After an hour, the happy grandmother even let me hold Tia myself.

By now my niece is two, and a sibling is on its way, so my mother will get to double her joy as a grandmother. Even though she complains my sister waited way too long to have kids, I'd say instead my sister did things just right. Each time Tia arrives at my parents' house, my mom greets her with a joyful holler. I love going back home to play Auntie myself, but there's nothing more special than watching my mother transformed. I'm sure she would agree that no matter how long it took Baby T to come along, the angel was well worth the wait.

~D.R. Ransdell

12

What Does a Grandmother Know?

A grandmother is a mother who has a second chance.
~Author Unknown

We were beginning to think we would be senile before we had grandchildren. We had even adjusted to the thought. On the plane flying out to visit our daughter Anna and her husband Sam and see their new house, I whispered to my husband, "I've got to learn to be patient. With the new house and new jobs, it will be at least a couple more years before they start trying to get pregnant." I was happy just to see them and their new house.

Then came the shock, presented with our daughter and son-in-law's wily smiles, in a restaurant that evening halfway across the country. In the booth midway through dinner, they nodded to each other and then handed us one of the "thank you" cards I had given them when Anna and Sam became engaged. Odd, I thought, as I pulled the card out of the envelope. What did they have to thank us for at that moment?

Cream colored, with names engraved in navy. There was "Anna and Sam" at the top as I remembered, but there was something else inked in. Suddenly my husband and I noticed below their names, "AND???" printed in large block letters with many question marks. Larry, grandpa-to-be started pounding the table; I was speechless and weepy. We couldn't control ourselves. We would not be senile after all, but we were acting like it in public.

We ordered dessert all around. They showed us the sonogram. "Isn't our child beautiful?" asked my son-in-law about the picture of a blur the size of a grain of rice.

"Can you tell the sex yet?" I asked.

"We don't want to know," they said emphatically in unison. We could only imagine how much planning, discussing, and decision-making had preceded their telling us this fact with such certainty.

"Oh, of course… of course," we agreed. But visions of little boys and little girls floated above our melting chocolate and whipped cream desserts.

We spent the next four days celebrating with the parents-to-be Sworn to secrecy, we returned home with the news securely tucked into our private chambers. But at night, I lay in bed thinking of Anna when she was born and how lovely it would be to have a girl again. Then I would switch and think how nice it would be to know what a little boy would be like. After flipping back and forth in my mind, I would fall asleep loving the mystery of not knowing, not caring in the least what sex the baby would be.

When Anna called a few days later and invited me to fly back cross-country in less than a month for her twenty-week sonogram, at first I said I couldn't take more time off. What a dummy, I thought, as I put the phone down. I called her right back after my brain clicked in. Of course, I'd come. How wonderful to be invited. So I moved my schedule around and spent hours on the phone making reservations.

I was thrilled. This most private of daughters, whose tiny body I had last seen naked more than twenty years ago, had invited me into the next stage of her pregnancy, into the small sonogram room, into the world of the roaming wand of the technician. I knew nothing about this technology. It hadn't existed when this daughter of mine was born. How could I not have answered immediately, "Of course I'll come."?

I flew back across the country and we appeared promptly at the doctor's office at 8:45 on a Wednesday morning. Sam, my son-in-law, always the avid golfer, was ecstatic when he found a signed golf ball and a quarter on the way into the office. "A great sign," he whispered on the way in.

I was once again in my nervous state. They didn't want to know the sex of the child. What if I saw it by mistake? Could I ever keep it to myself? And what of my son-in-law, the doctor? Wouldn't he see everything? And what was the etiquette in a sonogram room? And how do you act in situations like this? Besides the sex of this baby, there were a million other things I didn't know.

The room was tiny and dark, the technician funny and relaxed, yet concentrating and serious. Monitors registered everything as she moved the sonogram wand over my daughter's gelatinized growing abdomen. There was truly a child there—fingers, toes, a baby sucking a thumb, ribs, spine. The parents-to-be were calm and quiet; I was trying to keep my excitement under control. Only the clicking of measurements could be heard and the tiny less-than-a-pound baby's heartbeat booming. "Yup, normal, yup, normal, see the ribs, see the spine," the tech kept saying.

How could she use the word "normal" for what I was watching? I was with this miracle of a daughter of mine, looking into the miracle of her growing womb, looking at the miracle of tiny hands and big eyes in a tiny face. No way in the world is this just "normal." Everything in that dark room seemed miraculous to me.

Suddenly, my son-in-law said, "Okay, everyone turn away. She's moving toward the kidneys." And so we did turn away. At least I did and saw nothing. And again we heard, "Yup, normal... Yup, normal..."

"Heartbeat's 158, right where it should be," the tech said after telling us it was all right to turn around again. She gave us sonogram pictures and promised not to tell the doctor what the sex was. "I don't even write it in the chart," she said. "Docs forget and slip all the time," she said. Did she know, we asked. "Of course," she whispered, with a wink.

The appointment with the doctor was short, routine, upbeat.

After the appointment, we went to lunch before Anna had to go to a meeting. After she left, Sam and I kept eating and schmoozing. "I know what the sex is," I said over dahl.

"So do I," he said, over his naan. "How do you know?" he asked.

"The heartbeat," I said. "How do you know? Did you look?"

"I did not look," he retorted emphatically. "I'm guessing from the heartbeat, too. So what do you think it is?"

"A girl definitely," I said, "because the heartbeat was so fast." I didn't bother telling him that when I was pregnant with his wife, the doctors kept saying a fast heartbeat was a sign of a girl.

He stared at me. "Absolutely not," he said, "that heartbeat tells me it's a boy." My heartbeat is a lot faster than your daughter's," he said. "Wanna bet me an Indian lunch?" I am not a betting woman. Also, I thought it best not to argue with a doctor son-in-law so we continued eating and savoring the moment and the mystery.

"Well," he said, as we got up to leave, "one of us has to be right."

The best part was that we would not be senile before we found out. Four months later, after the fastest trip to the airport we had ever made, and racing to the hospital with a cab driver who thought we were crazy, our son-in-law came down the hospital corridor smiling. "It's a boy, seven pounds." Our healthy grandson was born without complication.

I ran down the hall to Anna's delivery room. We were both crying. I hugged her, looked over at the perfect child next to her, and whispered, "Did you know?"

"I didn't. I promise," she said. "We all thought this little fella would be a girl. You convinced us."

What does a grandmother know about the sex of a grandchild anyway?

~Davi Walders

13

From Sad to Glad

One of the most powerful handclasps is that of a new grandbaby
around the finger of a grandfather.
~Joy Hargrove

I was cleaning up my office desk, getting ready to go home, when my phone rang. Drat, I thought, just when I was geared up to get out of work on time for a change. I answered it immediately and was determined to make quick work of whoever had the nerve to call right at five o'clock.

"Hello," I said gruffly into the receiver.

"The baby died."

"What?" I asked, sure I had a kook on the phone.

"The baby died. They don't know how," the voice whispered. In that instant I recognized my older daughter Jennifer's voice. A million thoughts went through my mind at once. She was alone, she was five and a half months pregnant and she was in shock. My heart felt like a knife had gone through it.

I managed to stop my body from shaking and talk to her. "Jen, where are you? What happened? Dad and I will be there as soon as we can," I blurted out all in one breath.

"I went to the doctor for my check-up and he couldn't find a heartbeat so he sent me for an ultrasound. Then he told me the baby had just died and he didn't know why. I have to go to the hospital tonight for either a delivery or a D&C. Can you come down?" With this she started to sob.

"We're on our way, Jen," I consoled her, holding back the tears. "Try to stay calm. It shouldn't take more than an hour to get there."

"I need Ed," she whimpered, referring to her husband, who was serving in the Navy and was away on maneuvers out to sea.

"Don't worry. We'll get the Red Cross to find him. Everything will be okay. You'll see."

I wish I had more to offer my daughter, who was a hundred miles away in San Diego.

My husband Paul and I rushed down the freeway in heavy traffic. To say that he obeyed the speed limit would be a lie. As we travelled we were both lost in our own thoughts. I was so sad that I would never hold this grandchild in my arms. Sad and puzzled that another pregnancy had ended in a miscarriage for my daughter. Jen and Ed already had Payton, who was three. We were looking forward to a girl, our second grandchild.

The next few days were are a blur. Jennifer was lucky that she wasn't far enough along that she had to endure a stillborn delivery; she had a D&C. Both sets of grandparents sat outside labor and delivery praying all would go well. That night we took a weak and sad Jennifer home. We made urgent calls to the Red Cross and within a day we heard footsteps on her porch. In rushed Ed, who took Jennifer in his arms as they both cried. We silently left for home so they could cope with their grief alone.

A year later Jennifer was pregnant again. She was nervous during her pregnancy and her doctor gave her reassurances that all was going well. I hoped that I would have another grandchild to cuddle and coo, but this time we didn't care if it was a boy or a girl, we just wanted a healthy baby.

The November morning arrived sunny and clear in sunny Southern California and about 10:00 a.m., our phone rang again. This time it was good news.

"Mom, I'm in labor. Can you and Dad come down and be here with us? Both sides of the family are coming: Ed's parents, his grandma and grandpa, his sister, our best friends, Paige and Jeff too."

"We'll be there as soon as we pick up your sister Mary. I know she'll want to come too. Thank goodness Ed is home with you. Now don't go waiting for us. If you're not there, we'll go directly to the hospital," I said.

A happy group convened at the Sharp Hospital for Women in San Diego. We were having a family celebration in the maternity visitor area, joyously awaiting the outcome of the birth drama unfolding in the adjoining room. I hoped by dinnertime I would be holding my new grandbaby in my arms. I couldn't wait to meet him or her.

After several hours Jennifer's labor slowed way down. There were anxious looks and much pacing. The party mood abruptly came to a halt. Would this end in another sad day reminiscent of the previous year? The clock ticked away. I started praying. All of a sudden there was a flurry of activity; Ed disappeared with a nurse for what seemed like an eternity. Then he sent for Payton to join him. We all held our breath.

Soon Payton, age four, was carried out by Ed who placed him on a small table in the middle of the room. He grinned and held up his hands like he was conducting an orchestra.

"Hey everybody," said Ed. "Payton has something he wants to say."

With that Payton announced, "I just met my new baby sister!"

Tears and congratulations flowed freely. Grandparents hugged grandparents, friends hugged family. The cloud of sadness from the year before was forgotten when my granddaughter Emily arrived, a beautiful healthy bundle of joy.

~Sallie A. Rodman

Woven with Love

Grandmas never run out of hugs or cookies.
~Author Unknown

"Have any grandchildren, yet?" acquaintances would ask. "You'd better get busy or you'll be too old to keep up with grandkids." This bit of wisdom was usually followed by a brag book unfolded before me with adorable photos of chubby-faced cherubs in Easter outfits, kids clad in Winnie the Pooh pajamas tearing into Santa's packages, or a little dumpling planting a soggy kiss on Granny's cheek.

I often listened to friends reminisce about the special bond they had with their grandmothers; however, I had never experienced that relationship. My grandmothers were faded photos on my mother's dressing table, and stories shared by my parents of their childhood. Both my grandmothers died long before I was born—my maternal grandmother died giving birth to her eighth child.

From the time I rocked my babies in the old wooden rocker, handed down through three generations, I dreamed of sitting in the same rocker spoiling grandbabies.

As the years quickly sped by, my husband and I were proud of the talents and accomplishments of our children as they each excelled in their chosen professions—marriage and family on hold.

Many of our friends had grandkids in high school, while others were celebrating the birth of great-grandchildren.

Though at times it seemed there was a missing fabric in the crazy quilt of our lives, I loved the trips our kids invited us to take with them: Christmas in snowy Colorado, misty, early mornings on the cliffs of Maine, chairlift rides along the mountain range of Vermont.

Then, in her mid-thirties, our daughter announced she had met the man of her dreams. In a beautiful Christmastime wedding, our family increased—not by one but by three. Her new husband came with a bonus, a daughter and a son. Instant grandma!

The world of karate opened to me when the grandkids asked, "Grandma, you're coming to my next match, aren't you?" When they earned their black belts, I cheered the loudest.

Through the years my brag book grew fatter with vacation, birthday parties, and holiday photos. The grandkids' favorite gift under the Christmas tree each year? Christmas pokes. Instead of stockings, I stitched each of them a bag from holiday fabrics and ribbons to hold small toys and candies. One of my favorite stories from my mom was of her mother hand-stitching gift bags from flour sacks she trimmed with cotton lace. She had called them pokes.

Clouds sweep into every life, and one of our darkest made its appearance when our grandson was diagnosed with a non-malignant brain tumor. Following many surgeries, we spent long hours next to his hospital bed. When he lost his hair to chemo treatments, his dad shaved away his own mane of dark hair. We all wore yellow wristbands, and when asked about the band, I shared my grandson's brave battle. After years of intense treatments, his tumor was finally under control.

Our lives took another unexpected turn one Sunday morning after the young adult Sunday School class my husband taught. One of the young ladies asked if she could speak with him. Thinking it was a question about the lesson, he was surprised and humbled when she said, "Will you be my dad?" She had previously shared with us the difficult time she had growing up.

We instantly added a wonderful daughter and two more fabulous grandkids to our family. With these new additions, we were introduced to the exciting world of show animals as we sat for hours on backless bleachers at county fairs. It didn't matter if their animals won trophies. The pride we felt from our grandkids' dedication to hard work couldn't be measured. And who was called when an animal escaped from its pen? Grandpa!

When word got around about that special adoption, we were asked to be grandparents for two other beautiful baby girls. We were instantly transported back to the fantasy world of Disney characters and Barbie dolls. I began another brag book.

We don't know if our family is complete, but if other fabrics are added, they too, will be stitched with love and gratitude into the warmth of our family quilt.

~Joy Faire Stewart

15

On Becoming a Grandmother

Perfect love sometimes does not come until the first grandchild.
~Welsh Proverb

I thought I was prepared. I was a mother, after all. I already knew what it meant to love someone so much it hurt. I understood the old adage that to be a parent is to walk around forever with your heart outside your body. I had written in my journal, revealing all the emotions I'd discovered tag-teaming in my heart: happiness, melancholy, anxiety, joy, anticipation, worry. I had seen the ultrasound pictures. I'd crocheted a soft, fuzzy blue blanket, patiently undoing all my bungled stitches and doing them over so it would be a perfect square. I had memorized the verses in Psalm 139 that tell how God wonderfully forms us in our mother's womb. I had prayed for this child and for his parents daily since I learned of his existence. I had written letters to his mom and dad, assuring them how proud I was of them both, how I'd be as supportive as I knew how to be, how they would be excellent parents.

I'd prayed for myself, too. I'd wrestled with the idea that I was going to be a grandmother. Shouldn't I be wiser first? Or sweeter? Or at the very least, a better cook? How exactly did one cram for this event? I had even admitted to myself that I would soon be sleeping with someone's grandfather. That idea took a little getting used to, let me tell you!

I had bragged to my friends. I had celebrated with my mother. I had gifted my daughter-in-law with maternity clothes and bought the most irresistible little stuffed puppy for the baby.

I had done all of that. I thought I was prepared.

The day he was born, I rode along with his other grandparents to the hospital to meet our mutual little descendant for the first time. We were told to wait in the hallway while the nurses finished up whatever they were doing with him and his mother in the room. While I waited, I studied the instructional posters on the walls, filled with advice for new parents. I remembered how challenging those first few days could be. Given the hospital rules, I fully expected that my first sight of my little grandson would be in his plastic baby bed and I was prepared. But when I turned around, I instantly knew that no amount of groundwork could have prepared me for that moment. Instead of the expected baby bed, I was beholding my own firstborn carrying his firstborn in his arms.

I came unglued. Part of me was carried back twenty-six years to the day I first laid eyes on my son. But those twenty-six years had passed in an instant, and here I was looking at the next generation, with the same dark skin and the same head full of thick, dark hair. He was beautiful and I was smitten. I didn't even try to check the tears running down my cheeks as I held him in my arms and hugged his dad as tight as I could with the baby between us. What a cherished moment!

This little boy is about to turn three years old and now has a baby brother. Every day brings new adventures, new things to learn, new memories to make, and new opportunities to wonder at the marvelous work of our Creator. These little guys have taught me that sometimes stopping to watch ducks is more important than getting in out of the rain. They've uncovered my own impatient ways, the ones I thought I had overcome. They've reminded me that time spent cuddling a sleeping baby in a rocking chair trumps pretty much anything.

Most of all, I've come to realize that no matter how hard I tried, I could not have prepared to love someone so profusely, or to learn so much from someone so small.

~Terrie Todd

16

Ready or Not

Grandparents are similar to a piece of string—handy to have around and easily wrapped around the fingers of their grandchildren.
~Author Unknown

Bent over, leaning on a cane, I walked into my daughter's hospital room and croaked in the oldest voice I could muster, "Gayla, look what you've done to me!" As we laughed and hugged one another, in came the nurse, carrying the baby. She placed her into my waiting arms.

At the age of forty-four, I was not ready to become a grandmother. But it was inevitable. After all, I had become a mother at the age of nineteen. When my daughter announced that she was expecting her first child, my initial reaction was, "This can't be! I'm not old enough to be a grandmother! My hair isn't even gray!"

The months flew by, and on a hot summer day in 1983, the call came, "You have a granddaughter! When can you get here?"

I decided to dress the part on my first visit. Conspiring with my husband (who I felt was too young to be a grandfather), I wrapped a shawl around my shoulders, put on a hat with a veil, and perched a pair of wire rim glasses low on my nose. We drove the sixty miles to the hospital to meet our first grandchild, Susanna Claire.

The moment I laid eyes on my granddaughter, it was love at first sight. Becoming a grandmother was suddenly the highest station in life a woman could attain.

As she learned to walk and talk and use the telephone, I looked forward to her calls, "Hi, Gramma! It's me, Susanna Claire." Those words were music to my ears.

She started school, and soon I received her kindergarten picture—blue eyes, blond hair in pigtails. I thought, somewhere I have seen another little girl who looks just exactly like Susanna Claire. I wonder who it could be?

I couldn't rest, knowing somewhere in my boxes and boxes of pictures there was another little girl who was the mirror image of my granddaughter. I hauled the boxes out and started going through more than forty years of photographs I had accumulated.

"Yes, here it is! This is the picture I've been looking for!" It was my own first grade picture—blue eyes, blond hair in French braids. The face shape, the nose, the chin, the grin, were identical. I began to laugh in astonishment, as I realized that my granddaughter and I could have passed for identical twins at the age of five or six. I couldn't wait to show her the photos, which I placed in a double frame for display.

As the years passed, I looked forward to her visits, watching her grow and mature. She claimed the sleigh bed in the peach bedroom for overnights. "Gramma, I sleep so well in that bed!" Early on, she began begging for a special breakfast, "Gramma, do you think we could have waffles with strawberries and real whipped cream?"

"Of course, sweetie, anything for you," has always been, and still is, my answer as she approaches her twenty-seventh birthday, still asking for waffles, strawberries, and real whipped cream on her overnights.

I'm so glad I became a grandmother at that early age of forty-four! Since then, seven more grandchildren have found their place in my heart. I wouldn't trade the years of occupying such a fulfilling role for anything the world could offer.

~Margaret M. Marty

A Grandma's Heart

When a child is born, so are grandmothers.
~Judith Levy

She doesn't know my name. In fact, I can definitively say that she doesn't even know who I am. To her, I am just another pair of arms that hug her and hold her snugly against me while she sleeps. But I know her.

Her name is Karaleen, she is one week old, and she is my granddaughter. I can't believe she is here. I can't believe how beautiful and perfect she is in every way possible. Most of all, I can't believe she is my grandchild.

My husband Walter and I spent the day at the hospital. My son Jeff urged us to go home. "I'll call you when the doctor says something is about to happen," he assured us. Reluctantly, we left.

As we awaited Karaleen's arrival, I kept trying to imagine what it would be like to hold my very own grandchild. But when Jeff placed the baby in my arms shortly after her birth, I can truthfully say that even if I had another whole year to try to imagine the feeling, I wouldn't have been able to do it. There was no way for me to know what it was like until that little one was placed in my arms for the very first time.

I looked into her eyes and she gazed softly back at me. Jeff was standing in front of me. When he spoke, she turned and steadied her gaze on her daddy. She turned her head and again stared directly back at me. We connected immediately, linked by love—and genes!

I wondered: What will she look like, and what will she be like? I remembered asking myself those very same questions as a new mom nearly thirty years ago. I was overcome with emotion and tears spilled onto my face and raced down towards my chin. It was Grandma wearing her heart on her sleeve.

As tiny as she is, Karaleen has already provided insight into her personality. She was due at the end of the month but came two weeks early. At midnight, the doctor said she could be born any minute. Once again, she arrived on her own schedule at 3:27 a.m.

Twelve hours before Karaleen was born, my daughter-in-law Katie was on a monitor that tracked her contractions and Kara's heartbeat. The nurse came in while we were there; we got to hear Karaleen's heartbeat but it was almost drowned out by the pounding of this grandma's heart.

Karaleen, without having ever uttered a word, has captured my heart—a grandma's heart.

~Donna Lowich

18

Ready for Stardust

Nobody can do for little children what grandparents do.
Grandparents sort of sprinkle stardust over the lives of little children.
~Alex Haley

I don't think of myself as a crybaby, though I've whimpered at weddings. Oh, all right, I've sobbed at funerals, and sniveled at graduations. Who doesn't? And, of course, everybody cries at sad movies. Why, I recall once dispatching an annoyed boyfriend to the restroom for tissues when I couldn't stop bawling at the conclusion of *Carousel*.

But when tears trickled down my cheeks in the foyer of St. John Romanian Orthodox Church, everybody in attendance cast a curious glance my way. I mean, who cries at christenings, aside from infants? I felt relieved when baby Kendra obliged with some howls when she was plunged into the baptismal basin, grateful that she'd diverted attention from me. I fished in my purse for a handkerchief to blot my cheeks dry. My step-granddaughter and I had wailed for different reasons. I suspect she just felt cold, while I felt... old.

I'd never expected to become a grandmother, least of all in my seventies. My son, an only child, while still in his teens had told me he didn't anticipate being a dad. A decade later he married a woman who shared his doubts about offspring. The two happily raised cats.

I'd adjusted to a grandchild-free life easily. As a therapist I'd worked for years with infants and toddlers so hadn't missed out on singing lullabies or reading *Curious George*. At high school reunions when former classmates shuffled through photos of grandchildren, I'd nodded politely as they bragged about how beautiful, brilliant and perfectly behaved all their descendants turned out to be. I'd talk about my dogs, and pretend not to see pity fill their eyes when they realized I had no grandchildren of my own.

Then, in my sixties, I met and married a man who had enough grandchildren to fill my calendar pages with birthday reminders. Unfortunately, they all lived half a continent away. I felt a few jealous pangs when girlfriends talked of taking their granddaughters to see *The Nutcracker*, or out for banana splits. Nonetheless, I admitted that babysitting grandkids probably wouldn't be something I'd really relish.

Occasionally we'd see the kids at a family gathering, a graduation or a wedding. My husband claimed he didn't know how to relate to the younger ones, though.

"I never know what to say when I see them," Ken complained. "I can play chess with the older ones, but what in the world do you say to a five-year-old?"

I laughed. "Just invite the child to tell you a story. A five-year-old always has a tale to tell, even if it's just a rehash of 'The Three Bears.' You'll see."

Ken looked doubtful. I noticed that the next time we saw his grandkids, one or two blinked up at him with shining eyes. He'd smile for a minute and then turn away. Still uncomfortable, he didn't ask them to tell stories. Maybe he wasn't interested in hearing about Goldilocks. Though the children called me Grandma Terri, they didn't linger near me for long. I guessed they figured I was just a granny-come-lately, not a real grandma at all.

Then Kendra came along. Ken's middle son, Rick, married in his forties, and his wife, Angela, gave birth last year just weeks after my husband succumbed to cancer. This blessed child was his namesake. At eight months she already had her grandpa's twinkling blue eyes and lopsided smile.

I traveled to Arizona for her christening. I couldn't stop grinning when Rick introduced me to the priest as the grandmother. It was just a few minutes later that it struck me that this baby would be my own bona fide grandchild. I started to plan how I'd get to play with her whenever I could get down to Arizona or lure her parents to Washington. I'd remember every birthday, every Christmas. That's when my grin turned into a grimace and I burst into tears. I'd suddenly realized I wouldn't live long enough to snivel as she graduated from high school. I wouldn't be around to whimper at Kendra's wedding.

I finally pulled myself together. I didn't need to worry about the distant future. I could seize each chance to "grandma" as it came. I could send toys and games and books and cards. I could post photos on my Facebook page. I could display the holiday cards I'd get addressed to "Grandma." I could bore my friends at high school reunions with tales of her antics.

After the christening, one of Ken's old friends approached.

"Were you crying because you missed Ken?"

"Yes," I admitted, crossing my fingers.

It was just a little fib, a little white lie. I missed my husband. Certainly I wish he'd been there with me. But in my heart I knew I cried for all those lost years when I'd never had a chance to sprinkle stardust over grandchildren's lives the way my own grandmothers had over mine.

She's just turned one, but Kendra better watch out. Stardust will be drifting her way soon. I'm prepared to babysit. So she'd better be prepared to see *The Nutcracker* and to eat banana splits. When she gets a little older, I'll rent a video of *Carousel* and we can sniffle together. In the meantime, she can tell me stories. After all, I've waited far too long to find out what happened to Goldilocks.

And though I'm not a crybaby, she shouldn't be surprised if I tear up a little when I give her a welcome hug… or more than a little when it's time to kiss her goodbye.

~Terri Elders

19

A Different Bike Ride

Love is the poetry of the senses.
~Honoré de Balzac

"I just went for a bike ride with my grandson. He giggled as he sat in the basket." Outwardly, I cheered for my friend's joy. But deep inside, a bit of envy trickled in. She can take her grandson everywhere she wants. She can read to him, take him to the park, and watch all his sporting events and graduations.

The thought crossed my mind that should I become a grandmother someday, I'd never be able to achieve that kind of joy. Without eyesight, what would I have to offer my grandchildren?

I dismissed the quandary until the day we received the phone call from my son. "It's a beautiful girl. She weighs 8 pounds, 9 ounces and has lots of black hair."

I jumped to my feet, my heart beating fast at the good news. Hubby and I rushed to the hospital. He held my hand as we walked down the long corridors. Although he was guiding me, my steps went ahead of his.

Once in the room, I could hardly contain my squeal. "Can I hold her?"

I leaned toward the bed and my daughter-in-law placed the warm bundle in my hands. She didn't move, and as her tiny head rested on my arm, I brushed my fingertips across her silky hair, then down to her soft forehead.

That's when a wave of emotions crashed into me. I'll never know what she looks like. I'll never see how her smile makes her face shine. I'll never know if she's looking at me or reaching for me.

Will she know her grandma is limited? What will she expect of me?

Tears burned my eyes. I let some trickle down, and everyone thought they were from joy, but the sudden reality that my grandmother days would be filled with frustration and unfulfilled wishes crushed me.

Months flew by as she cooed and giggled—a delight to my soul. Then at almost one year old, her steps began. Hubby leaned toward me. "She's taking one or two steps toward you."

I extended my arms toward her and her little hand grabbed my index finger.

"Good job, you did it!" Weeks later, those steps multiplied, and running became her favorite thing.

"If you ever need it, I can keep her and take care of her," I said hesitantly to my son and daughter-in-law. Their immediate acceptance gave me such comfort. Then, the time came when I had her all to myself.

I felt for her blouse. "C'mon, sweet thing," I said as I put her on my lap and pinned a couple of small jingle bells to her shirt. She hopped off and my ears followed the sound, telling me where she was.

With each week, each month, she learned to handle her Nana. When navigating through the house, I held my hand out and immediately, her little hand slipped into mine. She doesn't know it, but she now leads me around.

Delighted, I let her take me any place she chooses. We often stop and sit on the floor, cross-legged. That's when all my senses are devoted to her. The books I read to her are my own inventions, my own stories that slip from my mind, exercising the words she already knows.

Sometimes we kneel and I teach her prayers, simple and with few words. I point to parts of the body, and she names them all in English. After a few repetitions, she learns each in Spanish.

Snack time comes about often. "Now the bananas," I say to her while she watches from her high chair. As I chop the pineapple and add blueberries, I talk to her. Then, all ingredients go in the blender for her favorite smoothie. Once I pour it in her cup, I find a straw in the drawer and put it inside; then I grope and find the middle of the tray. As her little fingers hold the cup, in her singsong tone she says, "Thank you, Nana."

"No, sweet baby," my heart wants to say. "Thank you for showing me the joy of being your Nana."

I sing songs to her while I change her diaper and when I get her dressed. Sometimes, I learn the clothes I put on her don't match. She doesn't seem to care, nor do I, because we concentrate on serious playing. And when I accidently bump into an object she stops, and in a high-pitched, angelic voice she asks, "You okay, Nana?"

At twenty months old, does she already know the importance of compassion?

I grope for my shoes, unable to find them. "Nana's shoes," she says as she quickly finds them and attempts to put them on my feet. Did she already learn to help those in need?

When she hands me something, she first calls my name, then places the item in my hand. Without me teaching her, did she learn to overcome her Nana's limitations?

One afternoon, thunder roared outside and we listened with awe. I pointed toward the sky and told her about the clouds. When the storm subsided, I scooped her in my arms and walked outside into a drizzling rain. "Look up, baby girl," I said. "That's rain. Feel how it tickles your face?"

I inhaled an exaggerated deep breath. "Smell that? That's the scent of a wet earth. It's good and fresh."

She mimics all I do, singing the songs I teach her and naming the shapes I hold in my hands. We go back and forth as she rides on my back, and she giggles when her Nana bucks like a horse.

Before naptime, she sits on my lap and I run my fingers across the delicate features of her small face. My mind registers her contour.

"Tickle me, Nana," she pleads. And when I do, I hear her giggle and my heart sees the beauty of her innocence.

My love for her increases as I dismiss my blindness. When she visits, I get on my knees and open my arms to her. It's not long before the pitter-patter sound of her footsteps draws closer and closer until she launches herself into my arms. I hold her tight and we're together, united by that special bond we can both see.

I plan to take her on lots of bike rides too, different than most. And while she sits in the basket of love, I'll point to another kind of scenery—lack of sight doesn't have to keep us from seeing the joy in little things, the wonder in this world, or the beauty that love can bring.

~Janet Perez Eckles

Evan

It's such a grand thing to be a mother of a mother —
that's why the world calls her grandmother.
~Author Unknown

It isn't supposed to be like this. I longed for my only daughter's child. At thirty-one years old, finally, she is pregnant. A grandson is on his way. We are euphoric as we celebrate her seventh month, believing that if he were born early, he would be okay. Then we lose him.

The worst phone call of my life starts with my son-in-law's devastated voice. "Mom. We lost Dylan." I can't breathe. I can't believe. I sink to the stairway, able only to cry, "No, no, no."

My teenage son sits by me, puts his arm around me and says, "God is here, Mom." He consoles me the only way he knows, saying to me the words I said to him many times, thinking at the time that he didn't really hear. My husband stands by waiting to see what he can do.

We plunge into action, packing fresh jeans, energy bars, water, only wanting to get on the road for the hour's journey to Salem, Oregon, where Tricia had gone in for her regular OB check-up. They couldn't find a heartbeat. No heartbeat. The baby is dead before he can even be born.

I enter the birth center. I don't have to identify myself. A nurse leaning against the curved, beige reception counter, with framed pictures of newborn babies, live newborn babies, watches me frantically enter the automatic double doors. She turns immediately toward the welcoming, wide blue hallway and speaks to someone waiting just outside an open, oversize exam room door. "She's here. The mother is here." She says it as if I have some answer, as if there were something I could do to lessen this tragedy.

Supported by her husband, Tricia, normally a strong, confident woman, stumbles out of the exam room into my arms. "I can't do it, Mom. I just can't do it."

Explanations come in a blur from unknown voices.

"We need to induce labor so she can deliver the baby."

"It's better for her than a cesarean."

"It will be more difficult emotionally, but better."

All I can think about is my own baby, grown and facing her own overwhelming grief. I hold her tight and tell her, "You can. You can do this. You are strong, and I am here. God is here." Chris's words are still with me, encouraging me to believe what is difficult to believe because how could this happen if God is really here. I want so badly to help Tricia hold on, be strong, when I can barely manage words.

For three days I wade through Tricia being distant, Tricia clinging, Tricia being brave, Tricia breaking down. I notice a picture of a single rose, a faded picture cut from a magazine and framed in construction paper, on Tricia's birthing room door. No pictures are on the other doors. It is a warning to those who enter that the baby is gone. It is cruel that she must be here in the hall meant for joyful people waiting for their babies. In her large, beige and blue room, with soft lights meant for welcoming a newborn startled to be in the world of light and sound, she waits for her ordeal to end.

I sleep on a window seat, in a chair by Tricia, on the floor. On the third day Dylan is born. On the fifth day, we have a funeral. It's not supposed to be like this.

Tricia recovers, physically. In the next two years, two more pregnancies end in the fourth and fifth months. We lose hope. Tricia's marriage ends. Tricia works out a life on her own, grieving her losses but growing stronger again. I love being Tricia's mother, but have to face never being grandmother to her child.

One year passes, then two years and Tricia meets Rob. A strong, tall quiet man, he blends with our family seamlessly. Then Tricia is again pregnant.

I share with my daughter the joy that comes with this new hope, but also the fear. Doctors are cautious, so we have 3-D ultrasounds from the first trimester. In the waiting room before the first one, the delay is long, Tricia is bordering frantic, so I, flailing for some way to distract her, suggest the alphabet game. We take turns coming up with baby names for our letter of the alphabet. I start. "A for Alan."

Rob goes next. "B for Brandon."

Tricia, laughing at the ridiculousness as we three adults sit across from each other in the two rows of plaid, upholstered chairs playing a kid's game, takes "C for Chris."

I pause at "D for…"

"Dylan," Tricia says firmly. She does not forget her firstborn.

We wear out the baby names and go on to movie titles. "A for *Armageddon*." "B for *Bourne Identity*." We're still naming when the ultrasound tech leads us back to her roomy curtained cubicle full of equipment standing and hanging on all sides. As she prepares Tricia's tummy, she helps out when we're stuck on "Y" with "*Yours, Mine & Ours*."

We hear the baby's heartbeat, but as head measurements take a long time with several repeats, the mood in the room darkens to fit with the lowered lights. Finally, the tech says she wants the doctor to double-check her measurements.

We pretend we're not worried. The doctor says some of the measurements of the baby's brain are abnormal, but that it could mean nothing. He also says we're having a boy. We keep trying to pretend we aren't worried. For seven months we pretend.

On a cold, February morning, Tricia delivers an eight-pound, breathing, healthy red-headed boy. We name him Evan.

Now, a year later, when Evan sees his Grammie, he holds out his arms and toddles hurriedly but unsteadily to me. I scoop him up and his little arms tighten around my neck. I still cry almost every time at the sight of the little boy I thought I would never hold, never change, never hear cry. Is this where God is?

~Sallie Wagner Brown

Grandmothers

Making a Difference

21

Solid Rangers

Uncles and aunts, and cousins, are all very well, and fathers and mothers
are not to be despised; but a grandmother, at holiday time, is worth them all.
~Fanny Fern

t had been more than twenty years since I had gone back to my mother's for Christmas. After I had children, and then grandchildren, the holiday was spent where the children were. But in 1987, my mother was unable to travel, so my daughters and I decided to spend Christmas with her. My stepfather had recently passed away and we couldn't bear the thought of her being alone.

My grandsons were Chris, five, and Ben, seven months. They were the children of my older daughter Karen and her husband Ralph.

We left for Ferriday, Louisiana on the day before Christmas Eve. We took two cars for the trip from Orlando, Florida. My younger daughter Linda and I were in one car, with Karen, Ralph and the boys in the other, except when Chris "visited" our car.

Even though we got an early start, we didn't arrive until nearly eleven o'clock that night, and by the time we decided on sleeping arrangements, made up roll-aways, and got everyone settled, it was nearly one in the morning. The adults were still sleeping soundly when the boys were awake and hungry. It wasn't yet eight o'clock when Karen, Linda, and I met in the kitchen and started to make breakfast.

I was standing at the stove in my mother's kitchen when Karen whispered, "Mom, I know you were really good at hiding Christmas presents from us when we were small, but Ralph and I can't find the stuff from your house."

"Stuff from my house?"

"You know. In the front bedroom closet?" Her eyes widened in panic.

Linda, not one to let a conversation go unheard, came over. "What are you two whispering about?" I looked over my shoulder to see that Chris was trying to hear our discussion, too. I motioned for the girls to follow me.

In the guest bedroom, I turned to Karen. "I wasn't supposed to get the presents from the closet, was I? I thought you got them."

"No, remember I asked you to bring them? We were looking for them because Ralph wanted to start wrapping while we made breakfast."

Oh, no. I thought she got those things. My breathing was shallow and I was suddenly cold.

"Karen, I'm sorry I didn't understand. What's back there? How hard would it be to find the same things here?"

"Ben's presents aren't a problem. But Chris expects one thing in particular—a special set of walkie-talkies. They're called Sonic Rangers, but he calls them Solid Rangers. That's all he's talked about for weeks. The stores at home are sold out. What are the chances of finding them in a small town like this?"

I vaguely remembered Chris talking about solid-something in the car, but I hadn't paid attention at the time.

Linda's face registered shock as she began to understand the situation. "Mom, could you and I drive to Monroe or Jackson? How long would it take?"

"We could. But if we go to Monroe and don't find them, it'll be too late to go somewhere else."

"Mom, Chris will be brokenhearted if he doesn't get those Solid Rangers. We promised him Santa would find us here. We even wrote a letter to Santa explaining where we'd be. We have to have those walkie-talkies."

"I know, sweetie. Let me think a minute."

Ralph came in and we explained the situation.

"I'm so sorry about this, Ralph. I don't know how I could have been so oblivious."

Ralph said, "It was just a misunderstanding, Mom. It could have happened to anybody."

I knew he was trying to make me feel better, but the look on his face showed how troubled he was.

I thought about the options. The longer I thought, the more I knew there was only one answer—get the toys from the closet in my house. If only I could. I reached for the phone book and started dialing.

"What are you doing?" asked Karen.

"I'm calling airlines."

"But there aren't any airports near here."

"There's New Orleans. I can drive down and fly home. If I can get a return flight tonight, we'll be all right."

"But what are the chances of getting there and back on the same day? Even if you can, that'll cost a fortune."

"Well, it was my mistake and I'm the one who needs to fix it. If I can get the flights, that seems like the only thing to do."

"Mom, you can't be serious," said Ralph.

"Yes, I am. I'm willing to do anything in my power to make sure that little boy isn't disappointed in the morning."

On my third call, I found a roundtrip from New Orleans to Orlando that would work, if I could be quick enough in Orlando. I'd have barely enough time to take a cab from the airport to my house, retrieve the packages, and get back to the airport in time for the return flight. Once in New Orleans, I'd then have to drive back up to Ferriday. It was going to be a long day.

I left as soon as I could get dressed. The drive time to New Orleans was ordinarily about four hours, but I knew the roads would be busy with people trying to reach their destinations before the end of the day.

At the airport in New Orleans, I went directly to the ticket counter. When I asked to buy the round-trip tickets, the agent looked up with surprise. "You don't want to return tonight, do you? Didn't you mean another day?"

"No, I need to get back here tonight."

"There's got to be a story here." She raised her eyebrows expectantly.

I told her about the forgotten toys and she said, "You're some determined grandmother, and you're lucky that today is Christmas Eve. If you'd wanted to do this yesterday, you'd have been out of luck. All the flights were full."

In Orlando, I got a cab, explained my mission to the driver and off we went. At my house, I rushed to the closet in the front bedroom. Sure enough, there sat two large bags of toys. I grabbed them and returned to the cab. We got back to the airport with only minutes to spare before the flight boarded.

The drive back to Ferriday was magical; people everywhere seemed to have stepped out of a Norman Rockwell painting, radiating merriment and good wishes. Grandma Santa was "over the hills and through the woods" making her delivery.

I made it back to Mother's at around two in the morning, with only hours to spare. Ralph and Karen still had wrapping and preparing to do.

I was the last one to join the family gathered around the tree on Christmas morning. Chris greeted me with, "Look, Grandma! Santa found me. He brought me Solid Rangers."

"He sure did, Chris." Winks and grins were shared around the room.

A few days later, as we used the Solid Rangers to talk between the cars during the drive home, I knew that flight had been worth every penny.

~Bettie Wailes

22

Sheryl's Gift

When you are sorrowful look again in your heart, and you shall see that in truth you are weeping for that which has been your delight.
~Kahlil Gibran

My eyes filled with tears as I held the strand of yellow, clay beads—a present from my dear friend, Sheryl, decades earlier. I pictured her radiant smile and envisioned her crouched in the garden wearing a gauzy white dress, violet larkspur all around. In the year since her death, when passing a place I associated with her, I still cried. Now, more tears came. Stroking each smooth cylindrical bead I wished, like the genie in the bottle, doing so would bring her back.

I lay the jewelry on the counter. It was time to pick up Aley, Sheryl's seven-year-old granddaughter, for our date. As soon as I arrived she ran toward me, yelling my name in glee. After embracing her, I passed a lavender envelope of remembrance to her father and gave him a long, knowing, heartfelt hug.

Over the past sixteen months, Aley and I waded into rivers and played in parks. We went to movies and theater, fabric and pet stores, Mardi Gras parades, and libraries. We talked about school, friends, family, and her grandmother. She told me she liked to go to my house. When I asked why, she said "'Cuz it feels good there." In my home she gathered frog and turtle figurines and brought them to life with her imagination. It was where we played old maid, watched Woody

Woodpecker cartoons, crafted Christmas ornaments, and dyed Easter eggs with yellow onion skins.

Today, when I felt her squirm beside me, I knew she was ready to go on our outing.

First, we went to the botanical garden where, with the sweet scent of viburnum wafting around us, she had my fifty-five-year-old body crawl over and under and through the arches and tunnels in the children's area. Next, lunch at Dixie Café, the place we'd eaten several times before and came to see as "our special place." Then the movie *Alice in Wonderland*—which I wouldn't have seen otherwise, but really enjoyed. After that, back to our café to top off the day with dessert.

Old Beatles music serenaded us from the sound system as we sat across the booth from each other on vinyl-covered seats. We played "Which of these Five Stylized Line Drawings of Fish Looks Exactly Like the Fish on Top?" on her paper place mat, using a waxy red crayon. I always loved that game. Crayons, too.

She wanted strawberry shortcake; I followed suit. When the desserts came, and after asking her, I scooped most of my whipped cream onto hers. She took a bite and made a big "yum." Looking at her dessert, and scooping up her next bite, she asked, "If Mommy and Daddy die, can I live with you?"

My mind raced. I recalled Sheryl during her chemo treatments, her bald head covered with a crocheted cap, asking me if I wanted to spend time with her granddaughter. It came out of the blue, and I spent several weeks thinking about it. But I never thought about Aley living with us. I wanted to check with my husband, but she needed a response now.

Still thinking, I heard the me that adores her say, "Yes."

My breathing returned. Noticing that she was spooning into the same bite, I was thankful only seconds had passed. I took another breath, smiled big, and added, "I don't think that will happen, but of course you can, sweetheart."

Lifting the spoon to her mouth, she continued.

"Or I could live with Grandma. My other grandma."

Dang. I don't want her to live with her grandmother. I want her to live with us! Shouldn't have taken so long to reply.

My mind filled with all the things I love about Aley. She skips in hallways and sings in the car. When the music in a store moves her, she dances. I want her spontaneous and joyful nature to rub off on me. She's inquisitive — often asking a question to further her intellectual curiosity. Answering her is stimulating. I was privy to witnessing her enchantment with homonyms and watched her progress from sounding out words phonetically, to reading every sign on the road, to pulling a Khalil Gibran book from her purse and reading it to me. Also, raising only one son, I never got any glitz. With Aley come cute colorful girly dresses and glittery shoes.

She offered me part of the cake beneath her strawberries and, after finishing it, I took her home. Continuing on to my house I thought about a recent conversation with a friend who also missed Sheryl. She asked if I was enjoying Aley-time. I said yes, adding that I hadn't realized how good it would be for me.

Her reply was, "Sheryl did."

The beads were lying on the kitchen counter when I got home. I held them close to my heart and kissed them.

~LeAynne Snell

Granny's Cedar Chest

They say genes skip generations. Maybe that's why
grandparents find their grandchildren so likeable.
~Joan McIntosh

Although the brass trim has tarnished over the decades, the wood of my grandmother's cedar chest retains a soft, warm glow and the faint scent of cedar still wafts upward when the lid opens. A treasure trove of family heirlooms lies within the cedar chest and my own talismans mingle with Granny's keepsakes. The worn baby shawl with hand-stitched edging remains within, along with a candy tin filled with dime store jewelry that a young Hazel Hayward wore when she worked as a telephone operator.

Yellowed, thin clippings and brittle photographs capture fragments of lives and preserve moments of the past. I can open any of the albums and thumb through to watch my own life unfold in Kodak clarity. Through these old photographs I can also catch a momentary glimpse of the past, of the world that once was reality.

There are too many items to count, to tally, but there is one artifact that is most important, a single item that has the most meaning for me because it sparked my career as a writer and sustains it. The manuscript is fragile and the ink is faded, the ink that was once stark, fresh black on new pages written over with great care. One corner of the faded manuscript remains tied with a red ribbon now softened to a dusky pink by time. I can read the title and the entire work with ease although my fingers handle the precious paper with a light touch so that I do not destroy my Granny's one work as a writer, the Class Prophecy she penned in 1912.

Class prophecies were the vogue in the year that the Titanic sank beneath the waters of the north Atlantic and hers is written in the flowery, delicious style of the times. Most graduating classes had one, the work of a single student that attempted to foretell the future of their classmates.

Written in the first person, my grandmother's work lives and breathes life into the long dead youth who finished school with her that spring. I was fourteen, little younger than she when I first read it. Then, as now, I was awed by the power of the words, the unknown gift of my grandmother.

My own yearning to become a writer came early and I scribbled stories as soon as I learned how to hold a pencil. As a teenager, I hoped that someday I might write words that could touch others but it was a secret dream I kept close.

Granny knew me, however, almost as well as her own heart and so she opened the cedar chest to reveal that old manuscript. I read it with amazement, unaware that the grandmother who wore aprons over her house dresses, the woman whose hands were gnarled and worn with years of toil, had once shared my dream. Dust motes floated in the afternoon sunlight that filled the bedroom that my father once shared with his brother, and tears burned in my eyes as I asked why she had not become a writer.

"I couldn't." Her words were soft and simple but they spoke volumes. She couldn't; she had gone to work soon after that eighth grade graduation. By the time that the World War involved America, she had been a telephone operator. Later, after dial phones eliminated many operators, she went to work in a hospital laundry, a job she held until soon after my birth. She had also raised three sons, sent two of them off to World War II, and buried a husband. She married again in an autumn romance to my beloved Pop, the grandfather connected to me through love if not blood.

I stared at this remarkable little woman, unable to speak... but she could. "I couldn't but you should."

Her words were both benediction and challenge. It was a gauntlet tossed down to spur me and it has. Had she been able to attend high school or college, she might have become a noted writer but there is no "might" or "could" in real life. She had not but I could.

My dream had once been hers and on that day the torch was passed from one generation to another. I made a promise that I would not marry until I finished my education—high school and college. And, I made a vow that I would strive to take words and make them sing, that I could succeed.

The road to becoming a full-time writer has been long and filled with obstacles, but when tempted to falter, I would remember that manuscript, that dream and press onward.

Granny's cedar chest now graces my living room. Within its burnished depths, that manuscript remains, testament to a dream and foundation to my career as a writer.

She couldn't but I have—because of her dream.

~Lee Ann Sontheimer Murphy

24

Brandon's New Life

> *He conquers who endures.*
> ~Persius

see the skateboard every time I walk into our garage — a sad reminder of another time. It was left at our house by our grandson one Christmas. He will not use it again. Brandon is now a quadriplegic confined to a wheelchair.

One Sunday around 1:30 a.m. our phone gave a shrill ring. My husband and I both sat up in bed and I dived for the phone. "Brandon had an accident," our son said. "The doctor says he's paralyzed."

While running on an inflatable obstacle at an after-prom party, fifteen-year-old Brandon fell, landing on his head. Instantly he lost feeling in his legs. One of the chaperones, a doctor, kept him still until the paramedics arrived.

Later that Sunday I flew 800 miles to be with Brandon and, because I am a retired nurse, the family asked me to stay with him during his time in a rehabilitation hospital. I didn't doubt that I could learn to help care for Brandon, yet nothing prepared me for those almost three months we spent together. As Brandon learned to deal with his new life as a quadriplegic, I learned there are no limits to a teenager's perseverance and endurance.

The rehab nurses taught me to suction Brandon's tracheotomy. While I knew I was helping him get rid of unwanted secretions, seeing him gag and choke on the catheter unnerved me. Twice a day I helped get Brandon in a sling, lower him into a wheelchair, and take him to physical therapy. There, the therapists and I got the sling under him again and lifted him to the mat where his lifeless limbs were exercised. If the whole process seemed tedious to me, what did it seem like to Brandon? However, he didn't complain.

Three times a day Brandon and I went together to the dining room where I attempted to feed him. But often waves of nausea came over him, and we had to leave before I got two bites in his mouth.

While Brandon spent time in rehab, his high school friends came in droves and I learned many of their names. They didn't seem threatened by the respirator or IVs attached to Brandon. After a few visits they would even help suction and turn him.

Every evening after the nurses had settled Brandon for sleep, he and I watched a movie — the same one every night, *Gladiator*. It was the story of a young warrior in ancient times who had many battles to fight to gain victory over his enemies. We forgot catheters, IVs and wheelchairs as the young man on the TV screen slew the villains in his path. After an exhausting day of physical therapy and breathing treatments, we both needed the escape.

Most nights I slept in the same room with Brandon. As I listened to his even breathing, I begged God to heal his bruised spinal cord. And in dreams, I pictured the tiny nerves reconnecting and sensation returning to my grandson's legs and feet. But over time my prayer changed and I said, "God, help Brandon to find a purpose for this new life. Please give him a cause to live for."

"We're going to the zoo on Friday. Want to come along, Brandon?" The occupational therapist stuck her head around the door of Brandon's room one morning. The zoo? Was she crazy? She wasn't joking. The patients, most of them on respirators, with tubes and catheters of every description, were wheeled into vans and taken to the city zoo for an outing. As the sun baked down on Brandon's pale face, I pushed him in his wheelchair on a gravel path and through dull eyes he gazed at polar bears and giraffes. I understood the concept — the patients needed to get away from the hospital, yet the whole process seemed like a lot of work to me.

But Brandon got the idea, and the next week we piled into a van with other patients bound for miniature golf. How can these people hit a golf ball when most of them can't even lift a fork to their mouths, I wondered. Again Brandon gave it his best swing. The laughs we shared during those games had nothing to do with golf. For a few minutes Brandon forgot the limitations of a wheelchair and, like any teen, enjoyed the outdoors with friends.

As part of Brandon's physical therapy, he was encouraged to dig with a hand trowel in a tiny plot of ground built level with his wheelchair. He and I laughed as his weak hand made a few scratches in the black dirt. "This is what you've always wanted to do, isn't it?" I said as I watched. How many teenage boys want to plant garden seeds? Yet, uncomplaining, Brandon dug until the trowel dropped from his exhausted hand.

One day the therapist announced that we'd spend the afternoon on the front steps of the hospital and, with Brandon in the chair, I learned the fine art of getting him up and down stairs in his wheelchair. For two hours I huffed and puffed, jerking, and jostling Brandon in his chair. That night we both fell into bed exhausted.

Soon Brandon's time in the rehab hospital ended. He returned to his home and high school. I also went home knowing life for neither of us would ever be the same. And I continued to pray our grandson would find purpose and meaning for his life as he viewed it from a wheelchair.

My prayer was answered recently when, through misty eyes, I watched a confident, handsome young man, with plans for his future, maneuver his wheelchair across a stage to receive his college degree.

~Jewell Johnson

25

Chicken Soup
for the Soul

Becoming a Second Generation Parent

Life is what happens while you are busy making other plans.
~John Lennon

My husband Paul and I sat across the courtroom from his son Andrew and his girlfriend Tammy. Our lawyer sat beside us, the familiar yellow legal pad and expandable folder in front of her.

Andrew's extremely short hair was dyed black. Small sores and scabs peppered Tammy's arms and face; she'd been scratching at imaginary insects crawling on her skin again.

These sights did not compare though with the smell... their water had been shut off for almost an entire year. How they had lived in those conditions for so long was incomprehensible to Paul and me. The stench slapped us in the face the moment they entered and I stifled a gag as we rose to our feet as the judge entered.

After a small recess, the judge made his ruling. Two and a half million grandparents in this country are raising their grandchildren. Paul and I had just been added to those numbers.

Three years ago, I had my life planned. I was finishing my teaching degree, a dream I had had since I was a child. I had married a wonderful man whose children were already adults, and I had my daughter, Sarah, a high school sophomore. Life wasn't perfect but it was going along at a steady pace.

And then we got the phone call.

Andrew was Paul's older child and since we had been together, Paul had battled with Andrew over his substance abuse. We knew Andrew had a problem, but until he wanted to change, there wasn't anything we could do. It seemed as though he was getting his life on track that year; he had a decent construction job and he and his long-time girlfriend, Tammy, had just had a baby boy.

Unfortunately, we only saw Andrew and Sam a couple of times in the next few months. Andrew would give us excuses as to why we couldn't come by or take Sam for a visit. As new grandparents, Paul and I were hurt but optimistic that we could mend the rift in our family over time.

In February of 2007, I got a call from Child Protective Services. What they told me still makes me shudder, thinking of how Paul and I had been so oblivious to all the signs. The caseworker told us that Sam had tested positive for methamphetamines and THC (the drug in marijuana) at birth and had been taken away from Andrew and Tammy. Andrew hadn't even mentioned that Paul and I existed, and instead signed over temporary custody to Tammy's parents.

That same month everything changed when Tammy's parents tested positive for substance abuse as well. "We can either place Sam with you, or he will go into foster care," the caseworker told me in a matter-of-fact way.

I stood there with the phone clutched tightly in my hand staring at Paul's questioning face. "I understand," I choked out. "Could I call you back after I speak to my husband?" I hung up and turned to Paul. As I explained what she had told me, I could see Paul's heart breaking. "What should we do?" I asked him quietly.

"We really don't have any other choice but to bring him home with us," he answered, echoing my own thoughts.

A week later, we stood outside a small two-story house in the bitter north Texas wind. The yard was strewn with broken toys and trash. Dead weeds scratched against the side of the porch. The door's paint, blistered and peeling, reminded me of a three-day-old sunburn. I had never been to Tammy's parents' home, and its condition shocked me. This is where our grandson had been living?

As we entered the front room, my eyes quickly adjusted to the sight; a full-size bed, two playpens, and a small bassinet cluttered the small area. In the bassinet, shoved up against the television, a small bundle was squirming. I looked down into the crib to see Sam's blue eyes smiling up at me. "Why hello there, little one," I greeted him, and was quickly rewarded with a huge smile. I knew instantly that I would do whatever I could for this precious child.

We couldn't take him with us that day, which tore Paul and me to pieces. Over the next two weeks, along with my class schedule, Paul's work, and Sarah's school activities, we were also meeting with CPS, scheduling our own drug testing to prove we were clean, and trying to remember all the necessary items needed for a baby. At the end of March, just before Paul's birthday, Sam came home with us.

Andrew and Tammy had signed over temporary custody to Paul and me, and our hope was that this crisis would be the shock they needed to get straight. However, by June it was evident that they had no intention of changing their lifestyle or getting clean to get Sam back. Our CPS caseworker suggested we find a lawyer and Paul and I agreed.

In May of 2008, the judge awarded us full custody of Sam. Through research, I discovered that babies born to mothers addicted to meth can seem sluggish and have uncontrollable tremors. I learned that these babies have a higher risk of stroke before being born. Luckily, Sam is relatively healthy, and Paul and I monitor him closely for any signs that his development is lagging behind that of other children his age. While his development was slow in the beginning, he is now an active, happy three-year-old. Unfortunately, not enough research has been done on the long-term effects of methamphetamines on children.

Thankfully, Paul and I managed to weather this storm without any major damage to our marriage, but getting Sam came at a cost. Paul, who had dreams of retiring once I began teaching, had to change jobs to support the costs of a new baby. I had hoped to finish college in 2008, but I wasn't able to take summer classes and care for Sam at the same time. While our life hasn't worked out the way we planned, Paul and I would not have it any other way. We are amazed at how this little guy makes us feel both old and young at the same time. And while we might have to postpone our retirement plans of travel and relaxation, our new adventures with Sam will be priceless.

~Christine Long

A Little Pink Sock

Grandmas hold our tiny hands for just a little while, but our hearts forever.
~Author Unknown

I found the sock under the den sofa. It was tiny—tinier than I could have imagined—and pink. So I knew it had to belong to Carly.

Something about the size of that sock—an anklet with ribbing—stopped me in my tracks. It reminded me of just how small and vulnerable this youngest granddaughter is—and of her relative scale in this big old world.

Carly is the baby of our family—the youngest grandchild who, at four, is constantly thrust into the larger world of her own big sister, a mighty five, and her assorted cousins. She gravitates towards Hannah, the presumably omnipotent oldest cousin who can save this little girl with the huge blue eyes from all peril.

When the grandkids are together for family parties and holidays, Carly somehow looks even smaller. She seems to disappear in the mêlée, trying desperately to keep up, and succeeding only some of the time. That's when she turns to Hannah, as supplicant.

What Carly doesn't say aloud is "Save me!" But something about the way she looks imploringly at her biggest cousin says it all.

I held that pink sock in my hand and started to remember how it felt to be small, vulnerable, and thrust into the world. I, too, was the baby of the family. I also was short—always the kid who was first in line when the line was based on height. I was the kid who had to strain to look over the head of the kid in front of me.

But back to Carly.

I suspect that her place in the extended family will have an impact on her personality and her sense of self. I suspect that less isn't always more when it comes to mingling with the "big guys," as this diminutive little girl calls her family confrères.

And how they treat this littlest one tells me a great deal about who these grandchildren are. Reactions to Carly range from tender to tough, with some of the boy cousins being a bit menacing, no doubt a reaction to their place in the world.

I wish I could save Carly from her fears—she is terrified of bees, large dogs and more recently, new places. When we took her to a gigantic stadium recently for a kiddie show, she froze when she saw the crowds, the lights and heard the din.

"I want to leave now!" she said emphatically, and not even her brave big sister could reassure her that all would be fine.

So Carly and I spent the first half of the show wandering the perimeter of the stadium. She clutched my hand every time she heard the distant roar of the crowd, and begged not to ever have to go into that "bad place" again.

How quickly we forget that the fears of the young are not rational, not reasonable and never predictable. Stages and phases come and go, bravery with them. What once was terrifying—the roller coaster, thunder, the ocean—can become thrilling. And what was thrilling can turn ho-hum.

Because we are so far from the stage of life when planet Earth seems a place inhabited by giants—when dogs and birds and even bugs can be menacing—it's sometimes tough to get into the heads of the very young among us. "This won't hurt you!" we attempt, but the words can't chase the demons. A hug may. A hasty retreat from the perceived danger may. And scooping up the fearful one in your arms almost always does the trick.

I'm planning to return Carly's sock to her the next time I see her—which can never be soon enough.

Meanwhile, I'm keeping it near me as a reminder of what we grandmothers owe our young.

Safety. A sense of being watched over. Loving arms.

And the awareness that every child deserves a hand on the long, tough journey to becoming a "big guy."

~Sally Schwartz Friedman

27

Not a Poem

A grandchild fills a space in your heart that you never knew was empty.
~Author Unknown

I cannot write
the poem about my grandson
for it would be saccharin and oozing
with obnoxious superlatives

I would have to leave out the part
that describes how his little foot fits
so soundly into the palm of my hand
that I want to place it inside my chest

I cannot write the poem
about my grandson
no one would want to read it

no one wants to know
how he charmed the other children
at the park today
and splashed in his bath
with joyful abandon

no one wants to hear about
the startling blue of his eyes

the feathers of his fair hair
the silk of his cheek

I cannot write this poem
because I do know
that other people
have grandchildren too
who crawl into their laps
book in hand and
snuggle in

but
this one
this little boy
can crack open my heart with his perfection
can make me laugh with his antics
can make me ache
for what I cannot give him

a mother
and
a poem

~Jane Ebihara

Editor's Note: Jane's thirty-three-year-old daughter-in-law died of cancer when her son, Jane's only grandchild, was three months old. The baby is now a toddler and thrives in the arms of his loving father with the help of a devoted village of family and friends.

28

Passages in Stone

Little children, headache; big children, heartache.
~Italian Proverb

When couples hike in all kinds of weather and terrain they develop a special intimacy built on those experiences. They learn about each other in an environment far removed from normal domestic life. There is not a lot of veneer on a person when he or she is wet and cold and struggling to continue on a long trail. They learn each other's quirks related to preparation, and each other's facility to recuperate from pain, as well as the strength they pull up from deep inside when the trail is hardest and the going most difficult.

Shirley and I hiked together for six wonderful years in many diverse locations in the West. We were older when we met; she was a grandmother and I was in my fifties. We forged a relationship built on weekend hiking trips that gave us plenty of satisfaction and also showed us a lot of fine country that we never would have seen otherwise. It also grew in us that special intimacy borne of hard hours on the trail.

On every trip Shirley would collect a couple of stones. These were not stones of any geologic value, but rather rocks with interesting shapes and swirls or those with varied colors or patterns. When we would reach the summit, or were halfway, or even when taking a needed rest, she would peruse the ground looking for stones of interest. She would pick one up and run it through her fingers, turning it over and around on her palm to inspect it in detail. If the stone met the standards of some ineffable criteria, she deposited it in her daypack for transport back home.

Two fates awaited these stones on our return. A stone could be deposited in the great urn by the fireplace that held other stones from other trips, or, if it was special enough, it was set aside for Chad, the younger of her two grandsons by her son Danny. When Chad was six or seven he started to enjoy looking at rocks with Grandma, whether it was at a family outing at the beach or in the mountains.

So it was that Shirley shared these stones with Chad. They held them and inspected them and Shirley would relate the story of their origin in detail. She would describe where the stone was from and what the weather was like, what the trip had entailed. Chad enjoyed this and it gave his grandma a chance to interact with him and to look inside the boy as he grew. It also allowed Chad a look inside his grandmother, whether or not he knew or appreciated it at the time.

The stone collection also kept the connection between Shirley and Chad intact as Chad grew up. Shirley never felt she had enough time with her grandsons, so when the opportunity presented itself, Shirley would use the stones to connect to Chad.

And so they appeared, stone after stone. Small rough stones came from the high passes of Yosemite, and rounded stones came from its watercourses and waterfalls. From Death Valley came samples from the low salt flats of Badwater to the high trails in the Panamint Mountains, and from the craters of Ubehebe. We gathered them from every area of the Pinnacles National Monument; from beaches at Morro Bay to the coast at Malibu, from the Los Padres to the San Gabriel Mountains came small pieces of wonder to hold and describe. She gathered them where we hiked in Southern California: in the Cuyamaca and Laguna mountains, the wonderful Anza-Borrego Desert, and in Palm Springs.

One hot summer day we were on a hiking trail above Donner Canyon on Mount Diablo east of San Francisco. It was dry and dusty and we were pushing a real sweat as we trudged our way higher up the slope with Shirley out in front. She stopped at a turn on the trail and looked down at something in front of her. She bent over and picked up a small dark stone with three bands across it. She first ran her fingers over it and then studied it as it lay in the palm of her hand. Then, with a look of sadness that she tried to conceal from me, she slowly tossed it off to the side of the trail.

Things change, and time moves on. Chad was now almost a teenager, and the wonder over his grandmother's stones and the stories of where they came from was now of little interest to him. He had crossed a threshold leading to adulthood and the door of that threshold was closed forever; gone with it was the portal that had connected Chad and Shirley in such an illuminating way these last six years.

The look on Shirley's face was one of pain and resignation. I walked up the trail to her side and there in the sun-drenched day we embraced. For everyone, feelings of anguish come to us like this throughout our lives. We need to see these passages for what they are, appreciate them for what they were, and then let them go. There is beauty in what is brief, and for those formative years that were so important to Shirley, those stones gave her special access to the young man growing up before her.

We stood there for a second on the trail sharing the moment. We turned and, lifting our faces from the stones at our feet, gazed over the canyon spreading out below us as the peaks and ridges rose up into the blue sky above. Then we continued up the trail to whatever awaited us there.

At home, the urn of stones sits by the fireplace.

~Laudizen King

29

Life

A grandmother is a babysitter who watches the kids instead of the television.
~Author Unknown

"Hurry up! We're going to miss the bus," I heard my seven-year-old grandson yell to his younger sister. She came hurrying out of the bathroom just in time to grab her school bag and run out the door to the waiting bus.

"Whew!" I said out loud to myself, crumbling into the nearest chair with a sigh. I had forgotten how difficult it is to get two children ready for school in the morning. I reached for my cold cup of cocoa and decided to drink it that way rather than get up on my already tired feet to make a fresh cup. I finished reading the Charlotte newspaper, with my feet up on the footstool, keeping an ear out for the "little one" who was still asleep.

A little while later, while I was in the kitchen washing up the breakfast dishes, I heard soft footsteps coming down the stairs very slowly. I went around the corner into the foyer where I was greeted with a sleepy, "Hungry, Nonie!"

I swooped the little guy up and carried him to the kitchen stool that had his name on the back. He plopped himself down. Then the curly blond-headed toddler looked at me with sparkling blue eyes and flashed a smile that went straight to my heart—a heart that he had owned since the day he was born almost three years ago.

"Life, Nonie," he said, pointing to one of the three boxes of cereal in the open cabinet.

I poured some of the cereal into his Thomas the Tank Engine bowl and asked if he wanted milk in his cereal. He replied, "Cup, Nonie," as if I should know that he wanted his cereal dry and that the milk went in his cup.

I watched him carefully pick up squares of Life with his long thin fingers, hesitating before he plucked each one from the bowl. He seemed determined to select just the right one each time.

I thought of the surgeon's long fingers—at this moment performing a thyroidectomy on his mother, my daughter. I could only pray that the surgeon was as precise and careful as my grandson, who innocently ate his breakfast while his mother began her fight against the cancer that had recently been diagnosed.

The quiet toddler finished off his bowl of Life cereal, then proceeded to empty his Thomas cup, drinking all the cold milk—down to the last drop. He wiped his mouth on his *Cars* pajama sleeve, looked up at me and said "Queen, Nonie!"

I had been forewarned that the movie *Cars* was his favorite movie, but that he called it "Queen" for some unknown reason. It was already in the DVD player, ready to go.

I washed his long fingers carefully, then lifted this precious child into my arms, holding him close to my chest so he wouldn't see the tears in my eyes.

Four months later, I was again with these wonderful children. The older two were eating a not-so-healthy breakfast of donuts and orange juice, while the little toddler was still asleep in the next room. I was trying to adjust the picture on the television set when I sensed someone behind me. Turning around, I saw my little grandson, rubbing the sleepiness from his eyes. He stopped, cocked his head to one side, looked up at me and asked, "Where is my mama?"

I happily replied, "She's somewhere in Disney World, running the marathon that I am trying to find on the TV. When your healthy mother gets back, she and your daddy are going to take all of you to the park to ride the rides."

He smiled and crawled into my lap with a sigh. I pray that I can keep him safe and this close to me forever!

~Frances R. Ruffin

Her Turn

Kindness, like a boomerang, always returns.
~Author Unknown

The first time I met them, I was nervous. I didn't know what to expect but I desperately wanted their approval. The prospect of meeting my future in-laws was enough to make me seriously doubt my qualifications. Would they like me? Would they measure me against the possibility of better offers for their grandson? Would they secretly wish for someone else, or would they actually welcome me into the family? Instead of sizing me up and down, Jack pulled me in for a great big hug and Joan handed me a beautiful afghan—handmade, with special colors and patterns chosen just for me.

I have to admit; at first their gestures were a little foreign to me. Not having spent much time with my own grandparents growing up, I didn't quite know how to respond to their generosity. The time and energy Joan had poured into my blanket both honored and inspired me. No one had ever given me a gift like that and I was humbled by the weight of the warmth it offered. Each stitch symbolized a moment of time she had spent thinking of me, and every intricate design embodied another gesture of unexpected kindness.

Jack and Joan were no strangers to welcoming others into their family. After raising five children of their own, they adopted another little boy—their grandson, my future husband. Selflessly putting aside plans for retirement, they took on another generation of PTA meetings, slumber parties, Boy Scouts, and private school tuition.

The kitchen table became another neighborhood hangout, and the stove rarely cooled between indulgent homemade feasts. Love wafted through the air in the form of lingering aromas of fried chicken, biscuits and gravy, and Joan's infamous coffee-glazed doughnuts. I've been told several stories of late night doughnut feeds that would have provided enough nourishment for a small country.

While they'd only say, "He was no trouble at all," I'm forever indebted to them for their years of servitude and self-sacrifice. Their lessons of love shaped my husband into the man he is now. Together, the two of them showed him what a home founded on grace and unlimited acceptance looks like. They taught him to have integrity and helped him create unending memories of laughter and adventure. Their faith provided an anchor of hope and their patience formed a foundation of gentle leadership that guides our marriage today.

Over thirty years ago, they stepped into a difficult situation, and altered history. With no regard for themselves, they created a potential that will reach generations to come. When they choose to take in their grandson, they chose to adopt me as well. When they changed his life, they forever transformed mine too. I couldn't be more thankful for the example they have given us. They have shown us what it looks like to stand firm in conviction, persevere with patience, and commit in spite of uncertainty. I'm always moved by their gracious understanding and constant support, and our children and grandchildren will be blessed because of a decision Jack and Joan made decades before they existed.

This last year Jack lost his battle with heart disease and medical complications, and left Joan to carry on without him. The house is empty now, and Joan is alone for the first time in her life—without the responsibility of caring for children, grandchildren, or an ailing husband. Her tears are many and her heartache is raw and unbearable at times. Still, she remains steadfast in expectation and confident in hope. Somehow, her care and concern for her family continues, as she prays blessings and guidance over all of us. She daily seeks to wrap her tenderness and attention around us, and never ceases to offer encouragement and support when we need it most.

Although we could never come close to repaying the depth of her compassion and affection, it's her turn to be adopted now. It's her turn to be pulled in and comforted; and like the afghans she has meticulously stitched for others, it's her turn to be wrapped in the safety and security of those who cherish her. When the chill of love lost pierces her heart, it's her turn to be taken in and consoled. Jack's departure is an experience that can't be mended this side of Heaven, but my fervent prayer is that her years of unconditional love and moments of immeasurable pain will be met by a blanket of peace that wraps around her soul and gently begins to heal her heart.

Thank you Joan, for adopting your grandson, for welcoming me into the family, and for faithfully standing beside us. But, now, it's our turn to return the favor.

~Kara Johnson

31

Chicken Soup for the Soul

Grandma's Trade Secret

If nothing is going well, call your grandmother.
~Italian Proverb

n the African-American community, there is an old, albeit incorrect, notion that hair is like cholesterol—there are good and bad versions. Fortunately, as the granddaughter of the late Edna Tucker, I never paid much consideration to said labels because when Grandma Tucker did your hair the only possible way it could come out was good.

I didn't know how she did it; I only knew that when divine intervention (my grandma's hands) touched charcoal-colored wool (my hair), the end result would be one that defied logic. And, much to my delight, I also knew that I could depend on this. It was a constant. Like stars in the sky, cartoons on Saturday mornings, and first-day-of-school jitters.

It was a particularly hot and steamy evening in late August of 1989, and I was very, very concerned. As I snapped the new fluorescent-colored folders into my Trapper Keeper and then splayed my brand new outfit across the chair in my room, I mindfully kept one eye on what was going on outside. The clouds were dark and ominous, and the air was thick and heavy with humidity. On an ordinary day, this wouldn't have bothered me, but this was no ordinary day. I was, in fact, preparing for what I then considered to be a life-altering occurrence: junior high. And the prospect of facing this momentous experience with unruly hair that resembled—in my own words—"cotton candy poofs," was unthinkable. My mother, bless her heart, knew what was at stake here. "You'd better call Grandma," she said.

My mother was spot on because no one could do hair like Grandma. Grandma's prowess in the hair beautification department was like the eighth wonder of the world. No, Grandma wasn't a card-carrying hairdresser, but as the mother of four daughters, she had certainly learned a trick or two.

"Grandma," I pleaded into the phone. "Can you come over and do my hair?"

She waited a beat, sighed, and then replied with a giggle, "Sure, sugar. I'm on my way."

I am not exaggerating when I say that my pulse returned to its normal rate as soon as I saw Grandma ambling up the walkway with her big black canvas tote bag filled with her arsenal of tools.

The enemy? Frizz. And it didn't stand a chance.

Having just washed and blown dry my hair, I sat patiently at the kitchen table as Grandma drew items from the bag and laid them before me on a pink cotton towel: A jar of pomade with a well-worn label; a black plastic comb; a few sheets of paper towel; a portable stove; and, last but certainly not least, a pressing comb. Anticipation welled up inside me as I watched my grandmother plug the tiny metal stove into a nearby outlet and place the pressing comb inside the stove's opening. As she waited for the pressing comb to heat up, she began to divide my hair into four sections and carefully apply the pomade. The sheer thought that, within an hour's time, my hair would become bone straight, silky, and shiny had my stomach turning over like a rotisserie chicken.

Finally, Grandma would run a piece of paper towel along the back of the comb and an ever-so-faint caramel line would appear: The comb was ready. She then proceeded to gently work the comb through various parts of my hair while I remained as still as a block of ice. I did manage to hold up a mirror from time to time in hopes of catching a glimpse of Grandma's trade secret, that indiscernible thing she did that made all her tools work that much better, but I was left scratching my head every time (no pun intended). Afterward, I helped Grandma pack up her things and we'd sit and chat about what I had considered to be items of utter importance: running track, algebra, and my crush on a boy named Billy. When the time came, I kissed her goodbye, most appreciative that my dark mane now danced about my shoulders—and that someone had tolerated my rambling about a boy whose name I am surprised I still remember.

It rained like the dickens on the first day of seventh grade, but my hair remained intact. I still have no idea how Grandma did it. My grandma passed away in 1991—a few years after that memorable humid evening, and a few years before I began to straighten my own hair. My mother and her sisters still maintain that the secret was in Grandma's wrist: "It was the way she turned the comb," my mother says, flicking her wrist with a closed fist.

I tend to agree. Sure, Grandma's wrist played a part. But her heart was in it, too.

~Courtney Conover

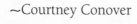

Chapter
4

Grandmothers

Grand Friends

32

The Day Nono Said Yes

*I don't intentionally spoil my grandkids. It's just that correcting them
often takes more energy than I have left.*
~Gene Perret

Some kids call their grandmother Nana but not us. We called our grandma Nono. An Irish immigrant who'd come here when her mother died, she'd seen bad times. She didn't smile much and seemed determined to instill the fear of God in her four granddaughters. Being the youngest, I'd been warned by my sisters not to make her mad. My two older sisters, Linda and Vicki, liked to tell me about the time Nono broke her hairbrush on Linda when they spent the weekend with my grandparents. It seems that Linda had found a Toni perm kit and gotten up in the middle of the night to perm Vicki's hair. Before Linda could finish the treatment, Nono woke up. Finding the two making quite a mess, she went into a rage, allegedly breaking her brush on Linda.

I needed no further convincing and was positive that we called her Nono because she was always saying "No! No!" to everything we did.

One day, when I was four and my sisters were at school, Nono babysat me. Mom was at one of her ladies' club luncheons or fashion shows.

After lunch, Nono put me in my crib although I was clearly outgrowing it. Outside my bedroom, I could hear her switch on her program, *As the World Turns*. She loved to see what that wicked

Lisa was up to and would gossip about her as if she lived in the neighborhood.

I was bored and not the least bit sleepy. I began to wiggle the bars on my well-worn crib. Having seen many years of use by my sisters and now me, they were loose. At first, they only wiggled from side to side, but I experimented. When I lifted the top bar a bit, the two vertical bars in the center dropped down almost an inch. Interesting! Next I used one hand to hold up the top bar while my other jiggled the loose bars below. First one bar and then the other pulled out of the top slot and into my crib. I couldn't believe it; I'd actually broken free! I could easily fit through the hole where the bars had been. I paused. That hairbrush story always made me consider carefully any actions that might set off Nono.

Yet the TV soap opera blared and I heard Nono direct a caustic remark at Lisa. What really compelled me to take a chance on my newfound freedom was the bag of Oreos Mom had in the kitchen drawer. I'd have to sneak past Nono in the living room but if I made it… Nirvana!

Getting out of the crib was a cinch. I was tall enough to step easily to the ground. These were my last steps as I reverted to my old crawl, hoping to evade Nono's eagle eyes.

Silently I crawled along the hallway carpet and saw Nono's side profile as she focused on our grainy black and white TV. As she stared, entranced by the small screen, I decided to go for it.

I would crawl beneath the piano bench alongside the wall nearest me. Once I got to the piano's front edge, I would be out of her line of vision. I proceeded slowly and silently, thankful for the TV's melodramatic dialogue for drowning out any sound my tiny movements might have made.

Under the bench, I proceeded undetected until I rounded the piano corner and rested on my haunches. I was hidden from view now.

The dining room opening was but a few short feet away from me now, but to get there I would have to move perilously close to the TV. The TV trance that had been my friend up to this moment now threatened to expose me. I froze as I heard the chair creak behind me.

Nono was out of her chair now. I pictured her in a rage above me, possibly with a hairbrush in hand.

I waited until I heard the flush of our large tank toilet. That was it. I seized my chance! Leaping up from my fearful crouch, I ran to the kitchen. Here my bare feet made sounds on the linoleum floor. I flattened my body behind the doorjamb as Nono returned to her comfortable chair.

I faced a veritable treasure trove… the cookie drawer! I waited for the laundry detergent commercial to end so as to assure Nono's total TV concentration.

Bob and Lisa were flirting so it was safe to make my move. Ever so gingerly I pulled the drawer open an inch or two. It dragged, making a rubbing sound. I stopped and waited for the yell to come. It didn't.

Instead, the soap stars bailed me out by raising their voices in one of their daily arguments. Quickly I pulled the drawer out another inch. The open bag of Oreos was clearly visible and my hand was small enough to reach into the partial opening and nab a handful of scrumptious cookies.

I could almost taste the creamy white filling as I lowered my anxious paw. The bag's opening required a gentle prying apart and I gladly obliged, creating the unmistakable crackle of a plastic bag. Just my luck, Lisa was taking a pregnant pause or exchanging a meaningful glance at that very moment. The TV that had served as my cover had abandoned me in my moment of need with its sudden, unexpected silence.

The dreaded yell paralyzed me. "What are you getting into?" Nono hollered.

"Oreos," was my terrified reply.

"Bring me some," she said, all anger mysteriously evaporating.

My eyes widened at the request. Was this a trap? Was there a hairbrush anywhere near the recliner?

"O-kay," I haltingly replied.

Grabbing four cookies, I entered the living room in a sort of death march toward my grandmother. She extended her long fingers toward me, taking just two of the cookies from my hand.

"Umm, these are good," she said after her first bite. "Get the bag."

"Okay," I replied in disbelief. Afraid to turn my back on her, I moonwalked back to the cookie drawer.

Two hours later, my sisters returned home from school. Three jaws dropped as they stared at me in Grandma's lap. She was telling me a story and laughing... giggling really... over a girlhood memory.

My fear of Nono was gone. My sisters remained wary but I'd seen the kid in her and now we could enjoy the pleasure of each other's company.

~Marsha Porter

The Snitch

Our grandchildren accept us for ourselves, without rebuke or effort to change us, as no one in our entire lives has ever done, not our parents, siblings, spouses, friends — and hardly ever our own grown children.
~Ruth Goode

My son and his family live in Australia, which makes being a grandma quite challenging. When the children were little, my husband and I were teachers and didn't have enough money to visit the kids very often. But every two years during our summer break I would fly to Sydney on the cheapest airfare available. Sometimes that meant thirty hours of flight with numerous stops and long layovers. But I didn't care. Whatever it took for me to be with my son, my Australian daughter-in-law and beautiful grandchildren was okay with me.

I sent lots of cards and called on holidays when the price was not excessive. It was hard because I so wanted to be a real grandma — able to bake cookies for the kids, tell them stories, answer their questions and be nearby for hugs and kisses.

When the children were six and eight years old, computers were becoming a new form of communication. I knew nothing of them, but the children did. During a visit they got very excited telling me that if I were to buy a computer, we could "talk" every day. It sounded too good to be true.

I went home, bought a computer and started learning how to use it. It wasn't easy but I would not give up until I mastered it.

Finally I learned how to send and receive e-mails. What a blessing! Soon I really was talking with my grandchildren nearly every day.

At first, when they were younger, they wrote about their school activities, friends and their hobbies. Once in a while they even "tattled" (or so they thought) on their mom and dad.

As they became older, Tracy wrote more openly. She would tell me when she had a problem and was upset. She would vent after having a disagreement with one of her parents and look to me for comfort or advice. She would describe her innermost thoughts and feelings.

I wondered if other children shared as much with a grandma who was right there with them, looking into their eyes. I wondered if maybe it was easier for a child to "talk" with someone who could not see her. Maybe there was an advantage to being some distance away. In any case it made me feel needed and trusted and loved.

But just about the time I began feeling pretty smug about being a great granny, I received an e-mail from Tracy telling me that her parents were going out of town and that she was planning to have a party at the house without telling them. I couldn't believe she was sharing this with me. This was a part of grandparenting no one had told me about. And I wasn't sure I could hold onto my ranking of greatness.

Did Tracy think I would keep her secret? Was she testing me? Deep down inside did she want me to tell her folks?

This was too much like parenting. I didn't want this much responsibility. And I certainly did not want to be a snitch. Weren't grandmas supposed to be the good guys—the ones with homemade goodies, comforting words and loving smiles? Grandmas weren't supposed to have to rat on their grandkids!

I pondered this dilemma for a couple days, wondering how Tracy would react if I told her mom and dad. Would she be furious with me? Would this be the end of our wonderful e-mail communication? Would my beautiful granddaughter stop loving me?

But if I said nothing there might be serious consequences and I would never forgive myself for being silent. So I called, talked with my daughter-in-law and waited for Tracy's reaction.

It wasn't long before Tracy sent me an e-mail telling me all about the new developments. There was no mention of my part in the situation. There was no anger. Instead it was as though Tracy expected me to do just as I had done.

Wow! Somehow I passed the test. And, even though there were thousands of miles between us, I could not have felt closer to my granddaughter.

Tracy is in college now and she e-mails me about her classes, the campus, her teachers and friends. I'm praying she doesn't get pregnant and ask me not to tell!

~Kay Conner Pliszka

Of Prune Pits and Pirate Ships

My grandson was visiting one day when he asked, "Gramma, do you know
how you and God are alike?"
I mentally polished my halo while I asked, "No, how are we alike?"
"You're both old," he replied.
~Author Unknown

"**O**ver here, best friend," he whispers. "I think he went this way." Dutifully I straighten my hat, adjust my weapon, and follow my leader into the grove of trees; bending, as he bends, to look for footprints; stopping, as he stops, to listen for sounds. We are on a hunt for tigers, or lions, or wolves, or any other fierce creature we believe inhabits the woods of our neighborhood park. We note the matted tuft of grass, the bent twig, the gouge on the tree. Surely a fierce animal has passed by.

What's that noise? We tiptoe down paths, looking behind us, and then slowly push forward, anticipating danger behind every turn. When a butterfly lights upon a cluster of wildflowers, we pause to observe the flutter of his dappled wings and the gentle sway of his body. I am with my best friend on safari, but I am also entering the world of imagination once again, learning to take slower steps and to marvel at the beauty that surrounds us.

For the past two years my grandson, Gage, arrived every week-day morning promptly at 7:00, backpack and stuffed animals in tow, a safari hat or some such gear for adventure, and a grin that would melt the coldest of hearts. I'm certain that if I checked in his back pocket, I'd find a ray of sunshine as well.

"Honey Nut Cheerios? Eggs?" I ask one morning, as we head to the kitchen for breakfast.

"Whatever you're having, best friend," he replies.

"Grape-Nuts?"

"Okay."

"Prunes?"

"What are they?"

"Try some."

"Can we plant prune seeds?"

"Sure, why not?"

Our endeavor to grow prunes from the prune pits proves to be fruitless, but we are an optimistic pair as our weekly inspections end with: "We'll check back next week." And then as we check the would-be plants one day, I notice him staring at me.

"What's the matter with your neck?" he asks.

I reach to feel the neck cords and the soft folds of skin. "Why?"

"It looks like a chicken."

"Well, Nana's a bit older than you," I say, trying to shrug off the observation. "Someday you'll have a chicken neck."

Gage grins. Best friends feel comfortable discussing anything that might seem indelicate.

Besides being hunters and planters, we are creators of the absurd. We build strange-looking snowmen with large bottoms and tiny heads and then carry on a conversation with them. We put puzzles together the wrong way so that arms stick out of heads and buildings lie atop trees, and we delight in the sheer ridiculousness of it all. Sometimes we drape a beach blanket across the dining room table and sit beneath, eating raisins and crackers and cheese, wondering if the cats will find us, or even better—scaly dragons. We sit in the grass and blow enormous soap bubbles, and when they land on our heads, we topple over, pretending that they have knocked us down. And all the while we shriek with laughter. With my best friend, my sense of whimsy is restored; my soul is set free. I have let go of the sensibility of old age and have embraced the reckless abandon of my youth.

Our imaginations take us on many adventures, but our favorite is rounding up pirates. Perched on cannons at an historic fort in Rhode Island, my friend and I aim toward the harbor at the bright green "pirate ship" filled with evil scallywags with long swords and sharp daggers who are ready to lay siege to the fort. Our cannon balls bombard the ship, and the fleeing pirates are rounded up and made to walk the plank or tossed in the brig. My partner slams the gate, locks it, and tosses the "key" into the ocean. We celebrate our victory with glasses of apple juice and animal crackers.

Gage might be a fierce hunter of animals, dragons, or pirates, but he is also a lover of nature. He never fails to remind me to "see" the world around us: the butterfly gently landing on the flowers, a bug crawling on a leaf, or a tiny hermit crab scurrying home beneath the rocks. We take delight in the weeping willow tree branches blowing delicately in the breeze, creating a magical waterfall as we sit beneath. We follow ants on their trek from rock to path to front yard. We watch with sadness as a seagull with one missing foot attempts to protect his dinner from scavenging companions. These things he observes with fascination and with open-mouth wonder.

While having a snack on my deck one day, Gage notices a bird darting in and out of a roof gutter. She must be feeding babies, he decides, and a check with the binoculars proves him correct, as he spots the tiny heads poking out from the gutter's opening. Each week we note the birds' activities and give a whoop and a holler when the fledglings finally leave the nest. Simple events in nature, all observed and appreciated by a young boy, are brought home to a grandmother who had often taken for granted those moments of wonder and delight.

I lost my best friend recently. Oh, he's not gone for good. It's just that our relationship has changed somewhat—perhaps a little, perhaps a lot. Time will tell. One thing, though, is certain: I'm not the same person. Having recently retired from teaching, I now find that I have become the student, learning valuable life lessons from a small boy.

Gage has begun a brand new adventure, a journey of learning. He sits in his seat in kindergarten and observes a new world that has opened up to him. I sit on my couch and think about prune pits and pirate ships. Though Gage's first year in school will likely be more exciting than any of our safaris and he will learn things of greater sophistication than the planting of prune pits, I pray that his delightful sense of imagination and love for nature's wonders will not be lost. The world is too beautiful and life is too brief.

Be well, best friend. May you have a wonderful journey. And should you ever get the urge to go on safari with your chicken-neck Nana, I'll be waiting, with our lunches packed and my safari hat in hand. If new baby birds are ready to fly from their nests, I will call. And I'll be sure to let you know when the prune pits are sprouting or if the Jolly Roger flag is flying in the harbor. I have the time now to notice. You taught me well.

~Gretchen Nilsen Lendrum

Adolescence Revisited

There is nothing wrong with today's teenager that twenty years won't cure.
~Author Unknown

You think you'll never forget. You assume that the "disappearing" phase was so painful that you'd remember it forever.... And then you don't.

When each of our three daughters got to be about twelve, there was an almost spooky sameness to their behavior. They were present, but absent. They were sitting with us at dinner, but clearly not happy to be, and much of the time, there was a palpable sullenness about them.

I was their favorite target. Everything about me was irritating at best, downright infuriating more of the time.

My clothes were wrong, my voice was annoying, my attitudes about everything were hopeless and there was the small matter of my being seen and heard by their friends—a capital crime.

"Don't talk!" Amy had once hissed at me as I was driving four of her shrieking friends somewhere. I felt stunned, but gritted my teeth and said nothing for the duration of that trip to some mall or movie.

Of course, everything—the remoteness, the craziness, the bubbling anger—marked the onset of a years-long condition officially called "adolescence," but unofficially, a test of parental endurance. I lived in that long, twisted tunnel for at least six consecutive years as one daughter would reemerge into the daylight, while her sister disappeared.

I even remember being sorry that we had carefully spaced our children to be two years apart. It meant no respite from the storms.

Just as startlingly, the girls became my very best friends at the exact moment when they were getting poised to leave us, something my husband and I devoutly wished for during the twelve- to fifteen-year-old sieges. But when the time came, in each instance, we actually wept. They were such marvelous companions, so smart and funny and wise, that we hated to let them go off to various campuses to find their way to young adulthood.

Then along came grandchildren, and I settled into the simple business of being adored by tiny people who thought I was absolutely wonderful just by virtue of my breathing in and out. Grandma could do no wrong because, I suppose, she saw only right in these delicious late midlife bonuses.

I figured the love-fest would go on and on. And it did for a lovely space of time. They would sit by my side, or better yet, on my lap. They would beg for nothing more than just grandpa and me. It was glorious and the kind of ego-boost that people no longer younger than springtime need in liberal doses.

And then adolescence hit the new generation. My three older grandkids—two boys, one girl—reminded me that the cycle was going to repeat itself, and that I would not be spared.

I barely noticed the subtle shift when they drifted into middle school. But by eighth grade, there was no mistaking it. They were sparing in what they said. They had turned inward, just as their mothers had at the same age. And when we visited, they sometimes wandered up the steps and into their rooms, plugged into their iPods with doors firmly closed. It seemed a perfect metaphor for their souls.

So I've retreated. Not easily. Not happily. But with a renewed awareness that these three are now people with ideas and values and yes, private lives.

I adore them. They know it.

In small ways, as the months fly by, I notice that they're starting to glide back to us, occasionally offering breathtaking glimpses of the adults they will become.

So I was just starting to exhale when we recently had a visit with our next oldest grandchild, the irrepressible guy who once loved just hanging out, and who shared jokes and school stuff and even... feelings.

Yet he seemed to have done a fast-fade, this dark-haired laughing boy. In his place was a lad with arms and legs that seemed to get in his way, a voice with the strangest range, and a distance that I'm sure wasn't there just a few months ago.

The message is clear: Another grandchild is about to wander off into that primeval forest of adolescence. Like his brother and his cousins, he will have to find his way through the thicket.

Of course, I'll be there on the sidelines, watching, praying, cheering him on.

And when he's finally ready to return, I'll be there, arms outstretched, waiting to welcome him back.

~Sally Schwartz Friedman

"You know I don't bring you candy, sweetheart. But now you're old enough for something better: stories about the trouble your mom got into when she was a kid."

ttyl

Computing is not about computers any more. It is about living.
~Nicholas Negroponte

"We threw a bash at LEGOLAND for my granddaughter's birthday," my girlfriend said and then passed a picture around. "Look at that sweet face." I glanced at it, then zipped up my jacket against the chill I felt inside. I played golf with three girlfriends and their chatter about grandchildren shouldn't have bothered me. But it did.

More pictures were passed around. "My Heather snuggles on my lap while we watch movies." "I had Tyler for a sleepover last weekend."

I swallowed the lump in my throat. My grandsons live in Wisconsin, 2,000 miles away from me in Southern California.

Phone calls often went like this: "How are you?" I'd ask.

"Fine," they'd say.

"What are you doing in school that's fun?"

"Nothing."

"How are your grades? What's your favorite class?" I'd ask, trying to keep them on the phone for a few more minutes.

I loved seeing them and flew there as often as I could. We baked cookies, visited Chuck E. Cheese, and played video games. I showered them with love, and them to me when we were together, but each passing year brought changes to their lives, and each trip ended much too soon. I'd ache to know who their current friends were, what movies they liked while they were still out in the theaters, whether they won or lost their latest baseball game.

Shortly after the new year began, I went to lunch with a different friend. She asked about Nick, fifteen, and Colton, ten.

"If you want to be part of their world, you have to use their technology," she said.

"Like what? I call them all the time," I protested. "And I visit as often as I can."

"What about e-mail? You can do that every day. My grandson lives on it. I'll bet your older grandson does too."

Driving home, I mulled it over. Questions popped into my head—did Nick have access to a computer? Would he think it dorky and weird to talk to his grandmother online? Would he even want to?

I called my daughter-in-law. "Nick's on my computer all the time," she said, "and has his own e-mail address. Colton isn't into the computer yet, but I'll tell Nick you called."

I hung up the phone and tried to put it out of my mind. After all, Nick was fifteen years old, with more important things to do than converse with his grandmother.

The next morning I sat down at my computer. There was an unusual address in my e-mail account with a subject line of "Hey." Could that be Nick? I clicked it open and devoured every word.

> *Hey its Nick,*
>
> *My mom told me that you wanted to keep in touch with me or something like that i cant exactly remember what she said. But ya im doing pretty good here accept they wont let me wrestle because I failed 1 class which was math and I was very surprised at that cause I thought I was good at math. But it is like 12:44 am here and I don't feel like going to sleep lol but ya e-mail me back*
>
> *Love ya lots,*
> *Nick*

I shot one right back, trying hard not to sound desperate for contact with him. I wanted to be cool. And I didn't correct his grammar, though I could have. I wanted to accept him for who he was, spelling mistakes and all.

> *Yo, Grandma B here,*
> *Nice to hear from you. Sad to hear that you can't wrestle cause you failed 1 class. Bummer. I was never very good at math. But if you thought you were, it's too bad that you didn't get a passing grade. How come you can't sleep at 12:44 a.m.? I'm snoring by that time.*
> *Love you double lots,*
> *Grandma B*

Pressing "send," I noticed the time. He was two hours ahead of me, so I pictured him roaming the halls in school, putting books in his locker, or poring over a textbook in study hall. How I wished I lived near enough to see his football games or wrestling matches. Now all I could do was wonder if he'd e-mail back. Did I dare to have even a sliver of hope that we could bridge the miles between us?

Later that day, a little ping sounded. I had mail.

> *Hey,*
> *Ya I hate that I cant wrestle. that camera you sent me is pretty sweet if you want to see the videos I took go to this... [link] Colton is the recorder lol i will be making tons more once summer comes and i can bike and skateboard and stuff like that.*
> *Love ya triple lots,*
> *Nick*

I clicked on the link. There he was skateboarding, flying high into the air and landing with a thud. It was awesome to see.

Nick e-mailed again.

> *Last night I went bowling and got 5 strikes in a row when*

they had good music and then a song I didn't like came on and
I got a gutter ball.

Often, his e-mails had weird letters in them, like ttyl or idk. It took me a while to figure out those meant "talk to you later," and "I don't know."

Months went by. Sometimes days passed before he responded to an e-mail, often apologizing for being so busy with schoolwork and sports. One day he attached photographs that I eagerly devoured. I felt like I was right there with him whenever I'd read an e-mail, watch a video, or see a picture.

Last week I saw my golfing friends again. One of them brought a picture of her granddaughter at a dance recital. I had one to share too. "Hey, look at the picture of Nick in his football uniform that he attached to his latest e-mail. Doesn't he look cool?"

It's been fun to learn the ways to stay connected in a teenager's world. Thanks to being open to a friend's suggestion and the willingness to change, this grandmother has learned a whole new way of relating to her grandsons.

~B.J. Taylor

37

Secret Smiles

*We should all have one person who knows how to bless us
despite the evidence. Grandmother was that person to me.*
~Phyllis Theroux

Crash! I stop sweeping the back patio. "Cody, what happened?"

"Nothin', Grandma."

"Are you bouncing that ball in my living room?"

Silence.

"Well?"

"I'm not now."

Cody is my first grandchild. He's a perpetual motion six-year-old. He's adorable and I love him from his sweaty head to his grubby toes. He makes me laugh and allows me to look at the world through his young, curious eyes. His gap-toothed grin melts my heart. Just when I think my old, exhausted body can't take another minute, he does something so sweet and caring that tears form in my eyes.

I pick up my leaf piles, toss them into the garbage can, and put the broom and dustpan away. I slide open the patio door and look for a first grader who is supposedly doing his homework. Silence is alleged to be golden, but this is too quiet. What's that kid done now? Where is he? What do I smell? Faint whiffs of peppermint linger in the air.

Hurrying into the living room, I glance at the glass shelves holding my treasures. Everything appears unscathed. All the porcelain figurines are in place. My eyes land on my favorite. The dancing girl's head sits at a jaunty angle and she looks quite sticky. Hidden behind a chair I spy an open jar of peppermint-scented paste.

Cody tiptoes into the room and throws his arms around my waist. "That girl's head sort of fell off, but I fixed it," he whispers. "Can this be our secret? And we won't tell my mom, okay? I'm really, really, really sorry, Grandma."

Cody's apology corrects my priorities. Treasures don't sit on shelves; they sneak up behind you and throw their arms around your waist. I can super-glue my dancing girl later. Right now it's hugging time.

• • •

Years later my daughter looks at my porcelain figurines on the shelves. "I've always liked this one best." She picks up the dancing girl. "Did you know there's a crack line around her neck?"

Nineteen-year-old Cody and I share a smile.

~Sharon Landeen

38

Letters to Mamaw

To send a letter is a good way to go somewhere
without moving anything but your heart.
~Phyllis Theroux

My grandmother's eightieth birthday was approaching and I was at a loss as to what to give her. She had recently moved into a nursing home and didn't have room for extra "stuff." She insisted that she didn't need a thing.

Finally, I came up with an idea. In her birthday card, I sent her a gift certificate for "A letter a week for the next year!" It was a big commitment. I've never been much of a letter writer, but now I was living far from home, and should be able to find plenty of news. Growing up just a mile from my grandparents, we'd always been close. I knew that she'd love to hear what was going on in my life.

The letter gift certificate was a huge hit. She got fifty-two letters that first year. Some were long and filled with homesickness. Others were short and newsy. More than once what she received was just a funny card with a few short lines. All showed her that I was thinking of her regularly.

As her next birthday rolled around, she asked for another letter gift certificate for her birthday. In fact, that's also what she wanted for her next eight birthdays.

For nine and a half years I wrote her. She was rarely able to write back. So much happened in those nine years! At first I wrote about the cold Michigan winters and working on my graduate degree. Then

I wrote about my pregnancy, which turned out to be twins! We lived in four different places during those years and I described them all. During the boys' preschool years I shared every funny thing they did and said, and as they grew they started adding "picture letters" to the envelope. I sent postcard letters from vacations.

I flew home annually to visit and soon realized that the entire nursing home staff knew all the details of my life, as more and more often they were reading the letters to her.

My last letter arrived the day after her death. I've always wanted relationships with no regrets. None of that "I wish I had told her I loved her" for me! I felt I had given her the best gift I could.

What I hadn't counted on was how her gift would come back full-circle to me.

Months later, while going through her things, my dad found a box full of her correspondence. It was filled with letters from me. Those letters are a journal of my life. Some were unremarkable. Others were filled with moments and pictures I had completely forgotten. Such as on May 22, 1997, when I told her that the twins were having Western day at preschool and that when I explained to three-year-old Ben that the boys would be dressing up as cowboys he asked, "Will the girls be dressing up as cows?" Funny, I don't remember that. In some ways it seems I missed those years due to motherly exhaustion. She saved those memories for me in my letters.

Life really does fly by. Loved ones come and go. But sometimes our gifts to others come back to us in unexpected ways. This is one of those times.

~Lisa Kulka

39

That's What Grandmothers Are For

Just about the time a woman thinks her work is done,
she becomes a grandmother.
~Edward H. Dreschnack

"Amy left several emotional calls for you on our answering machine while you were gone," announced my husband, Jim, as I walked in the door, exhausted after four hours of driving across the state. For the last three days I had accompanied my twelve-year-old granddaughter, Rachel, during her competition at the Florida State Science Fair where she won second place in Junior Chemistry. "Amy was extremely upset and crying when she left her messages," continued Jim. "She needed to talk to her Gram."

My mind raced. What could be wrong with this bubbly fourth grader who last week flew from her home in Maryland and spent her spring break with us in Florida? Just four days ago I had taken her to the airport for her return flight, and smiled when the busy airline employee handling the Unaccompanied Minor paperwork stared at my cute, blond granddaughter and remarked, "You are the most adorable little girl, in your denim hat with the big sunflower in front."

"That makes six compliments about my hat today, Gram," beamed Amy as we headed toward security. "Remember all the people who told me they liked it when we went shopping this morning?"

My thoughts returned to Jim's descriptions of Amy's frantic calls. I couldn't bear to listen to them.

"Why was she so upset?" I asked.

"She lost her sunflower hat on the plane and was so miserable she couldn't sleep. She had placed it on top of her bag of books, under the seat in front of her, and then realized it was missing while she was at the baggage carousel. She and her dad rushed back to the plane and had the attendants check around her seat but the hat was gone."

My heart sank.

"I have to leave," I told Jim as I grabbed my keys and headed toward the door.

"But you just got here after a long drive and you're exhausted. Where are you going?"

"On a mission."

I wondered where I could buy a big sunflower as I headed for the mall. I doubted the arts and crafts store would be open this late on Sunday evening, but it was. I raced down the aisles and right before closing I found their only big sunflower and bought it. I rushed home, rummaged through my collection of hats, and grabbed the denim one. I sewed the sunflower in front, smiled at the clone I'd created, and called Amy.

"I've replaced your hat, sweetie. Now, you can feel better and sleep tonight. I think this one's cuter than the other one."

"Oh, thank you Gram. I've been so sad since I lost my hat."

"Do you want me to send it or bring it to you?"

"Bring it with you when you visit this summer, so it won't get lost in the mail."

Unexpectedly, Amy's mother, Betsy, flew down for the weekend to celebrate my birthday and she was amazed when she saw the hat. "Let me take this back to Amy. She'll be thrilled!"

The next evening I checked my e-mails and discovered a video titled "The hat." I watched as Betsy sat on the floor, opened her suitcase, and handed the hat to speechless Amy.

"Did you find it?" asked five-year-old sister, Anna, thinking the replica was the lost hat.

Amy walked to a mirror, posed in the hat, then ran to the camera and gushed, "Gram, if you're watching this, I love you. And thank you, thank you, thank you for getting me another hat. I like it better than the other one!"

I was pleased I made my grandchild happy.

That's what grandmothers are for.

~Miriam Hill

40

Staying with Mammie

*Being grandparents sufficiently removes us from the responsibilities
so that we can be friends.*
~Allan Frome

My parents fretted and worried before boarding their flight to Orlando. It was the first time they had left their four-year-old daughter for an extended stay. They reassured themselves with the thought that I would not be with a stranger. I would be staying with my grandmother—and boy did I love my Mammie.

Who wouldn't? Imagine spending several days in a house with someone who lets you do anything you want. Malted Milk Balls for breakfast? No problem. Cheetos for lunch? Why not? Watching movies until midnight? Sure thing.

My stay at Mammie's was better than any fairy tale I had read about. Mammie brushed and styled my hair and gave me long back-rubs. She brought out an entire drawer of costume jewelry and photographed me wearing several strands of beads. Mammie and I painted with water, colored pictures with jumbo crayons, picked flowers, and sang nursery rhymes. I did what I wanted, ate what I wanted, and the majority of my requests were met with, "Sure, darling."

I was rocking in Mammie's oversized, orange chair, my hand in a box of animal crackers, when my luxury vacation came to an abrupt end. Mom and Dad were back.

My parents stood at the door, arms outstretched and ready to greet their first-born child. They expected hugs and kisses. They expected me to be anxious for their return and ready to go home with them.

Instead, they spent a few minutes gathering my belongings while I sat in Mammie's chair and cried. "I don't want to go home!" I sobbed. "I want to stay at Mammie's!"

I cried the entire thirty-minute drive home and then a little more once we went inside. I was not ready for rules, structure, and set bedtimes. I was not ready to leave Mammie's.

Mom and Dad said that it took almost a month to get me back on track after my vacation at my grandmother's house. I had a hard time going to bed, waking up, and eating vegetables. I longed for the good times I had at Mammie's.

Ever since, I have been well aware of the strong gravitational pull that exists between Mammie's house and me. I returned quite often as a youngster for overnight visits. In my teenage years, Mammie and I stayed up late playing *Yahtzee*, watching movies and completing Mad Libs. We laughed, ate ice cream sundaes, and laughed some more.

As a college student, I came home for visits, quickly checked in with my parents, and then drove to Mammie's. We drank several cups of coffee, watched Letterman, and talked about my college courses until the early morning hours. We thoroughly enjoyed each other's company and I always looked forward to my next visit.

Earlier this year, Mammie became ill with complications from an allergic reaction. She was hospitalized and then placed in a nursing home for physical therapy. It was almost two months before she was able to return home and get back to her old routine.

Mammie invited my husband and me over for dinner recently. It was the first time she had cooked for us since she had gotten sick. Mammie made potato soup, meatloaf, green beans, and biscuits. Everything was delicious and in a lot of ways, the visit felt like the old days. Being in Mammie's presence is so intoxicating that I tend to forget all about my responsibilities and work obligations.

When it was time to go home, I really wasn't ready to leave. It was approaching ten o'clock and I knew I needed to get ready for bed. And though I was reluctant, I didn't pout and cry in Mammie's chair or refuse to get in the car with my husband. But I know why the younger me resorted to such tantrums.

I am thirty years old and still drawn to Mammie's house. She makes me dinner. She makes me laugh. She makes me happy. And when I am at her house, her love makes me wish I could stay... and stay.

~Melissa Face

"They weren't kidding when they said
grandparents let grandchildren get away with most anything.
That was my mom. She's taking our kids to Macchu Picchu.
Right now."

Pizza Night

A grandmother is a little bit parent, a little bit teacher,
and a little bit best friend.
~Author Unknown

My first week at college was rough. I already had two quizzes to study for, a project to begin, and a pile of lecture notes to review. My financial aid was a mess, and my roommate wouldn't speak to me. Everything was unfamiliar, and I didn't know anyone. This was not how I had planned things.

While I was only three hours from home, it seemed much farther. I couldn't wait until the weekend.

Finally, it was Friday. I told my roommate I was going home. He actually acknowledged me by nodding his head once. If Western had a degree in video games, this guy would get an A. As I drove home, I prayed and asked the Lord to please take my mess and take control over it.

I got home and no one was there. "Great," I thought. "Just when I need them the most." Then, out of the blue, it occurred to me that I hadn't seen my grandmother in weeks even though she only lived ten minutes away.

Expecting no company, Grandma's porch light was out. I could see the light of the TV flickering in the window. I knocked at the door and heard Grandma coming to the door. Suddenly, I was blinded by the porch light and the door swung open. "Well, hello there! I sure didn't expect to see you," she exclaimed.

Pictures of all the grandkids crowded the mantle and every available space on every shelf in the living room. The ceramic pig that had given Grandpa the last smile I saw him smile sat on a shelf across the room from me. I still remembered giving it to him for Christmas more than fifteen years ago. The wooden duck our last pastor had carved for Grandma and Grandpa sat on yet another shelf. I could see into the kitchen from where I sat and noticed the door to the stairwell. That stairwell led to an upstairs adventure paradise for us grandkids for so many years.

I was already glad I had come to see Grandma. We talked about my week. I had so much to tell. I had been there for over an hour when Grandma asked me something I never thought I'd hear her ask. "I have a pizza in the freezer. You in the mood for pizza?" she asked.

"You like pizza, Grandma?"

"I love pizza, especially after I doctor it up!"

Grandma is well known for her cooking. I couldn't imagine what doctoring up a pizza meant to her.

As we added extra cheese, pepperoni, and peppers to the pizza, I realized I had never really had a conversation with Grandma until that night. My grandfather had passed away nearly fifteen years earlier, and I always regretted that I never really got to talk to Grandpa. I suddenly felt so blessed to have this evening with Grandma. The pizza turned out awesome. The best pizza I had ever had, in fact.

The thing I noticed about Grandma was that she really listened to me. Often, I find myself interrupting people to give advice. I realized that sometimes we just need to listen. Grandma would only occasionally say, "Just pray about it."

So I prayed about my situation all weekend. The next week was so much better. I didn't even go home that next weekend. I hadn't even realized that Western had such a beautiful campus. I had been blinded by my troubles but Jesus had removed the trouble. Now I could see.

I started making a point to get to Grandma's at least once a month for pizza. We still have those pizza nights four years later. I'm just thankful that the Lord led me to Grandma when I needed an ear. As the ways of the Lord often turn out, I got so much more.

~William Mark Baldwin

Grandmothers

The Name Game

They Call Me Bup

*A married daughter with children puts you in danger of
being catalogued as a first edition.*
~Author Unknown

When my daughter announced that she was going to
have a baby, I must confess I was mortified. Not that
she was only seventeen and pregnant, but that I was
going to be a grandmother at only thirty-nine! After all, grandmas
were supposed to be stodgy women wearing support stockings and
living quiet, conservative lives! I was newly single, svelte and enjoying the nightclub scene!

I did my best to be a supportive mother by helping Carey explore
all available options. When she decided to get married and raise the
baby, I also half-jokingly told her, "I don't want this child to call me
Grandma."

When twelve-pound, one-ounce Coltan was born that November,
I couldn't have been more delighted. It was love at first sight! I didn't
get to see Coltan nearly enough during the first several months of his
life due to the two-hour distance between us. When Carey and family
moved back to my city, however, I became a regular visitor to their
home. By this time, Coltan was beginning to walk and to talk.

During one evening visit, Coltan approached me with arms outstretched and a series of grunts indicating his desire for me to pick
him up. I encouraged his learning process by telling him to say "up."
After a few repetitions, the word "bup" came out of his mouth. This

resulted in much praise and, of course, a pickup with lots of hugs from his Mommy's Mom (still not Grandma)! In a phone conversation with Carey the next day, she told me Coltan had decided my name was "Bup." She said that after I left, Coltan walked around their house with his arms in the air saying "Bup" repeatedly, and very obviously looking for me.

That's how it began. Coltan, without intending to, had given me the most special nickname ever to replace the standard title of "Grandma." As he continued to call me "Bup" his sister, Sarah, arrived. And what did she call me when she started talking? You guessed it! Coltan is now twenty and Sarah is nineteen and both still call me "Bup," without hesitation and regardless of where we are or who can hear. But there's even more! Today Carey's third child, Alex, is turning six years old. I am also "Bup" to him.

I have now been "Bup" for nearly twenty years and have probably heard that word 10,000 times. Still, every time I hear my grandchildren call me "Bup," I am proud beyond words to be their grandma.

~Luann Warner

43

Chicken Soup
for the Soul

The Baby Babble Race

It's amazing how grandparents seem so young once you become one.
~Author Unknown

In our family there's a race to be the first name spoken by Baby Bella, our new granddaughter. While "Mamma" seems most logical, it is by no means guaranteed. Frankly, it's way too early since the baby is only six months old, but that hasn't stopped the campaigning. Star, my daughter, patiently mouths, "M-m-mamma." Often, I catch Joe, Bella's father, coaching the infant with "Daa-daa." Even my husband gets into the act, "Grandpa-chino!" (This was a friend's laughing reference to David's cappuccino habit. Who knew he'd embrace it?)

"Say Grandpa-chino!" he coos.

Boy, is he at the back of the bus. I'm no linguist, but shaping a "g" and four syllables is a tad unlikely. Bless his heart, he believes. Me? I'm biding my time. "Lola" is the Filipino term for grandmother. At age fifty-something, I appreciate the word's sexy sound and the whole "whatever-Lola-wants-Lola gets" connotation. So let's get it right the first time. Patience is required.

Everyone else is lined up at the starting gate, champing at the bit, with Mommy hoping to beat Daddy. The little mother comes seeking reassurance from me.

"What was my first word, Mom?" Star asks.

"Cookie."

I can't tell if Star's disappointment is from dashed hopes or the revelation of what it said about my own early mothering skills.

A few weeks later, Baby Bella links recognition to sound, looks at Star and says, "Mm... mm."

A true triumph for motherhood (or is it milk?), but we are surprised to find the paternal jury is not convinced.

Still dubious, Joe says, "She's just making sounds."

Star and I sneak smiles at each other and listen as Bella's daddy argues his position.

"'M-m-m' doesn't necessarily mean 'mommy.'"

Star and I again raise eyebrows at each other and Star throws out the other possibilities. "Yeah, she could be trying to say money or Monday or mammals."

I add, "Joe, you're right, maybe Bella is really asking, 'Hey, everybody, are we Mormons?'"

Cashing in his chips, Joe concedes, "Okay, I get it."

Now that the "first name uttered" competition is officially over, the din lowers within our Tower of Babble. We all have a sneaking suspicion "doggy" might win the silver.

Meanwhile, I often bring Bella into my bedroom for private coaching, "Okay, say L-L-Lola-Whom-I-Love-More-Than-Life-Itself."

~Suzette Martinez Standring

Name-Calling

Children are unpredictable.
You never know what inconsistency they're going to catch you in next.
~Franklin P. Jones

Hurrying down the church corridor, I approached a classroom to collect my three-year-old daughter, Kayla. Waving the picture she had colored, she bubbled with good humor as she grabbed for my hand. But before we turned to leave, her Sunday School teacher motioned us aside.

"I'm so sorry," the teacher put her arm around my shoulders. "I had no idea you and your husband both lost your mothers."

"What?" Perhaps I'd misunderstood her in the crowded confusion of the classroom.

"Your mothers," she repeated, louder. "We were discussing grandparents in our lesson this morning and Kayla mentioned that she doesn't have any grandmas."

"Why, Kayla," I admonished, "of course you do."

"No, I don't." Kayla shook her head with a wistful sigh. "The other kids gots grandmas." She splayed her open palms for woeful emphasis. "But all I gots is a Grammy and a Oma!"

~Carol McAdoo Rehme

Extra Grandma

Never have children, only grandchildren.
~Gore Vidal

y husband Sid and I were never able to have children.
I had always wanted a family and that longing deep-
ened after his death. He was all I had and when he
died I felt like I had lost my entire family.

On my journey to recovery, I never dreamed that I would finally
get the family I had always wished for—even though it was not how
I had envisioned that earlier in my life. A few years after Sid's death I
met Tom. We fell in love and when we married I suddenly inherited
four grown children and eight grandchildren.

But would his children like and accept me? I was very apprehen-
sive about that first meeting. My worries melted away when I realized
that they were more than willing to bring me into their family as a
stepmother. And when his daughters asked me if their children could
call me "Mimi," I was thrilled.

Tom was divorced, so I was also concerned about the fact that
the children already had two grandmothers. Would the little ones
understand how I fit into the family? Would they, too, be willing to
accept me?

At one of our first extended family gatherings, I noticed our six-
year-old grandson staring at me with a perplexed look. He seemed
to be contemplating something very serious. Suddenly, sporting a
big grin, he piped up and said "I know who you are! You are extra

grandma!" At that moment, I knew it was time to just relax and relish my new role.

We have all had a lot of fun joking about how I got to be a grandmother. I didn't have to change dirty diapers, stumble out of bed for a midnight feeding, suffer through teenage years, or pay for college and a wedding to get my wonderful grandchildren.

I always thought I would have children and then grandchildren in the usual manner. I have heard people say that when a door closes, God opens a window. Now I know what that means. I lost so much joy when Sid died, but now I have a new happy life filled with lots of unconditional love.

I am enjoying so many things I never got to experience before—like building block towers on the floor, reading bedtime stories or holding a tiny child who has fallen asleep peacefully in my arms. My refrigerator is covered with drawings, and my walls are decorated with photos of the kids. I find myself pulling out my brag book every chance I get, and loving it! I may be an instant "extra grandma," but I am just as proud as any other "regular" grandparent I know.

One of my friends has a sign displayed above her kitchen door that reads, "Some of my greatest blessings call me Mimi." I'd like to find one that says, "Some of my greatest blessings call me Mimi… and Extra Grandma."

~Melinda Richarz Lyons

Adopting Edna

A child needs a grandparent, anybody's grandparent,
to grow a little more securely into an unfamiliar world.
~Charles and Ann Morse

Finishing a run on a rather warm day, I stopped by the deli to buy a bottle of water. That's when I thought of it. A bowl of vanilla ice cream. That's when I thought of her.

Anyone who exercises knows the last thing your sweaty, exhausted body needs when you reach the finish line is ice cream. But she couldn't know that. Just like she couldn't fathom why I'd want to run on a scorching day in August. Or any day, for that matter. When I returned to her house, breathless and weary, the heaping helping of vanilla ice cream was her way of trying to cool me down. A grandmotherly thing to do.

Driving to upstate New York to meet her for the first time, I imagined what she'd be like. Bustling about her tidy kitchen, she'd have ruffles on her curtains and her apron. She'd stir butter and sugar into the carrots and keep the cookie jar filled. She'd knit afghans while she spun tales. She'd have a big heart and a lap that fit great-grandchildren.

When we arrived at her house, sure enough, she was everything I thought a grandmother would be. So I decided to adopt her. Although I didn't tell her right away.

"You can call me Gram," she said to me with a smile to her grandson, my husband at the time.

"I miss having a grandmother," I told her. "Both of mine died when I was young. I never got to know them that well."

"You'll get to know me," she replied.

And I did. Thanksgivings swirling with the sweet smell of pumpkin pie. Blizzards blustering outside her warm and cozy kitchen. Fans creaking louder than crickets on the Fourth of July.

She had an easy way about her that I admired. A quick smile that welcomed anyone who stopped by for a visit. A quiet way of listening that made the conversation flow. A steady temperament that seemed to calm those around her.

One day, as I sat at her kitchen table while she stirred pots and pans on the stove, I decided to tell her about my plan to adopt her.

"You can call me Gram," she said with a wink. "I already told you that."

As I would soon learn, she meant what she said. Just like a grandmother, she accepted me for who I was. For better or worse. So when my marriage to her grandson eventually ended, she was sad. But she was still there for me.

"Things don't always turn out like you plan," she said. Guess she had seen enough life to understand its disappointments. She had felt enough pain to know there are times you need comfort more than questions.

"You can call me Gram," she reminded me.

But keeping house by yourself in upstate New York, or anywhere, gets hard after a while. And so in time she moved to Rhode Island to be closer to her family. Every once in a while, I'd take my son to visit his great-grandmother. Sometimes when he was at school, I'd go alone. When I married again, I brought my new daughter along to visit.

"You can call me Great-Gram," she told my daughter.

It was never out of obligation that I went to see her. I came for her wisdom. When I went to visit her, I'd bring shortbread or green tea or Crackerjacks to brighten her day. In return, she'd give me something to think about.

When I was sad about the past, she'd remind me to think of the future. When the kids were loud and wild, she'd tell me to enjoy them. When I was worried about a problem at work or an argument with a friend, she'd tell me it would all work out. And it did. Always.

There was no better cure for my shortsightedness than her long view of life. Time and again, I'd see her eyes light up when she saw the kids. "Let them laugh," she'd say with a chuckle. "Let them play. Let them dance."

The last time I saw her, she was sleeping. She didn't hear me come into the room. She didn't notice I had brought the kids along. She didn't see the flower I left on her nightstand. "Kiss Great-Gram," I told the kids. And I did, too. "She's tired. She needs to rest."

Of all the things she taught me, I'd like to share this thought with you. Some think adoption is just for kids. I disagree. Adopt a grandfather. Adopt a grandmother. Someone who can tell you about the future because they've survived the past. Someone who understands how easy it is to see the trees and miss the forest. Someone who will remind you that yesterday's gone, tomorrow may be coming, but today is here.

~Rita Lussier

Grandma's the Name

Grandmas are moms with lots of frosting.
~Author Unknown

I am a fourth-generation writer and a first-generation "Grandma."
My own grandmother was called "Honie" by all of us, and
that started because she called us "honey," and we returned
the favor. Or so I thought. What actually is true is that Honie felt too
young to be called Grandma and so encouraged something less age-
related. Since her name was Helen, she contracted it to Honie.

That tradition continued with my own mother when I had my
children. Having a career in the glamorous field of writing and possessing a special talent, she considered these names: "Glamour" and
"Talent." I believe we all discouraged that, but there was a name waiting for her.

In addition to possessing talent, my mother also possessed a
pet Capuchin monkey named "Bomba." My children were quick to
realize that she was, in fact, Bomba's Momma, and that got shortened
to "Bomma." And she has been Bomma to all of her grandchildren
since.

Just as her own mother did, my mother felt too young to be
labeled with a name that implied generation seniority.

I forgive them both. It's not their fault that they lived through
a time when a woman's age was never a thing to discuss or disclose.
Thank goodness times have changed!

They didn't have the good fortune to live (or work) where aging and aging well are badges of honor.

How lucky I am to be working in a retirement home and seeing first-hand every day that age is irrelevant, and it's not how long one lives that matters, but how well one lives.

And that's why, when my darling first grandchild, Audrey Caroline, was born on November 5, I claimed the name of "Grandma" with as much pride as the men who planted the American flag on the moon.

I'm Grandma! I am Grand MA! And I have to say, it's the best title I've ever held... well, next to MOM, that is.

~Linda Williams Aber

48

Mommar's Girl

Other things may change us, but we start and end with the family.
~Anthony Brandt

She was only a few hours old when I first held her in my arms, but she was as beautiful as any baby ever born. Through tears, I studied everything about her, from her long eyelashes to her tiny, pink fingers. What a sight to behold. Jenny! I was overcome with the joy of her presence, awestruck by the miracle of this new life. My first grandchild.

Mommar. It's the funny name Jenny gave me. The name is not important, only the one who gave it to me and the relationship we shared.

My memories were interrupted as someone whispered, "It's your turn." The next thing I knew, I was being ushered to my seat in the front of the church. Music played softly as the sunset filtered through stained glass windows onto carefully arranged white flowers. All around me were friends and family who had come to celebrate this special occasion. They waited patiently as the wedding party strolled down the aisle in time to the music, yet all were anticipating the entrance of the bride — Jenny.

Where had the years gone? What had happened to those wonderful summers when she came for a two-week visit, but managed to stay for four? Those were the special days when we ate our lunch in the park, swam in the pool or played at the beach — the times we said prayers and sang songs at bedtime, and stole hugs and kisses at every opportunity.

Today it did not matter that she had been a teenage beauty queen and a star athlete. That was her past. Today was the beginning of her future—the first day of the rest of her life.

The organ music announced the moment everyone waited for—the entrance of the bride. As I looked back, the sight I beheld almost took my breath away, for coming down the aisle was the most beautiful bride I had ever seen. Her gown was unadorned, yet on her it was elegant beyond words. The smile on her face, even more beautiful than the flowers she carried, was the perfect final touch to such a vision.

She walked slowly, secure on the arm of her father. They were alike in so many ways. How proud he was of his wonderful daughter, but the tears in his eyes betrayed what was in his heart. They had always been best of pals and that would never change, but beneath their smiles, both knew from this day forward it would never be quite the same, for now there was another man in her life.

How long had it been since she and Zachary became engaged? I was one of the first people to whom she told the news. That evening I had just taken the ice cream out of the freezer when Jenny phoned to give me every detail—the lovely boat ride at sunset, their special dinner, the proposal on bended knee. It didn't matter to me the ice cream was melting or my guests were wondering what was taking so long. This conversation would be savored, it would be cherished, but it would not be rushed.

As I walked from the church, I wanted to be happy about the many times Jenny and I would be together in the future, the fun things we would do, the adult lives we would share. But before I could do that, I needed to take one moment, just one little moment, to acknowledge the final chapter in the story of the beautiful little girl and her Mommar.

~Joanne Wright Schulte

Mama

People who don't cherish their elderly
have forgotten whence they came and whither they go.
~Ramsey Clark

We buried my Mama today.
She wasn't really my mother
But, then again, she was.
The mother that bore me had died
When I was six months old,
And this wonderful grandmother
Took on the task as she turned fifty,
Of raising a motherless child.

I called her "Mama" just like most
Have called the mother of their youth.
But, when I got into my teens,
I was too "sophisticated"
To be heard calling her "Mama."
Thereafter, she was "Grandmother."
But still, she was a grand mother.

When I had grown up and married,
The first child that was born to us
Was rushed to be placed in her arms,
For there was no greater blessing

That I could give this little one
Than to entrust him, though briefly,
To this loving great-grandmother.

Another twenty years passed by
And she became the grandmother
To another generation.
I wrote, and called, and visited:
"Hi, Grandmother," I greeted her...
"It's me, Grandmother," when I phoned...
"Dear Grandmother," said my letters.

And then, the dreaded phone call came:
"She's gone," my aunt relayed to me.
I called the florist in her town.
"I want a spray with a big bow,
And a ribbon with just one word;"
It was then I broke down and cried,
And sobbed out the one word: "Mama,"
From a once-again motherless child.

~Henry Matthew Ward

50

She Called Me Grandma

Gone—flitted away,
Taken the stars from the night and the sun
From the day!
Gone, and a cloud in my heart.
~Alfred Tennyson

As I stare at the silver-framed picture another tear falls from my eye. Like a bright shining star the little girl came into our lives—a four-year-old daughter my son-in-law didn't know he had. Our family greeted her with open arms and we quickly settled into bi-weekly visits. Dates were marked on a calendar and we waited for her arrival with anticipation.

One weekend, we sat in a chair huddled against each other while I read a story—a story of a princess—and my heart skipped a beat when she called me Grandma for the first time.

At the grocery store, I gathered gummy snacks with Barbie pictures on the box, rainbow-colored cereal and coloring books. As in a dream, our lives changed instantly.

I study the smiling face from the picture and can hear laughter in my mind. Brown eyes look back at me—kind eyes like her dad's. She looks sedate, but the first pictures taken were of exaggerated poses, a scrunched-up face and clawing hands when she imitated a monster and finally the face with childlike innocence that I look at now. Sparkling lights twinkle from the Christmas tree behind her.

The purple velvet dress with an apple green sash reminds me of the *Nutcracker* ballet we went to that day.

Newly married, my daughter and son-in-law knew the mother only wanted money but they battled for consistent visitation. They fought through the unyielding legal system and became frustrated when their voices were not heard. The excuses came early. She was sick, she was visiting an aunt, she simply couldn't come. The court order meant nothing—the judge ignored the mother's actions. "Contempt" was a written word of no consequence, and the battle continued.

While ordering the cake for her fifth birthday I waited anxiously. I gripped the phone in my hand and wondered if the mother would show up at the pick-up point with my granddaughter. The phone rang.

"We've got her," said my daughter.

I breathed a sigh of relief as I bought the cake and picked out helium balloons. It was months before we found out where she really lived. On that happy birthday, she quickly discarded her shorts, pulled on a lavender dress with flowing tulle, donned a crown and clipped on pink, heart-shaped earrings. She pranced around the room in plastic slippers with a Disney princess pictured on the strap. Her friends and cousins surrounded her when she pulled off a pink plastic sheet to reveal a dollhouse taller than she.

"This is the best birthday of my whole life," she said.

Each weekend she entertained us. She chased her friends and cousins, splashed in a wading pool and played board games with her dad. Her happiness and sense of humor were infectious. We laughed as she painted a picture of her Barbie doll—a picture of exaggerated features with thick black eyelashes, a small body and wide skirt. She painted the face with a mixture of white and red and called the color "valilla."

Wearing a fringed skirt and red cowboy hat she rode on a metal horse at the Cowgirl Museum, painted pumpkins for Halloween, climbed on an alligator statue at the zoo and made a gingerbread house before Christmas. We took her to the *Nutcracker*, where her eyes grew large as she watched the ballerinas. During the intermission she kicked off her sparkled shoes and twirled in the carpeted foyer—her black tights wrinkled around slender ankles. She jumped and pointed her toes, leaping across the pale green carpet. At the end of the last scene she slumped her head onto her dad's lap and, like the ballerina, fell asleep. If only the dream had lasted.

We decorated her bedroom and made pink, polka dot curtains, painted furniture and stacked the shelves with Disney movies and books. The toy box overflowed. The last weekend I saw her, she was running up and down the stairs with a green and red stuffed parrot bouncing on her shoulder and a black pirate hat on her head. Behind her were friends and cousins wearing eye patches and similar hats. They wielded plastic swords and orchestrated mock battles in the hallway. If we had only known that her mom was already living in a different town, and preparing to move to another state, we would have held her tighter, whispered "I love you" more times, and been reluctant to let her go. Alas, we found out too late that she would be gone from our lives. The laughter echoes in our minds but the room with the polka dot curtains is empty. There will be no more bouncing on the bed, using her Barbie doll as a microphone, no more little hands moving furniture in the doll house and no more running down the stairs calling "Grandma" as she runs into my arms.

Today I hear the husky voice of my daughter. We tell each other she will find us one day as we layer her toys and her favorite purple dress in a box. On top is a picture book of the *Nutcracker*. We hope that if she returns, the contents will trigger memories of the happy times spent with us. We each wrote letters, letting her know how much we love her and we shed more tears than we knew were possible. The letters are tucked into the keepsake box.

Maybe one day my daughter will have children. Meanwhile, my arms are empty but I will remember that smile and the word that gave me so much joy—"Grandma."

~Ann Summerville

Comeuppance

We worry about what a child will become tomorrow,
yet we forget that he is someone today.
~Stacia Tauscher

Three young grandchildren were in my care for the day and I hoped no major catastrophes would occur. The usual chaos had temporarily halted and we gathered in the family room. The children amused themselves, at least for the moment.

Artistic Missy, age six, busily covered sheets of typing paper with pictures and designs. I didn't comment on the crayons and colored pencils scattered to the far corners of the room. Stephanie, age four, lugged in her big dollhouse and plunked it in the midst of the myriad of toys already spread out on the floor. Tiny pieces of doll furniture littered the carpet, adding to the already present obstacle course. Tommy, age three, kept busy by constantly flinging a tennis ball in an effort to make a "basket" through the roof of the dollhouse. Now and then Stephanie and Missy hollered at their pesky younger brother to quit bothering them but it didn't stop his Michael Jordan imitation.

I tuned out the name-calling and grabbed a chance to put my feet up in the big recliner chair to snatch a well-deserved break. Closing my eyes, I sighed gratefully for a day without unfortunate incidents. Suddenly a gap in the children's playful quarrelling alerted me. Missy, a precocious first grader, spouted orders to her younger sister.

"Stephanie," she commanded with authority, "you are never to use the F word or the S word."

166   The Name Game : *Comeuppance*

Appalled at the thought of foul language coming from the mouth of a six-year-old, my feet thumped to the ground. I lunged from my chair to take charge. Surely my precious grandchildren hadn't learned such crude language from their parents. Certainly not from their grandparents! I shook my finger in Stephanie's face to get her attention. "Just what kind of language do you think you're using, young lady?" I barked. "Bad language will not be tolerated in this house," I warned with every intention of sending Stephanie to her room until her parents returned.

Stephanie looked shocked. Tears filled her brown eyes and her lower lip quivered. Missy moved close to her sister, eyes wide and puzzled. "But Grandma," Missy offered, eager to defend her sister, "I just told Stephanie it's naughty to use the F and S words. She called me Stupid. Mommy says we aren't ever supposed to call anyone Fat or Stupid. I'm sorry."

A chagrined grandma had overlooked the infinite wisdom of parents and the uncorrupted innocence of children. The grandchildren obviously could manage very well without interference from a clueless grandmother. I mumbled an apology and slunk back to my chair.

~Barbara Brady

Chapter 6

Grandmothers

Through the Generations

No Greater Compliment

Grandchildren are God's way of compensating us for growing old.
~Mary H. Waldrip

ike nothing I had ever done before, writing my stories worked like magic, touching hearts along the way. And, it felt good to know I was leaving my memories behind, my individual fingerprint, for future generations. But, I never dreamed that the imprint was already taking place.

When I mailed the first envelope, a sense of doubt filled my head. "You're actually sending in your personal life story for all the world to see?" Maybe I was being a bit presumptuous, but this was a whole new venture for me. I was so excited, yet it was hard to explain why I was doing it. I wasn't getting paid and it was hard for me to type like I used to. With crippling rheumatoid arthritis hitting in my early thirties, I learned to swallow my pride and find alternative ways of doing things. Over the years, surgeries to correct deformities in my hands had been temporary. So, in order to get back to the keyboard, I resorted to typing with one hand, using the eraser end of a fat pencil like I used in first grade. It wasn't easy, but my brain adapted quickly, letting me know there were no more excuses. I had always wanted to be a writer and the time had come. Now, with thoughts of my disease getting progressively worse, I had a good reason to make it happen.

My life experiences gave me a lot to write about — scoliosis at age twelve, living with RA, going through a traumatic divorce, raising two children on my own, remarriage in my forties — and, now, being a grandmother. The more stories I put into the computer, the more stories formed in my head. Writing became such a huge part of my life I couldn't see myself ever not writing.

As time went on, some of my stories and articles were published in magazines, newspapers, online, and in newsletters. I found the market was there if I did my part right and didn't give up. A few of them even paid me, but the greatest reward for me was seeing my work in print. I didn't think it could get any better. I was wrong.

One day while my eight-year-old granddaughter, Taylor, was visiting, she asked if she could play games on my computer. I didn't have many games, so I showed her my Word file and told her how I write and save my stories on it. She was already my number one fan. I always called her when I got something published. Being a devoted animal lover, she especially liked the ones about my dogs. "Okay," she said. "Do you think I could write a story?"

Thrilled at the prospect, I said, "Sure you can!" I opened up a new page for her. "Think of a story you would like to tell and type it like you're talking to a friend." I left her alone to concentrate. Before long, she called for me and asked me to read what she had written. It was just a short paragraph about her dog, Maggie, but she was heading in the right direction. Then, I showed her how to name it and save it and told her to keep thinking of things to add to it. "You can add another paragraph on your next visit," I said. Seeing the sparkle in her eyes, I wondered where I would be today if I had starting writing at her age.

In a few weeks, Taylor was back and made a beeline for my computer room. I could see it in her eyes. She had something to add to her story. I waited a while before going back to check on her. When I did, she was in deep concentration, so I didn't dare disturb her. Instead, I watched from the doorway as tears filled my eyes. She was typing with my big pencil, eraser down, slowly pecking out every word.

I motioned for my husband in the other room. "Come and see what she's doing," I whispered.

He shook his head and smiled. "She's copying you, Linda. That's a real compliment."

I nodded, but couldn't say a word. My technique was different, but it didn't matter to her. That simple act showed me it wasn't how I typed, but that she wanted to do it like me. I had inspired her; now, she was inspiring me.

Sometimes I wish Taylor had known me when I played piano, crocheted, embroidered and typed eighty words per minute. But, she never knew that person and still believes in me. In the eyes of a child, she sees past my crippled hands and unorthodox attempts to get the job done. And because of that, I'll try harder not to let her down.

~Linda C. Defew

Silence Is Golden

There was no respect for youth when I was young, and now that I am old,
there is no respect for age — I missed it coming and going.
~J.B. Priestly

I feel the words forming on my lips, just itching to escape. And by a sheer effort of will, I stop myself. I do not — repeat, do not — tell Nancy why I earnestly believe that she's crazy to take her son — my beloved grandson — outdoors on this chilly night without a sweater or jacket.

It takes Herculean effort to zip my mouth shut instead of simply zipping little Sam into something warm. But I manage it. And each time I do it, I wonder whether I can ever do it again now that I'm a grandmother, presumably loaded with wisdom and experience.

Our three daughters who are all mothers themselves now, would tell you that I have far too many opinions about the care and feeding of their babes. They'd hint darkly that I'm that stereotypical interfering mother run amok as a grandmother.

Little do they know how much they're not hearing because I've forced an unnatural silence upon myself, willing certain "essential" hints never to be uttered. Hands-off is the challenge of this stage of life, and it's the dirty little secret that nobody had warned me about.

Sure, I'd heard all that lofty stuff about letting your adult children make their own mistakes, about how errors are almost always instructional. But that was B.G.: Before Grandchildren.

It's a far different thing to muzzle yourself as you watch a baby you love more than life itself being—well, mishandled. At least in your prudent and judicious view.

"Don't let Hannah negotiate her own bedtime!" I wanted to shout, not whisper, as I watched what I felt was a most unwise road to disaster on a recent evening.

But there I sat, lips sealed, as Jill and her daughter played out the ancient "I don't want to go to bed!" conflict before my anguished eyes.

Several times, smart little Hannah shot imploring looks at me as these two strong-willed females—my daughter and granddaughter—battled it out, with Jill, I felt, losing ground by the second.

My huge temptation, of course, was to substitute my judgment for Jill's. Hadn't I maneuvered my way through these skirmishes three times, once with Jill herself and twice more with her feisty sisters? Wasn't I "credentialed" by virtue of my having gotten through all this with daughters at least as oppositional as little Hannah?

I was not. And that's the crux of it.

No matter how wise and all-knowing we grandparents think we are—no matter how awesome our perspective, how brilliant our insights—never is silence as golden as when your child, now a parent, is working her way through a conflict.

I've already been sorely tested. On issues from whether aerobic exercise is wise in the last trimester of pregnancy, to how much strained applesauce a growing baby should be urged to eat, the moments have come fast and furious when my own fount of wisdom has been shut down by a glance, a cross word, a "thanks but no thanks" response to my brilliance.

Nancy clearly doesn't welcome my gratuitous advice about how to dress Sam for the elements any more than Jill appreciates my bedtime psychology or my lacerating point of view as to why little Isaiah needs more fresh air. Amy has steadfastly resisted my brilliance on the merits of fresh applesauce over the kind that comes in jars for one of our younger grandchildren.

There is no market, these days, for my piercing opinions on discipline, nutrition or the importance of ballet in a little girl's life.

It's not the way I thought things would be. It never is.

Motherhood/grandmotherhood, I dare to suggest, was easier a generation ago when new mothers were younger and when society somehow allowed grandmothers more slack.

I can also vividly remember my own mother getting advice from her own stern mother, Grandmom Goldberg, whose wisdom came from the shtetls of Russia. It seems to me that my mother listened, more often than not.

But I've just about memorized the chief commandment of contemporary grandparenthood: "Thou shalt not give advice to the parents of your grandchildren."

The reasons are obvious, rational and right. But the heart may struggle to accept what the head knows. So like most grandparents, I sometimes stumble on the road to wisdom. Then I pick myself up, dust myself off, and try again to do the hardest work in the world: keep my opinions to myself.

I remind myself of the powerful reasons to butt out, I practice primitive control devices like counting to ten, or I just beat a hasty retreat from the crisis at hand.

And when all else fails, I remind myself of this eternal verity about adult children: Even though, once upon a time, you changed their diapers and taught them how to tie their shoes, they won't listen to you anyway.

~Sally Schwartz Friedman

"Mom, texting me 'helpful suggestions' about the kids is not the same as keeping quiet."

How Can We Make
Grams Cry This Year?

*Grandma always made you feel she had been waiting to see just you all day
and now the day was complete.*

~Marcy DeMaree

Once a year, my brother, sister and I, together with my three cousins, have a common goal — to make our grandmother cry. Yes, it sounds cruel, but let me explain.

Over the years, we've created a tradition with our grandmother, who we call Grams. It is one of those traditions that wasn't planned — it just happened. The tradition takes place on the day before Christmas every year and it has for many, many years.

As I mentioned, our goal is to make Grams cry. In our family, there are six grandkids who are all relatively close in age. Growing up we got together once or twice a year, typically in the summer and at Christmas. Our family was and is still very close. We enjoy playing cards, watching movies, and spending time together laughing and telling silly stories.

Since we were young, our Grams spoiled us rotten. You could tell she loved it. When we were younger, she always had a chocolate bar or a pack of bubble gum in her purse when she came to visit. She loves to make us happy and when she is really happy, she cries with tears of joy. You really know how full of joy she is when the tears arrive.

Back in the 1980s, when the three older grandkids (myself and two of my cousins) were in grades six and seven, we decided we wanted to find a Christmas present for Grams. On December 24th, our parents packed us in the car and we headed for the mall. After spending over two hours searching every possible store that had potential gifts, we found this funky lamp. It had a bunch of thin clear plastic strands that you placed into the top of the lamp. To all of us in our preteens, this was the coolest possible present we could give Grams. I'm almost positive our parents thought we were nuts. It is the thought that counts, so we put all our savings together and bought Grams the funky lamp.

On Christmas morning, after some initial presents were opened, all the grandkids gathered around Grams and the square, wrapped box. She ripped off the wrapping paper and as her eyes saw the picture on the side of the box, she laughed a big strong laugh. At the same time, she was overwhelmed by the fact that her young grandkids had gone out of their way to find her a unique gift. In a very short period of time, her laughter turned to tears. We all gave her a big hug and a kiss.

A year later on Christmas Eve, after hours of searching, we found an owl figurine we thought she would like. We all remembered she had an owl figurine on her coffee table and we figured she would love to start a collection. Again, this made her cry with tears of joy. We later found out owls weren't really her favorite. Someone else had given the original owl on her coffee table to her, thinking she liked them too.

By the third year, our quest to find Grams a present was the highlight of our Christmas. I think it was in the third year we realized our gifts had consistently made her cry. We had a new challenge on our hands, in addition to the hours of searching the mall every Christmas Eve, trying to get consensus from six grandkids on one present. We all began to learn endurance, negotiation and the power of giving, more and more every year.

As we got older, we needed to get more creative. We even got proactive and started planning before Christmas Eve so we weren't scrambling at the last minute.

If you are curious about some of things we gave our Grams, here is a short list. Over the years, we became smarter at picking specific presents that would result in tears of joy:

- A lamp that contained an illuminated rose in a clear box
- An electric massager for her chair
- A T-shirt with all our handprints on it
- A stocking full of bath soaps and perfumes
- A picture of all six grandkids with Santa
- A calendar with pictures of the grandkids in every month plus all our special days were labeled — birthdays, holidays, anniversaries, etc.
- A digital photo frame with a variety of pictures of all the grandkids
- Individual pictures of all the grandkids wearing red hats (in honour of her membership with the Red Hat Society)
- A variety of pictures of all the grandkids with the letters G, R, A, M, S made in various ways
- A theme gift of "Sweet Treats" — we all gave her different kinds of her favorite sweet things

Over the years, our Grams has been through a lot of hardships and I have always been amazed by her ability to overcome challenges. She has faced cancer more than once, survived a near fatal car accident in the late 1990s and lost her husband at a young age.

Of course, she still lives in her own home and drives her own car. She recently enrolled in driver's education so she could pass a required road test to keep her driver's license.

She still gets out to see her friends to play cards every week and when we are all together, she is the one wanting to stay up late and play cards. She has more energy than I ever will have. She keeps up to date with all the major tennis, golf and curling events, and at age eighty-seven, she bought a wide screen TV and contemplated whether or not to get the five-year extended warranty.

Our Grams is an inspiration for how life should be enjoyed every moment and every day. We all should have tears of joy for each day we are alive.

~Aaron Solly

55

Return to Heart Mountain

I will permit no man to narrow and degrade my soul by making me hate him.
~Booker T. Washington

ike a little kid who gets too excited waiting to ride a roller coaster, I feel like I might throw up. I have been looking forward to this and yet, my emotions alternate between complete euphoria and an overwhelming desire to turn the car around. I'm scared, but I can't turn back. There is too much riding on this venture and so I continue driving into the unknown at sixty-five miles per hour.

It feels like my husband, Mike, and I have been driving on this rural Wyoming highway for hours, when in reality barely twenty minutes have passed since we left our motel in Cody. The land before me is beautiful, but I am unable to appreciate it because I am so preoccupied with what is about to happen. My hands take on a life of their own, fidgeting with the seatbelt, the window, my sunglasses. My eyes search the road for any sign of our destination. In my hand I hold the directions given to me by my grandma. The frayed edges are becoming damp in my sweaty hands.

"Is that it?" Mike asks. I follow his gaze and almost miss seeing a small brown sign with faded white lettering on the side of the road.

This is Heart Mountain Relocation Camp. This is our destination and the reason for our trip. We have come to visit the site of the internment camp where my grandma spent three years of her life locked up like a prisoner during World War II simply because she was the "wrong" race.

"That's it!" I yell, but we have already missed our turn.

"Don't worry, I'm turning around," Mike says. He reaches over and pats my leg, both to reassure me and to make me sit back down in my seat.

"Here it is," Mike says as he exits onto a small dirt road. I stare at the land, devoid of any markers that would hint at its importance, as we slowly make our way towards the camp.

The humming sound of gravel under the tires of our car has a calming effect, but it can't drown the sound of my heartbeat in my ears or ease the tightness in my throat. I catch myself leaning forward, silently urging the car to go faster. The remnants of the camp come into view and I want to be there now. I need to be there.

We pull off onto what might have once been a dirt road, but is now nothing more than a path overgrown with weeds. There are no other cars around and even the birds that chirped non-stop since we arrived in Cody seem to have disappeared. As we park the car I sink back into my seat, unable to move.

Three buildings loom before me, the remains of my grandma's former prison, fenced in by a chain link fence. A thin line of barbed wire tops the fence and the sight of it sickens me.

They were fenced in like cattle, I think. And guarded like criminals in their own country.

The buildings are predictably worn down, but after years of staring at pictures of the camp in textbooks, I recognize them. I recognize the black tar paper that barely kept out the wind and snow. I recognize the tiny windows in the walls.

In the far distance, I can see a tower made of bricks. I know from my grandma's stories that it used to be a part of the internee hospital. It is infamous in my family because it is in that hospital that my grandma's first daughter died when she was less than a day old, a baby whose only day on earth was spent behind barbed wire fences.

I am no longer afraid. Instead, I feel the resentment my grandma has been holding onto for half a century collect in a lump in my throat. The reality of what happened to her so many years ago hits me harder as I stare at the same landscape my grandma stared at for three long years. I am angry. Big salty tears blur my vision and I lose sight of my surroundings.

"Are you ready?" Mike asks quietly when minutes after we have parked we are still sitting in the car.

I nod my head, but still don't move. Mike gets out of the car and I take little notice of him as he rummages through the trunk. My eyes are glued to the tower. Mike opens my car door and I jump at the sound.

"Come on," he urges as he pushes my camera into my hands. Suddenly, I am out of the car, brushing past Mike and running towards the buildings. I remember why I am here. This place, so desolate and run down, is a piece of my history. I am here to remember those who lost their lives and lost their years in this place. I am here to document what's left of their prison. I have brought years of resentment and anger with me and I intend to leave them here. I have come in my grandma's stead to make peace with the past that has held our family captive for too long. I have come for closure.

The land feels empty and eerie, but in a strange way it also feels welcoming, like it has been waiting for me. I move reverently among the buildings, snapping photographs and lightly tracing my fingers over the walls. I try to wrap my head around what I am feeling, but words escape me. I feel pain. I feel connected. I feel peace.

As I look through the lens of my camera I feel myself willing the buildings to give up their stories. For an hour I silently wander back and forth, taking pictures and taking it all in. As I walk, I can literally feel myself change. I unclench my fists and the anger that Grandma had felt, the anger that she had passed on to me, seems to drop to the ground like pebbles.

I close my eyes and take a breath.

"We forgive you," I whisper, and as my words are carried away with the breeze the roots of resentment that had kept my family tied to Heart Mountain begin to untangle themselves from the ground. I bend down and pick up a two small white rocks from the dirt. I am taking home a piece of this place: one rock for me and one for Grandma.

As we slowly drive away from the site, I turn around in my seat and stick my head out of the window desperate to watch it until it completely disappears. The wind whips my hair around my head in a frenzied dance. Years ago my grandma had lived here as a prisoner in her own country, forced to give up everything she owned. Today, I had walked the grounds offering forgiveness for the past and gaining closure in return. I did it for myself. I did it for my family. I did it for Grandma.

~Jessie Miyeko Santala

Two Peas in a Pod

There is a bit of insanity in dancing that does everybody a great deal of good.
~Edwin Denby

When my granddaughter Emily was five she was a go-getter who tried my patience to the limit. With big blue eyes the size of saucers and blond hair that looked like it was combed with an eggbeater, she was a whirlwind in motion. After one of her visits, I would head for the bottle of aspirin and fill the tub with hot water for a bubble bath, some medication and meditation.

During one particular visit, she was in rare form. She had twirled into a lamp and broken it, stuck her toe into the nightlight and burned it, and clogged the toilet by flushing a napkin down it, all in the course of twenty-four hours.

She was up at the crack of dawn the next morning and found my cosmetics. I was practically scared out of my wits when a small ghoulish form in full make-up crawled into bed with me. I was ready to scold her, but my heart melted when Emily said, "Nana, you always look so pretty. Would you teach me to wear make-up just like you do?"

I decided that day we would do a craft project together to keep Emily out of mischief and maybe this time we would bond a little. I sat at the kitchen table with scrapbooking tools of every description, papers in various hues of the rainbow and scissors that cut every which way. I was working hard at lining up letters on a page while Emily twirled around the room in circles.

"Emily, please sit down!" I practically yelled across the kitchen. "I'm getting a headache watching you."

"But, Nana, I love to see the colors in my skirt go round and round," she replied.

Pushing on my temples, I tried to will away the throb that was building behind my eyes.

"Emily, you're not helping Nana's headache," I cautioned.

"What's wrong, Nana? I'm just twirling. I'm not hurting anything."

Why did Emily drive me crazy? I had done fine with my own children but this granddaughter was getting on my nerves. I must be a terrible grandmother, I thought as I lay in bed that night listening to her hum to herself. Why couldn't she sit still? Where had I gone wrong? I was more determined than ever to make her visit a happy experience. Maybe we would form a connection. Living two hours away, I didn't get to see her as often as I would have liked.

The next morning I gave up on scrapbooking and let Emily play dress-up with my costume jewelry and old evening dresses. Heels, purses, boas and scarves kept her busy the rest of the afternoon. As I busied myself in the kitchen, I watched her out of the corner of my eye. She seemed to have more fun tramping around the room singing than trying to do a craft project with me. I felt like the worst grandma in the world.

That evening I called Emily's mom, Jennifer.

"Jen, I'm just doing terrible as a grandmother," I confessed.

"What makes you say that, Mom?"

"Well, I can't seem to relate to Emily. She's a bundle of energy and never sits still long enough for us to get to know one another," I said, practically in tears.

My daughter began to chuckle, "Mom, you don't get it, do you?"

"What?" I asked.

"She's you! You two are exactly alike—two peas in a pod."

"Me? You're kidding, right? I'm not like her."

"Yes, Mom, you! You're both bundles of energy. You both like glittery clothes, shiny jewelry, and are drama queens at heart. Give yourself a chance."

"A drama queen? Really!" I couldn't believe my ears.

I paused to think. Could it be? Was she right? She had made some good points. I had to admit it—maybe she was right on.

"You know, Jen, I just didn't see it. I may have been going about this all wrong. I have an idea that might work. We'll talk again tomorrow night," I said, gently hanging up the phone.

The next day I decided to try a different approach. I dragged out the Karaoke machine and Emily's eyes lit up. She loved to sing and dance, just as I had at her age. I remembered the feel of the conical toe shoes in ballet class and the sound of tap clicks on the wooden floor of the dance studio. I was never happier than when I was singing or dancing. I loved make-up and wearing bling.

"Emily, would you like it if Nana put on a show with you?" I asked.

"Oh goodie," she said, clapping her hands and jumping up and down.

We moved the furniture around and hung up a sheet in the entry hall. We used the tiled foyer as our stage. Then we proceeded to put on a wild floorshow, complete with improvised costumes, lots of beads and make-up. The afternoon flew by as we glided and stomped across the floor. Emily and I moved to the beat of the Stones, and giggled and hugged when we took our bows. It felt good to feel so young and alive again. Maybe I wasn't such a bad grandma after all.

"Can we do it again tomorrow, Nana?"

"Sure," I replied. I had found the magic key. That night in bed we cuddled and recollected our day. I got a big kiss goodnight and an extra long hug.

Emily and I got bolder as the week went on. We danced to Chubby Checker, Herman's Hermits, Buddy Holly, and did our own version of *Grease*. Emily didn't know where I got all the material, but little did she know her Nana was once a hoppin' and boppin' teenager.

Ten years have gone by and Emily has lived in Japan and Washington. Even though she is far away she sends me pictures of funky clothes she likes, via e-mail. I see her pictures on Facebook and I mail her glittery costume jewelry that I find.

Our love has evolved over time and we are now in sync. I can relate to her and I love her enthusiastic approach to life. What was once so annoying to me is now as refreshing as the baths I used to take when she left. Emily is a sophomore in high school and is moving back to our area this year. She now does performances in local theater and in her school's talent show. I can't wait to be there in person. I'll be the one cheering in the front row. I know when she bows she'll blow a special kiss just for me. We're two peas in a pod.

~Sallie A. Rodman

Chicken Soup
for the Soul.

Great Expectations

If the family were a fruit, it would be an orange, a circle of sections,
held together but separable — each segment distinct.
~Letty Cottin Pogrebin

"**H**e's seventeen!" my daughter fairly shouted over the phone lines. My mind went back seventeen years to a sad day in November. Janie was only fourteen and had returned home from a summer staying at her married brother's house. Her father and I had worried about our high-spirited daughter getting into trouble if she stayed home alone all summer.

It would seem that Janie had already gotten into trouble before she went to stay with her brother, as it was obvious that she was pregnant. "They put ads in the paper," Janie told me. "We call them and then we talk to them and if they're okay, I let them adopt the baby."

I knew nothing about adopting out newborn babies but would soon learn more than I ever thought I would ever want to know.

Janie did choose the parents to adopt her baby and on a cold night in November she gave birth to her son. As the adoptive parents and their family cheered and shared their joy over their newborn son, Janie and I sat alone in the delivery room, the birth over. I felt as if we were no longer needed. All I could do was hold on to Janie with all my strength.

We got through it together.

Through the years I prayed every week at church for this grandson. "Please let him be having a good life. Let his parents be loving and good. Let him grow into a strong, well-adjusted young man," I would silently ask my Lord.

Fourteen was entirely too young to be raising a baby. Janie moved on. She got married. She had another child, a daughter.

I lavished all the pent-up grandmotherly urges in me on my beautiful granddaughter, Katie. I took her on long weekends, arranging interesting and educational activities, attending live musicals, nature walks, swimming at the local beach. I loved being a grandmother. It is the best thing about grandparenting: a child to love, enjoy and send home to proper parents come the right time.

Somewhere some other woman was the grandmother to my first grandchild. "Please let him be having a good life. Let his parents be loving and good. Let him grow into a strong, well-adjusted young man" was still my silent prayer. "Let him have a grandmother who enjoys being with him the way I enjoy being with Katie," I would add after a weekend with my beloved granddaughter.

Katie began attending school and Janie would tell me that she was trying to find her firstborn son. It had been a modern adoption. Janie was entitled to periodic pictures upon request. I knew that the baby boy born on that sad November night was a teenager by now. I wondered what sorts of things a grandmother would do with a teenage grandson. "Please let him be having a good life. Let his parents be loving and good. Let him grow into a strong, well-adjusted young man. Let him have a grandmother who enjoys being with him the way I enjoy being with Katie. Let Janie and I find him someday," was my longer silent prayer.

Janie found him. The adoptive mother sent Janie pictures of young Charles. Charles looked so much like Janie it took my breath away. He looked more like Janie than even Katie.

There were several pictures sent along, including a short letter from Charles's adoptive mother. It's hard to ascertain such things from pictures, I suppose, but judging by the activities in the pictures: carving pumpkins, playing on the beach, riding a bike, one could ascertain by the smile and relaxed manner Charles displayed in the pictures that he was happy and well-adjusted. I closed my eyes and thanked the Lord.

For he looked like he was having a good life. His parents looked as if they were loving and good. He certainly appeared to be a strong, well-adjusted young man. I recalled the joyful noises in the hospital the night he was born. I was certain he had a grandmother who enjoyed being with him the way I enjoyed being with Katie. And now, Janie and I have found him. We learned he has two younger siblings, also adopted.

It will be a few years before we meet Charles in person. Janie says he's still too young to confuse him with the introduction of another family. Someday he'll meet Katie and Janie and me. Then I will be a grandmother who will enjoy being with him the way I enjoy being with Katie.

~Patricia Fish

58

Grandma's Legacy

*That which seems the height of absurdity in one generation
often becomes the height of wisdom in another.*
~Adlai Stevenson

The spring he turned eleven, my husband's parents asked his grandmother to watch him when they left for a sunny Florida vacation. That first afternoon, as he did every day, Ron played ball in his Brooklyn schoolyard with a dozen other pre-adolescent boys. Suddenly, Gram appeared behind the chain link fence—an embarrassing act of enormous proportions—and to his horror, presented him with hot chocolate.

Humiliation swept over him. Hiding behind an air of nonchalance, he turned his back and dribbled the ball to the farthest end of the yard, and shot two successive hoops.

"Ronchkinyoo!" Undeterred, Gram proceeded to call over to him, using the Eastern European form of nicknaming the children. "Ronchkinyoo, what vegetable do you want for dinner on Thursday?"

The dinner menu for four days hence was the last thing on Ron's mind, as remote as his chance of ever kissing Ellen Goldberg.

But while Ronchkinyoo was ready then to swear to his snickering friends that he had never met this crazed woman who pretended to know him, forty years later her memory makes him smile. He reminisces about that special woman who nurtured him with boundless devotion, who so easily accepted the fact that her grandson only saw the aging woman with swollen legs and a double chin. She allowed him to playfully flick the bat-like flab arms, never letting on that not long before she had been a young woman who was kissed by men.

That question, "Ronchkinyoo, what vegetable do you want for dinner on Thursday?" had, in time, distilled into a legacy, for Ron became a cross between being a grandma hen and the manager who plans ahead.

"We'll need to get Jonathan a new winter coat," Ron says when school breaks for the summer. "Do you want a window seat or an aisle when we go to the Bahamas?" he asks when he calls me at the office five months before the trip.

I often let out a deep sigh of exasperation. The last-minute person in me must cope with the client presentation due tomorrow, and the overdue wrapping of a baby gift for a friend who managed to beat the biological clock a year ago.

But on a snow-filled Sunday, when I'm ready to say "no more" to long-term planning, Gram's nurturing shadow reappears.

I have risen early. Six hours later I am still punching the keyboard when Ron shows up with a lunch plate of mixed greens and blue cheese dressing, the way I like it. He places it at my elbow. "You should eat something," he says, and kisses the top of my head.

And I raise my eyes from the glaring screen, my heart overflowing at the tenderness of his nurturing. And I think of his Gram who taught him all those years ago about loving and giving.

~Talia Carner

59

Grandma's Challah

If God had intended us to follow recipes,
He wouldn't have given us grandmothers.
~Linda Henley

My grandma came all the way from New York to visit us in California when I was ten. She was going to teach me how to make her marvelous challah bread.

After she settled in we set out all the ingredients, a huge bowl, and a big mixing spoon. I grabbed a pencil and paper and stood poised, ready to scribble down the recipe as she made the dough.

She measured one cup of hot water. She dropped in two small blocks of yeast and a large pinch of sugar.

A pinch — about a teaspoon, maybe two. I wrote it down.

"While the yeast is growing fluffy, we can start with the flour."

I held out a measuring cup. Grandma waved it aside and dipped her hands into the flour canister. She scooped out six handfuls and piled them right onto the big wooden breadboard.

My mouth dropped open. "Wait, Grandma!" I shoveled the pile into the measuring cup, dumping them one by one into the big bowl.

Almost exactly six cups. Check. Got it.

Grandma dumped the flour back onto the board. A white cloud poofed up into our faces. "A little of this…" She added a small handful of sugar. "And a bissel of that." In went three shakes of salt. Grandma stared at the pile, pursing her lips thoughtfully. She added another handful of flour.

"Grandma, I need to measure the flour before you add it."

Grandma smiled and wiped stray flour from my cheek. "What's important is how the dough feels. That's how you know how much flour to use." She made a well in the center of the flour and added four eggs. I stared, amazed, as she deftly mixed those eggs into the flour—nothing oozed out the side. She made the well deeper, then added the frothy yeast mix.

Grandma kneaded the soft, yellow dough, gently punching and turning, punching and turning. "Come Bubbalah, you try it now." She took my hands into her large, wrinkled ones. Together we kneaded the dough into a smooth, satiny ball.

"Squeeze here gently." Grandma guided my hand slowly into the yellow dough. "This is what challah dough should feel like."

"It's kind of soft," I said.

"Soft, but not too soft." Grandma's gray-blue eyes stared into mine. "What else?"

I squeezed again. "It's squishy, like rubber."

Grandma's eyes twinkled. "Exactly!" She put her nose near the dough and sniffed deeply. "Ahh!" she murmured.

"Ahh!" I looked at Grandma. I really wanted to sample the dough before we baked it.

Grandma saw me licking my lips and poked my tummy. "Okay, Little Dough Girl, you can have a small taste."

I popped a thimble-sized piece in my mouth. "It doesn't taste like challah," I said, scrunching up my nose.

Grandma just smiled. She scooped up the soft pile and plopped it into the bottom of a huge blue bowl, then covered it with a kitchen towel.

"Now what, Grandma?"

"Now the dough takes a nap."

"A nap?"

Grandma nodded. "It has to rise up big and puffy until it fills the bowl to the top."

"How long a nap does it need?"

Grandma looked at the kitchen clock above our sink. "It will rest for one hour." She looked at me. "How about we make this kitchen sparkling bright for your mama?"

My bottom lip puckered out. "Aw, Grandma." But she had already begun piling the cups and spoons from our baking into the sink with the leftover lunch dishes.

"I'll wash, you dry." She tossed me a towel. There was no arguing with Grandma. We spent the entire hour scrubbing every inch of that kitchen, from some leftover tomato sauce that had somehow found its way to the ceiling to the lima bean hiding in the corner behind the kitchen table.

"Excellent!" Grandma beamed as she surveyed the spotless room. "We're done, and so is the challah dough."

I ran over and peeled the towel from the bowl. My jaw dropped open. "Grandma, it filled up the whole bowl!"

"Now we punch it down and braid it." Grandma made a fist with her right hand. I did the same.

What fun it was to push my fist into that billowy soft dough until my whole hand disappeared, then slowly pull it out with a noisy thwerp.

"What's next, Grandma?"

"We make long logs." Grandma divided the dough into four parts. "See?" she said, rolling one part gently between her palms.

I watched as the blob of dough lengthened into a roly-poly snake.

"Your turn." Grandma smiled as she placed the next blob into my eager hands. My snakes were short and lumpy, but Grandma praised them as the best she'd ever seen. With a few well-placed squeezes from her magic fingers, my dough looked just like hers. I reached for the last blob.

"Wait, Bubbalah. That one has a special job. We have to braid these three first. Do you know how to braid?"

My mom had taught me how to braid yarn when I was eight. But how do you braid squishy, floppy dough snakes? "Right over left, left over right?"

"So smart you are!" Grandma laid the dough strips side by side. Starting at one end, she took the right strip and placed it over the middle one. "Right over left." Next she took the left strip and placed it over the one now in the middle. "Left over right."

"Just like with yarn!" I laughed. Grandma let me finish. The challah lay on the board, pale and skinny. Grandma took the last blob of dough and divided it into three smaller snakes. I quickly braided it for her and she placed it right on top of the bigger challah. Then she pulled off two small balls of dough from the end.

"These will be the sweet little birdies to guard the challah and make it rise big and tall." Grandma fashioned two perfect little birds and nestled them on the top braid. She carefully moved the challah onto a cookie sheet and covered it with the towel.

"Time for another nap, Grandma?"

"Yes dear, for the challah and for me, too." Grandma set the timer and sat down in our big, comfy recliner. I helped her put her feet up, then went to get my Nancy Drew book.

Grandma snored slightly while I cheered on Nancy and her dad.

"Time to turn on the oven."

I looked up. Grandma was on her way to the kitchen. The timer buzzed as the oven grew hot. I uncovered the dough.

"Grandma!" The challah had grown as large as the cookie sheet. We popped it into the oven. The smell of the baking bread filled the kitchen.

"Mmm," said my mom as she came in the front door. I ran to help her put away the groceries.

"Yum!" said Dad a short time later as he came home from work.

The timer buzzed once more. Grandma took out our golden brown challah.

"That has got to be the best looking challah in the whole world!" Dad gave me a big hug. "I haven't had a homemade challah since…"

He looked at Grandma, then back at me. "Well, not since way before you were born."

Grandma came over and we joined in a great big hug, all braided together, just like the challah.

~Marcia Berneger

60

Memories

*A memory is what is left when something happens
and does not completely unhappen.*
~Edward de Bono

"Sunrise, sunset, sunrise, sunset, swiftly through the years." The melody from *Fiddler on the Roof* continues to float through my mind. Where have all the years gone? It seems like only yesterday that my granddaughter, Amanda, was that energetic, exuberant little girl who ran with outstretched arms to greet me at the airport, then lifted a tear-stained face for one more kiss when our visit was over and it was time for me to leave.

Living hundreds of miles away made those visits few and far between—only once or twice a year but oh, so precious to me. That's why when my husband suggested we retire in Texas, it was a no-brainer for me. I missed being close to family and all those hugs and kisses.

Yet, now living just a few blocks away, I sense a distance has grown between Amanda and me. It has been a long time since I've gotten a hug without asking. Granted, Amanda isn't a little girl anymore. She has become an attractive young woman. Her long, lustrous dark curls frame her rich chocolate eyes that twinkle with delight when she laughs. Her Texas sun-bronzed skin adds one more touch to her beauty.

I know Amanda is beautiful inside as well, but I wonder, does she know it? I sense a struggle within. What is it about those teen years that may have caused a rift between us? Is the generation gap too difficult to bridge? How do we break down the invisible wall I feel standing between us? Now in just a few short days, Amanda will be stepping into that monumental year—the year we all seem to eagerly long for as our rite-of-passage to adulthood. What can I do to show Amanda she is special on her twenty-first birthday?

Memories of other special events nudged me as I pulled out the stack of family photo albums tucked away in the cupboard and began to turn back the pages of time. What if I made a unique album just for her—one with pictures of the three of us together that would tell her, "Thanks for all the wonderful memories."

Beside each picture, David and I took turns writing our thoughts about what those moments meant to us. As I gazed at the snapshot of when I held her at three weeks old, I told her, "It was love at first sight for me." Dancing with her in his arms while still in their pajamas one Christmas morning, the look of total contentment on Grandpa's face told her, "I could have danced all night."

As the album quickly fills with wonderful memories of summer vacations, Christmas and other holidays throughout the years I wonder if this effort will be enough. Leaving Amanda's gift with our daughter for their family weekend-getaway celebration, I knew I'd have to wait to find out when they returned.

That evening the phone rang and I heard words that were music to my ears. "Grandma—I had to call you before we left! I love my album! It is so awesome—you made me cry. I love you."

Tears filled my eyes as I answered, "I love you too, Amanda. Happy twenty-first birthday!"

~Karen R. Kilby

A Working Woman

*A lot of what passes for depression these days
is nothing more than a body saying that it needs work.*
~Geoffrey Norman

Grandma pulled the quilts she'd made out of the trunk, like she did every time I came to visit. "Did you see this one last time?" she asked, as she held one up that was sewn in bright primary colors, pieced together to form one large star.

"The Lone Star. I remember that one. The colors are beautiful," I answered.

"I figured you might like that one since you live in Texas now."

She lifted several more quilts out of the trunk and unfolded another one.

"How about this embroidered one?" Grandma smoothed her hands over a quilt that featured blocks embroidered with the birds of all fifty states. "I can't remember if I got that one out or not."

"Yes, we talked about that one. I didn't know you did embroidery until you showed it to me. It's fine work."

Grandma smiled at the compliment but looked frustrated. It didn't appear that she would be able to rest until she could show me a quilt I hadn't yet seen. I could tell she was tiring herself from lifting the quilts out of the trunk and spreading them out. I stood up to help, but she waved me back to my chair.

"You can see them better from back there. You just stay put."

I wondered how much more time we would spend looking at

the quilts. My visit wouldn't be long, and I had hoped our talk would center on our family. Grandma was able to summon up wonderful memories of the distant past, and she would regale me with detailed stories of her childhood if she was in the mood. I had even brought a pad and pen with me, hoping to write down some of the things she said in order to chronicle them for future generations. But we seemed to be stuck on the quilts.

"Now I know I've finished some since you were here last. They've got to be in this stack."

I thought maybe if I pried her away from the living room we might get a chance to talk about something else. "Grandma, how about we take a break and I'll take you out to lunch somewhere?"

"Oh, I don't think so dear. My hair's a mess and I'm not dressed for it."

"Well how about if I run out and pick something up for us?"

"That would be fine. While you're gone I'll try to figure out which of these you haven't seen."

Grandma turned back to the pile of quilts, while I slung my purse over my shoulder and headed for my car. I couldn't figure out why she was so fixated on the quilts. She always liked to show them off, but I'd never seen her unable to focus on anything else.

As I sat in line at the drive-up window, it came to me so suddenly and so simply that I wondered how I had missed it. Grandma had been a busy farmwoman all her life. Her days had been filled with chores like feeding the chickens, tending to her vegetable garden and cooking meals for her family. She measured her worth by how much hard work she did each day. My grandfather died several years earlier and now Grandma lived in a small apartment. Her quilts were now her contribution to the world, and she needed to show them to anyone who came by to prove that she was still providing something of value. I knew what I needed to do when I returned to her apartment with our lunches in a sack. I left my pen and pad in the car—I knew I wouldn't need them.

When Grandma opened her door I saw she had set out glasses, silverware and napkins for our fast food meal at her small kitchen table.

"Would you mind if we took our sandwiches into the living room to eat?" I asked. "We don't want to get food on the quilts, but we could see them while we're eating and I can ask you questions about them."

Grandmother's eyes sparkled. "Well, I think that's a great idea," she said, as she started for the living room. "And while you were gone I think I found a couple I've finished since you came last time."

I smiled and grabbed the sack of food and followed her. My questions about family could wait for another day.

~Nancy Hatten

62

Full of Grace

The robbed that smiles, steals something from the thief.
~William Shakespeare

"I don't feel right about this," I whispered to one of my cousins. She nodded in agreement and tucked an errant hair behind her ear. I twisted my fingers in the napkin on my lap, not wanting to be the first to touch the food. Turkey, mashed potatoes with gravy, stuffing and green bean casserole called to me, but their siren song seemed muted. I sighed and waited for one of the older adults to start.

Thanksgiving usually meant laughter and stuffed bellies; however, this year was different. My family sat around the candlelit table staring at our feast. No words, no sounds of utensils clinking, only unmet gazes and shifting in seats. Everyone had a full plate, everyone except for Grandma.

After conquering throat cancer, the radiation treatment intended to provide life-saving therapy took away one of her greatest pleasures, eating. Grandma had received her feeding tube a few weeks earlier and this was the first of many food-focused holidays to come. I couldn't imagine what it would be like to never taste buttery rolls or pumpkin pie again.

The fabric in my hands was now more origami than napkin when my dad began to pray. A small ripple of relief passed through me for the few seconds of just having to listen. By the time he reached, "Amen," concern thundered around me again. This felt wrong.

My cousin Molly pierced the silence with a raise of her glass, "To Nat."

We all followed her lead, one crystal goblet at a time.

"Your courage and strength inspire us all," she continued.

Unshed tears sparkled as Grandma smiled and said, "Thank you. Please, please eat."

And with that, we all began to feast. Conversations erupted around the room while Grandma laughed and talked with us all. She graciously asked questions about the food, wondering if the stuffing was too dry or if the sweet potatoes had too many marshmallows. Cancer would take away her ability to eat, but not her gift of being the ultimate hostess.

The evening went on as normal Thanksgivings do, with rounds of *Pictionary* and jokes told over dessert. By the time the night was over, I felt closer to my family than ever before. I learned that we gather together on holidays not to eat rich fare and complain of "food coma," but to support and share with one another. We celebrated my grandmother's courage, but we all learned a lesson in grace.

In the years following, my grandma continued to create meals for family events that were just as delicious, if not better, than before. Not once did I hear her lament about what she was missing. She told me once with a laugh, "I may not be able to eat, but I can still taste things."

Her spin on what could have been a chute into the depths of depression showed me the value of a positive attitude. Instead of obsessing about what she lost, she channeled her focus into becoming a champion of taste. She discovered new recipes and made improvements on old ones, all the while surviving after a life-altering blow. With a selfless heart, she prepared what she could not have for the sole purpose of making us happy. She inspired me to learn to cook and helped me find the secret ingredient to make everything come together: love.

~Hilary Heskett

Chapter
7

Grandmothers

Grand Fun

63

An "Aha Moment"

There's no place like home except Grandma's.
~Author Unknown

When my grandson was born, it was love at first sight. Tears of joy flooded my face as Randy's tiny fingers gripped mine. A proud grandma, I couldn't help but point out his sparkling dark brown eyes, handsome features and cute little grin. Whenever anyone suggested that he looked like me, I agreed wholeheartedly.

The older he got, the more I bragged. So handsome. And smart? It was obvious he was destined to be a rocket scientist. Or maybe an engineer. Did you see how he stacked those blocks? What a genius.

Time has a way of slipping by. An honor student and star athlete, Randy makes me proud. Now that he's almost a teenager he's become preoccupied with iPods, Xbox, cell phones and texting. Before I can hold a conversation with him, I have to remove the headphone from his ears. Our one-on-one time seems to be dwindling.

My recent foot surgery had me off my feet for several months. Randy lives next door and surprised me when he showed up every day after school to see if I needed help. We watched TV and played game after game of *Clue* just like old times.

Some afternoons he'd flop on the couch, and we'd talk about sports, summer and the future. He was so attentive, I worried he knew something I didn't. It was just foot surgery, right?

Every afternoon before he left, he asked to use my laptop. One day I peeked over his shoulder to see what he was working on. With a sheepish grin, he admitted he was chatting with friends on MySpace.

"That's my girlfriend," he said pointing to a cute little girl with long brown hair.

"You're way too young for that, but I love her dimples."

For two weeks, he visited non-stop. When he found out Grandpa was leaving for a trap shoot, he even offered to spend the weekend. What a wonderful grandson. Smiling, I caught myself remembering when he used to call and ask, "Are you thinking what I'm thinking? Come and get me."

One day, Randy's visits stopped as abruptly as they'd started. I assumed it was because I'd graduated to a walking boot and didn't need as much help. A week went by without us seeing each other. I knew he was busy with the new school year and sports, but I missed his company.

His mother checked on me daily. One day she called and said, "Well, I'm glad Randy's grades have improved."

"How can you do better than an A?" I asked.

She explained his study habits and marks had gone downhill since he'd started middle school. He'd put more effort into texting girls and making new friends than he had on homework. Thanks to online monitoring, she noticed his marks slipping well before progress reports came out.

Knowing he was capable of more, she'd taken away his electronic privileges, including his cell phone and computer. When she'd finished the litany of his punishment, there was silence on my end.

Finally, she said, "Mom, are you there?"

I chuckled, and then broke out in fits of laughter.

"Mom, what's going on?"

Choking back giggles, I said, "I've just had an aha moment. That explains our bonding the past few weeks. It wasn't my charming company after all. It was my wireless connection."

Randy must've heard his mother's end of the conversation

because he stopped by later that afternoon and said, "Grandma, are you doing okay?"

Trying to hide my smile I said, "Yes honey. And so are you."

~Alice Muschany

64

Serious Business

At the height of laughter, the universe is
flung into a kaleidoscope of new possibilities.
~Jean Houston

"That's right, now shimmy a little. Bend forward and just kind of drop into it." My grandmother moved as she spoke, twitching her shoulders from side to side and leaning forward, pantomiming how to delicately plop one's chest into the cups of a waiting bra. Around us the pink dressing room glowed cheerfully. Standing there half-dressed, looking at Nan sitting like royalty on the tiny stool with a mountain of candy-colored bras draped across her, I caught the giggles.

"What's so funny?" she demanded, her wrinkled hands sorting deftly through the scraps of fabric on her lap. "And what is this?"

Nan held up a leopard print bra with black lace on the edges. At twenty-one I was still embarrassed for her to see my more risqué selections.

"I'm just trying that on for size," I muttered, grabbing it from her hand and throwing it over one of the hooks on the opposite wall. Turning my back, I pulled on another option, a turquoise bra with tiny white polka dots that reminded me of a bikini from the '60s.

"Looks like a swimsuit," Nan decreed. "Next."

I slipped out of the offending underwear and put on a blue bra with tiny pink flowers embroidered across the bands.

"Bland," Nan opined, waving at me to take it off as soon as possible. "Besides, those flowers will make your shirt look lumpy."

I tried on a bright white bra ("boring"), a lilac bra printed with bumblebees ("childish") and a mustard-colored bra ("downright ugly") before Nan stopped passing me any more options.

"It's time for the leopard print," she announced, still tucking the rejected garments back onto their hangers.

I looked up in surprise. Normally Nan was against anything even remotely tacky and, in her book, leopard print and lace were probably in that category.

"Every girl needs a racy little something," she winked. "Though heaven help you if you think leopard print and lace is the way to go. If you want my advice, I'd say pick up a little something in black silk and call it a day."

Then Nan snapped her gum decisively and made me laugh all over again. In the dressing room next to us a woman chuckled and from across the small hallway I heard a delicate snort. An unsuspecting saleswoman wandered into the fray and asked if anyone needed help.

"Do you have anything in black silk?" my grandmother called, setting us all off again.

"I don't know what you're laughing about," Nan stage-whispered. "Bras are serious business."

I nodded, trying so hard not to laugh hysterically that I didn't trust myself to speak. I reached out and hugged her, holding tight while tiny lingerie hangers stabbed my ribs. She was right, bras were serious business. But just like everything else they were certainly more fun when she was around.

~Beth Morrissey

The Candy Drawer

All you need is love. But a little chocolate now and then doesn't hurt.
~Charles M. Schultz

The candy drawer was the upper right drawer of a wooden breakfront, located in a study off the living room. The drawer never closed easily, so a little push at the end, which came with a wooden squeak, was required. It was hard to sneak anything because it could be heard in other rooms. But since the drawer was opened frequently, closing it all the way really wasn't necessary.

I cannot remember the first time I discovered the candy drawer in my grandmother's house. It was just something that Gammy seemed to have always had, stocked full of candies and goodies for her grandchildren, visitors, and eventually, great-grandchild. Hershey's Kisses, lemon drops, Werther's Originals, M&M's (both peanut and plain) in mason jars, assorted chocolate miniatures, cough drops, sugar-free sweets, and anything else Gammy decided was needed made its way in at one time or another.

The contents of the drawer changed with the seasons. Almond Roca or sesame sticks at holiday time, Godiva chocolate around our mutual April 17th birthday, a bigger selection of fruit drops in the summer. Each stage of Gammy's and her loved ones' lives was reflected by the type of candy in the drawer. If one of us was especially concerned about sugar, calories, or fat, the candy drawer would be stocked accordingly. Although we never mentioned what to buy, Gammy, the official supplier of the candy drawer, just knew.

When my two sisters or I visited Gammy, which was often, we would always check the candy drawer as if it, too, were the reason for our visit. We didn't always eat the candy, but that didn't matter. The important thing was that it was there, and we found comfort in knowing that certain things remained a constant at Gammy's.

Though Gammy was an expert on nutrition many years before the rest of us cared about it, much less understood it, Gammy believed that moderation in anything, candy included, was okay—especially Hershey's Kisses. And an occasional Hershey's Kiss was one of the few indulgences that she allowed herself.

In December 1994, Gammy, who was eighty-five years old and in excellent health physically and mentally, was diagnosed with a terminal illness. She was told she had only six or maybe eight weeks to live. Though other people would perhaps eat whatever they wanted at that point, Gammy still felt that good nutrition would increase her quality of life. She continued to indulge in one or two Hershey's Kisses at a time before she read that chocolate was not good for her condition.

Gammy was still living alone, as she had for many years, but she realized that she would require daily assistance until the end of her life. What started out as a few hours a day of assistance was soon twenty-four. It was at this point that I became the supplier of the candy drawer. Although the drawer still held many of the regular goodies, I began to search for smaller lemon, raspberry, and other fruit drops that were easier for Gammy to enjoy, putting in the same thought and care that Gammy had always done for us.

The focus of the candy drawer shifted quickly. While the contents of the drawer still consisted of candy for family and friends, its main purpose was to make the companions' days and nights more enjoyable. I began to fill it with the kinds of candy that they enjoyed and soon began to request. As Gammy became sicker and required more care, the candy drawer was stocked quite frequently. And as always, it was usually open a crack, never quite closed.

Gammy outlived her prognosis of six to eight weeks by lasting twelve. Shortly after her death, one of my sisters and I were in Gammy's house, in the study that housed the candy drawer. We both looked fondly toward the candy drawer at the same time. With some hesitation, she opened the drawer and took out a few pieces of candy. We each opened a piece and began to cry. It was then that we realized that time would not change certain things. Although the candy drawer would no longer physically exist at Gammy's house, the tradition would live on in our hearts and now our homes. And very soon, a new generation would come to embrace and expect what we had.

~Karen Jameson

66

Just Wait Until You're a Mother

Before you begin on the journey of revenge, dig two graves.
~Proverb

When I was a teenager, my best friend's dad told us that eventually our parents would get even with us. "Someday you'll have kids just like you," he prophesized. Now I understand that one of the great pleasures of being a grandparent is fulfilling the unconscious desire to get even with our kids for their rebellious behavior. I believe the appropriate word is "payback."

Payback can be coupled with the obsession to bag the perfect Christmas gift for our grandchildren, a gift that separates the grandparent from the stodgy, practical, parental role. Searching the uttermost parts of the city, I find it, the ultimate testimony to a grandson's delight, a Frog Sanctuary! Here is my opportunity to be a hero to the grandchildren and gloat in silent, guileful abandon at the expression on their parents' faces.

As expected, the Frog Habitat is a blue ribbon hit on Christmas Day. There are, of course, a few unexpected setbacks. The tadpoles have to be ordered, and the order sheet hidden deep within the box at the time of purchase reveals two details. One is that you must pay extra for the tadpoles. Two, if it is the wrong time of year, you will wait several months for your tadpoles to arrive. I know that all things work for good if we are only willing to wait. Even an empty frog house sitting on the shelf holds the promise of pleasure to those who are patient. However, these are points difficult to explain to four- and six-year-old boys, especially when a significant part of their Christmas present doesn't arrive until April.

Finally, in the spring, my daughter calls me at work with a detailed description of their new family members. One she describes as really big and wild. "He acts like he wants to jump out of the water," she reports nervously. This one they dub Max. The second is lovingly referred to as puny and spindly. Appropriately, he is christened Peewee. She relays point by point the care instructions provided. I giggle under my breath as she stumbles over words like live crickets and mealworms when describing their dietary requirements.

Over the next few weeks I get a regular status report on the metamorphoses. Tails are exchanged for back legs. Nubs appear that quickly sprout front legs. Finally the day arrives when they move from the tadpole pond to the frog habitat. A perfect place to house small, agile, fast jumping little frogs, small frogs that need their home cleaned on a regular basis and seek every angle or opportunity for escape. What a lovely picture — frogs darting, daughter screaming, grandchildren laughing and scampering after small hopping green bodies. It does my heart good to know that I had a part in this picturesque scene.

Soon, though, tragedy strikes. Peewee loses his attractive green color and develops a slightly pale complexion. The concern for his health is justified when he is discovered in a rather stiff, prone position. The boys take it pretty well, much better than my daughter, who draws the duty of retrieving the small fishy body from its abode.

Miraculously a small tree frog appears on their doorstep. The timing is perfect and though we grieve the loss of poor Peewee, Max now has a new friend. Junior is small but wiry. Though half his size, Junior has a voracious appetite that puts poor Max to shame.

Everything is now status quo in the frog world. There is, however, one thing that I have not counted on. Vacation time arrives and it is obvious to all concerned that not only do frogs not travel well but they probably wouldn't be welcome houseguests. Since they need daily care, the most obvious caregiver is the grandmother who provided the darling critters. After all, Grandma must love frogs, right? She's the one who bought them. In a well-rehearsed speech, my daughter is quick to remind me of this. Suddenly this payback thing takes an objectionable turn.

Max and Junior arrive, complete with frog habitat, distilled water and mealworms. I am indoctrinated in the art of frog maintenance and dietary requirements. This includes the report of their love for sow bugs. They assure me I will have no trouble finding them outside under logs or bricks. I don't burst this bubble by revealing that Grandpa has recently declared war on every crawling insect within our property line. This chemical assault assures us of no homegrown delicacies for our houseguests.

I discover that Max and Junior are quite personable. Their tiny suction cup feet stick to the inside of the transparent domicile. The cute little throat and tummies move in and out against the plastic dome. I see the beady eyes watching, waiting, expectant, with one thing in mind: "I will escape."

Did you know that when you keep the worms in the refrigerator they go dormant, so they don't move around much until they warm up? What an educational gift! I also discover that there is a natural law that states: No matter how small, any hole large enough to fit a human hand also has enough space for a small slippery amphibian to pass through.

Cleaning the cage is a colorful event. Jumping in every direction, these two creatures might as well be a dozen. Finally, I complete my task. My hair is dripping, my damp clothes smell like fish, and the bathroom is destroyed. Nevertheless, Max and Junior are now clean, fed, and watered. Snuggled in their cozy refuge they are utterly safe and sound. This is what my limited perception tells me. Reality arrives as I check their haven and discover the top of the habitat is open and Junior has escaped. My worst fears have materialized. There are thousands of places a smart frog can hide. Fortunately, he is not one of the smart ones. Junior is located a few feet away sitting in a corner. Grandpa is coerced into his frog rescue mode and the runaway is returned to captivity.

Time grows short, and we know the grandchildren will return soon to reclaim their prize. This will not be too soon, as we have discovered that Max and Junior no longer have a desire for mealworms. The last several meals lay floating on their pond. I begin to panic, when Grandpa comes to the rescue with... sow bugs! Wow, do those frogs eat, and I am relieved. I might make it through this yet....

Vacation ends but my daughter seems to take her time coming after their pets. I am sure it's nothing personal. She sighs as she cleans their house, empties the water and prepares them for transportation. Though she lacks enthusiasm, I am sure it is due to vacation lag. Anyway, I am enthusiastic enough for both of us.

Perhaps they'd like a nice green snake, or maybe a set of drums.... The months pass quickly and the novelty of Max and Junior fades, as do my initial plans for revenge. But I'm not worried; Christmas is on its way once again. There is ample time to conceive another formidable and workable plan. After all, I do have a reputation to uphold.

~Valerie J. Frost

"Thanks again for staying with the kids while we're away.
Now you'll also get to enjoy the thoughtful gifts you gave them."

67

Watching Andrew

If your baby is "beautiful and perfect, never cries or fusses, sleeps on schedule and burps on demand, an angel all the time," you're the grandma.
~Teresa Bloomingdale

I am taking care of Andrew for the weekend. The house is quiet as he has just settled in for a nap. Looking around, the room is filled with signs of babyhood. Stuffed animals peek their heads from the toy box and the aroma of baby powder scents the room. I am on intimate terms with Big Bird. Winnie the Pooh and his friends are my friends, too. Last night Andrew and I had dinner with Jemima Puddle-Duck. At bedtime, we said good night to eight stuffed animals, each of which holds a significant place in Andrew's heart. Because my grandson doesn't like bathing alone, I climbed into the tub with him, his three rubber ducks, a couple of plastic balls and a wind-up turtle that swims.

Life with Andrew is never dull. From when I arrived yesterday, my world has moved in and out from real to make-believe. Such magical moments encourage one to shed the confines of conventionality and cross over to that sacred place where storybook bunnies talk, and Sesame Street is still populated with the same gang from my daughter's childhood: Bert and Ernie, Grover, Cookie Monster and Oscar the Grouch are our pals.

While Andrew naps, exhausted from a morning of new discoveries, a stroller ride into town and lunch at our favorite haunt, he sleeps off an apple juice hangover while I stretch out on his parents' bed.

Grandchildren are the jewels of life. Andrew is my link to a world I long ago abandoned when my daughter's baby carriage was disassembled and stored under a large quilt in the basement. When tricycles made way for two-wheelers, toy cars evolved into real automobiles and eventually, a beginner's driver's license. At sixteen, Elizabeth was out on the road, tooling about town, all piss and vinegar, as though she owned the world despite the fact she still hadn't mastered the art of making her bed.

Now, years later, her car houses a baby seat. She drives to and from appointments, no longer "burning rubber" as she did as a teen, but keeping a watchful eye on the rear view mirror, on the precious cargo she carries in the back: her son… my grandchild.

She admits that life is different now. The rooms of her home are decorated in a new motif: Toddler Eclectic. The doorways are adorned with safety gates, the walls are accented with peanut butter taupe and scrambled egg yellow with just a hint of apple sauce crust on the door knobs. She thinks it gives the house that cozy, lived-in look.

As Andrew grows, we who spend time with him and know him best have grown too, in ways that only happen when we allow ourselves to slip back to that enchanted place known as childhood — that place where the unexpected occurs daily and we, the adults, must trespass carefully so as not to interrupt the rhythm of miracles in the making. Just this morning, on our way to town, Andrew picked up a rock, studied it and handed it to me. Upon inspection, I saw nooks and crannies revealing hidden stone landscapes. Throughout the morning, other commonplace objects became new creations, born from the mind of a child and passed on to me for further scrutiny.

I think now of children whose imaginations are never stirred, who live with hunger, illness and daily struggles — children worn out emotionally before they even have the chance to explore the wonders of childhood. My heart aches for the cruelties and hardships inflicted on those little people. While Andrew sleeps, surrounded by Elmo and Barney, the inequity of human existence becomes disturbingly apparent and profound.

Soon, my grandson, refreshed from his nap, alerts me to the fact he is up and ready to resume his afternoon agenda. First, a diaper change is in order. Then, off we go in search of new delights: a puddle of water from last night's rain becomes a mirror of Andrew's reflection. An ant wending its way toward a crack in the sidewalk can hold his interest for at least five minutes. And oh that face he makes when he tastes a new flavor of ice cream, making his lips pucker as he savors each frosty bite. "Andrew," I tell him, "ice cream always tastes better when eaten with you." The afternoon beckons as we, two explorers on a mission, navigate the streets and gardens of his town, occasionally pausing to meet a neighborhood dog or cat out on a stroll. Surprises await us at every turn: mud pies become deliciously real, a lone bird on a telephone wire elicits squeals of delight. A fire truck racing down the road alerts him to stop and take notice. As evening approaches, we wend our way back home, to supper, bath and bedtime stories. Another day in the life of Andrew draws to a close and he is ready for sleep. His world has expanded. Mine is that much the richer for having Andrew in it.

But, wait... I hear a crash: a city of wooden blocks is suddenly demolished. Andrew and Piglet are sitting among the rubble having an important conversation. I've got to hurry. I don't want to miss a single word.

~Judith Marks-White

68

Jeffrey's Promise

You cannot do a kindness too soon,
for you never know how soon it will be too late.
~Ralph Waldo Emerson

One day, my three-year-old son Jeffrey was sitting on his Nana's lap, spinning the rings on the fingers of her left hand. "Nana," he asked, "where did you get these diamond rings?"

"My darling, I got these rings from your grampa," replied my mother.

Always inquisitive, Jeffrey asked "Why did he give you these rings?"

Nana replied, "Because he loves me so much."

A few hours later, as Jeffrey sat beside his Nana watching TV, Nana asked Grampa for a ride to the local bingo hall. Due to poor health and a back injury, my mother had to rely on others for transportation to her favorite pastime, bingo. Unfortunately, Grampa was settled in for the evening and was not feeling like going anywhere that night. Grampa politely said, "I don't think so, not tonight." Disappointed, Nana jokingly pouted her bottom lip.

Jeffrey, the consummate consoler, reached up to put his little hand on her cheek saying, "Don't worry, Nana. When I get big, I will take you to bingo and I will buy you diamonds, too."

As the years passed, my mother and I would reminisce about that day and Jeffrey's undying compassion for others. Occasionally, she would jokingly tease Jeffrey about his promises of bingo and diamonds. As Jeffrey got older, my mother and I would giggle about that day and reflect on how rapidly Jeffrey was growing to be such a fine young man. All the while, my mother harbored failing health and uncertainty as to whether she'd live to see Jeffrey's promise fulfilled.

Jeffrey was sixteen years old when he passed the test for a driver's license. With his newfound independence, he realized he could drive around town unrestricted. Just a few days later, he got his first paycheck from his very first job. A young man on a mission, he made his first purchase with his money and then made plans to give someone a ride.

That afternoon, he arrived at his grandmother's house with excitement, "I got my license! Are you ready to go to bingo, Nana?" Jeffrey proudly escorted Nana to his car and chauffeured her to the bingo hall. Before exiting the vehicle, he handed her a small box. My mother opened the box to reveal a diamond ring. While the diamond may have been small, the love it represented was immeasurable. Through the trials and tribulations of teenage life, Jeffrey never forgot his promise to his grandmother.

Six months later my mom passed away.

~Pam Rogers

69

The Magic Purse

No cowboy was ever faster on the draw than a grandparent
pulling a baby picture out of a wallet.
~Author Unknown

The purse was huge, straining at the seams, threatening to spill its guts. It scared me a bit, but it didn't scare Grandma. Standing less than five feet tall, she could sling "the monster" over her shoulder and run like crazy when the occasion called for it. Like when I'd let go of her hand in a crowded mall or just because she was glad to see me. One thing is sure; the weight of that purse was no match for a woman in hot pursuit of her grandchild! I wondered if it was magic, some clever sleight-of-hand trick that rendered it weightless at such times.

Once, I peeked into that bottomless pit and saw what looked like a large pile of tattered notes. Years later, I discovered that these were directions to the nearest amusement park, in fact, all of my favorite places, and also the closest emergency room. That our family affectionately referred to Grandma as "directionally disabled" seemed a moot point. The way I saw it, every diversion gave us more time to talk, laugh and just be together.

But I always wondered why the purse was so heavy. The first (and last) time I asked to hold it, it pulled me to the ground. On cue, Grandma plucked from it a box of bandages, gently soothed medicine on the scrape, applied an oversized bandage "so the whole thing is covered," and then topped it off with a kiss. I'm unsure which of the three remedies made it all better, but I suspect it was the kiss. And I couldn't figure how Grandma managed to find anything in her purse, since most of the contents lay buried beneath scads of tissues. Then again, at the sight of tears flowing from my eyes for any reason, she never failed to catch every drop.

In spite of my obsession with her purse, nothing much bothered me when I was with Grandma. We always had fun and she hardly ever got angry. Even when I repeatedly forgot my sunglasses, she'd pluck an extra pair from her purse and plop them over my eyes and ears. She even kept the first extra pair I wore—engraved with tiny teeth marks—in one of her memory trunks.

Whenever we got together, Grandma always had a little extra cash on hand. Funny thing, though, I never saw my grandma withdraw money from a wallet. Bound tight with a rubber band, her dollar bills instead strained to be free from a large wad of cash. I guess it didn't much matter; Grandma's smiles as she watched me bite into the sugary treats and play with the new toys she'd just bought were the important thing.

It's an understatement that Grandma's purse held more than the average number of items. One day as she removed from it a box of crayons, a coloring book and stickers, I could restrain my curiosity no longer. "Grandma, is your purse magic?" I asked. She chuckled, replying, "Why yes, I suppose it is!" And just like that, my long-held suspicions began to be confirmed.

That night, I tossed and turned in my bed, pondering everything I knew about the woman. I wondered if the monstrous purse was but one of many magical things about Grandma. I thought about how she was always there just when I needed her. Suddenly, I realized she was there for me even when she didn't have her purse!

I decided the next morning that I needed a slam-dunk clue. Yet even with the intervention of Lady Luck, I was seven before I solved the case. When the answer came, it was with such clarity that I imagined a light bulb floating cartoon-like above my head!

It happened as Grandma and I sat in a soda shop enjoying ice cream. The waitress had returned, asking if everything tasted okay and to leave the bill. That's when Grandma stopped eating. I noticed at once because Grandma never quit on ice cream until it was gone. Anyway, the two women started talking and at some point, Grandma grabbed her purse. After digging deep within, her hand came back out with, of all things, a wallet. As it burst open at the click of the snap, scores of photos—all of me—tumbled onto the table. Grandma gathered them up, shuffling the stack into some kind of order. Then, she placed the heap smack dab in front of the waitress.

The waitress, being a good sport, uttered the requisite "oohs" and "aahs," perhaps knowing that an abundant tip was in the making. Just as she looked at the last photo, Grandma again delved into her purse. Figuring it was time to pay for our ice cream, I piped up, asking, "Are you looking for your wad of dollar bills?" Grandma didn't answer, busily tugging at something beyond my sight. Finally, her efforts paid off as three small photo albums were dislodged from the purse. That's when the waitress had to sit down.

Fifteen minutes later, Grandma saw that her ice cream had melted and that mine was long gone. A smile crossed the waitress's face as she jumped up, offering to get us a new order. And don't you know when round two of our ice cream arrived, we got to meet a new waitress! So we ate the bonus round, and then headed to my house.

On the way home, I recalled how easily Grandma seemed to gather in the waitress. Until that day, I hadn't known it was because she wanted to share her secret stash of photos hidden in her purse. Ah, yes! She'd done this before. Could it be that she dabbled in the art of entrapment? I could barely say the word, let alone grasp its meaning, but that's what Mom and Dad called it. The tears streaming down their faces during my telling of the soda shop incident confused me because they were also laughing. Noticing that I was perplexed, they defined entrapment to me as trapping someone for a reason other than what is apparent. No need to worry, they told me, it's simply Grandma's hobby!

To this day I wonder if Grandma ever considered the remote possibility that the "victims" of her innocent hobby were eager to get on with their busy lives. Rushing here, rushing there, and too rushed to be detained by a grandmother eager to share a hidden portfolio of her grandchild. Then again, I suppose we all have our own priorities.

Eventually, the sad day came when I had to acknowledge that Grandma's purse hadn't been magical at all. It was at her funeral while everyone was laughing about the big purse she always carried. Since then, I often think of that purse and it brings a smile to my face every time. In the final analysis, it turns out that Grandma's purse was love. And that, my friends, is magic.

~P.S. Durham

"Rumor has it there was another grandchild once--
until she disappeared in Grandma's purse."

Brownies for Breakfast

*To become a grandparent is to enjoy one of the few pleasures in life
for which the consequences have already been paid.*
~Robert Brault, www.robertbrault.com

Chocolate brownies for breakfast? Surely a grandmother
could find a more nutritious meal for her much-loved
granddaughter. Not this grandma.

I had been a responsible mother. I cooked old-fashioned oatmeal for my children for breakfast, cut up countless carrot sticks for
snacks, and made certain that vegetables accompanied every meal.
I cooked from scratch, going so far as to make my own healthful,
preservative-free mixes for cakes, puddings, and other treats.

Now, though, I was a grandmother and reveling in the experience. When three-year-old Reynna asked for brownies for breakfast
after a sleepover at my house, I said, "Why not?"

I preheated the oven, greased a baking pan, and laid out the
ingredients.

We mixed up the batter from a store-bought mix, taking delight
in dabbing it on each other's chin and nose. (I had long since given
up making my own mixes.)

I stuck my finger into the rich batter, bringing up a swirl of
chocolate. I licked. "Mmm."

Reynna did the same. "It's good."

We repeated the process. With each lick, I promised myself — and
Reynna — that would be the last one. Soon, however, the bowl held

only a small bit of batter, not nearly enough to bake a pan of brownies. I grabbed two spoons, gave one to Reynna and kept one for myself.

We scraped the bottom of the bowl, savoring each spoonful.

"Grandma, should we tell Mommy?" Reynna asked.

I hugged her, heedless of the chocolate that now decorated our clothes and faces. "Why don't we keep this our secret?"

She hugged me back. "I love you, Grandma."

"I love you right back."

We cleaned up the mess, cleaned up ourselves, and grinned at each other over our special secret.

Brownies for breakfast. Why not?

~Jane McBride Choate

The Problem with Scandinavian Grandmothers

Grandparents are there to help the child get into mischief they haven't thought of yet.

~Gene Perret

"**S**he didn't!" my sister exclaimed, exhaling a cloud of blue cigarette smoke as she spoke.

"She did!" I said, rolling my eyes and nodding to emphasize the point. Anabel threw back her head, her long brown hair catching the breeze.

"I'm surprised she didn't get arrested!"

"I think people might have been a little nervous about making a citizen's arrest in the circumstances." We both laughed at the thought.

So here we all were, the family together for a weekend at my parents' holiday house in Norfolk on the windy east coast of England. It was autumn and the leaves were flying off the trees, swirling in the air all around us. The sky was cool blue, the end of summer not quite forgotten. My Danish grandmother, Anna, was visiting us and was now pottering about in the vegetable garden with an old trowel in search of potatoes. My grandfather, Per, had found an old armchair by the large windows in the sitting room and was smoking a cigar and playing chess against himself. Nobody in our family could give him much of a game. We sometimes tried, but it would always end in a short and bloody massacre of bishops, knights and rooks.

My boyfriend, Robert, had come up with me from London and this was his first introduction to the Scandinavian side of the family. It had all started so well. The previous evening we ate in the large dining room overlooking the garden. My mother had prepared a wonderful meal of roast beef with all the trimmings; Dad had produced an old French red wine and said, as he always did, that tonight was an auspicious night to drink it. We talked and relaxed and all slept a little late in the morning. After breakfast, we decided to take a walk along Holkham Beach. Robert, my mother, my grandmother and I all piled into the old car armed with Wellington boots and green Barbour coats, hats and gloves and, of course, the dog, Rogan.

We arrived at the beach at around eleven and this was where the "incident" occurred. Holkham is my favourite place in the world, with its ten miles of wide beach stretching out towards the North Sea. Pine woods and sandy paths line the coast; sand dunes run in front of them as far as the eye can see. It is wild and beautiful at any time of the year, and you can lose yourself in space within a few minutes of setting foot on the sand.

We wandered down the wooden boarded path through the woods, the cool scent of the sea filling our nostrils, the gray London smog clearing out of our lungs with every breath. Robert grasped my hand; it felt warm compared with the crisp breeze on my cheeks. My grandmother and mother walked behind us, a little more slowly, stopping to look at the trees from time to time and talking in Danish. After a while, we found a spot in the dunes and settled down to watch the world go by.

"Time for a swim," announced my grandmother lightly in her soft Danish accent.

"Really? Are you sure?" I said, pulling my coat tight around me and feeling the shiver of the North Sea. My grandparents have swum in the North Sea all their lives, mainly from the coast of Jutland, which is even further towards the North Pole than Norfolk. As children during the summer holidays, we would be marched into the sea by my grandfather with the clear instructions: "No squealing, no screaming—just walk right in without stopping and swim fast!" And that is what we did. To this day, I can walk into the coldest of seas without a moment of hesitation, without uttering a sound. However, more often than not, I choose not to.

My grandmother started to take off her coat and sweater. As she did this, Robert leant towards me with a grin, saying: "She's some lady, your grandmother." And then, at that moment, I realised what was about to happen. No, she wasn't going to, was she? Yes, she was. She was going to swim in the nude, in Norfolk, in England, in the middle of October. I lay back on the sand and looked upwards with a resolute stare. A moment later Robert fell back too, landing with a thud, and whispered, "Oh, my word!"

A small point I haven't yet mentioned was that the dunes were half a mile or so from the water's edge. Between us and the sea there was a large expanse of sand — a large expanse of sand where a naked octogenarian would be highly visible to the innocents of North Norfolk. My grandmother, her towel set over her shoulder in a somewhat cavalier fashion, set off alone in her "birthday suit." Rogan followed at a respectful distance. A couple in full Gortex stopped and rapidly diverted their route, calling their black Labrador to heel with a brusque instruction. A group of small boys building a sand castle stopped what they were doing and stared open-mouthed. One shouted: "Mummy, look!" Mummy looked and Mummy stared too. A young runner quickened his pace, veering violently towards the sea, the unexpected vision before him now surely seared in his mind forever.

After what seemed like an age, she finally reached the sea and had her swim. We watched her walking back, her ancient skin and breasts sagged and swayed with every step. She even stopped to pick up a shell or pebble that had caught her eye. Robert turned to me: "Does she always do that?" I thought for a moment.

"Well, only in Denmark where everyone does it."

"Actually, I think it's great," he said. "It's us with the hang-up about nudity."

"Perhaps," I replied, lowering my voice to a whisper, "but I think it may still be illegal in Norfolk!"

We both laughed.

"Come on," said Robert, getting up and starting to take off his coat.

"You are joking, aren't you?" I asked nervously.

~Elizabeth Bostock

Favorites

Most grandmas have a touch of the scallywag.
~Helen Thomson

At last, I'm escaping home. It's Friday night, and Daddy is driving me to Grandma's for my almost-weekly ritual of spending the weekend with her. All by myself. No little brothers distracting her with their antics. No baby sister cooing sweetly to be cuddled.

Just me... nine years old, and skinny as a rail with stringy brown hair that falls into my eyes. I wear shorts, a top that slips off my shoulder and my first pair of glasses. Dark brown-rimmed and thick lenses because I am horribly near-sighted. Although I now see more clearly, the glasses are just one more thing I don't like about myself. But that doesn't matter tonight—because I'm going to Grandma's, and she likes my glasses.

And she loves me best of all. I know because she whispered it to me once, cupping her hand to my ear so no one else heard. "You're my favorite, you know, because you're my first grandchild. You're special."

Going to Grandma's is like running away from home. Carrying my change of clothes in a paper grocery sack, I arrive at the three-room apartment where she's lived since Grandpa died. We hug hello, though I can barely reach my arms around Grandma's waist. She's a high-calorie cook—and it shows.

I push Daddy out the door. Now my escape is complete from

where I feel out of place and have no privacy, where I try to please Mama—but manage to draw an exasperated look at something I say or get underfoot as she cleans up messes left by my brothers or sister or dog.

At last, I sigh and begin my weekend adventure where Grandma will let me be whoever I want and do whatever I want.

"Want something to eat?" she asks.

"Yes, let's play restaurant." I scrounge through the table drawer to dig out the order book Grandma bought me. With a stubby pencil poised over the paper, I stand by Grandma seated at her gray, Formica-topped dining table.

"What would you like, ma'am?" I ask, using my grown-up voice.

"Hmm," she puts her finger to her cheek and taps it as if deciding what delicious feast she fancies today. "I'll have vegetable soup, a cheese sandwich and sweet tea with a slice of lemon." I scribble her order, poke the pencil behind my ear like the truck-stop waitress I imagine I am, and walk to the stove to prepare the fare.

While the soup warms, I take two more orders from imaginary customers and pull dishes off open shelves above the sink. Grandma lets me use her good dishes as long as I'm careful not to drop them and I return them clean at the end of my shift.

"Lunch is scrumptious," she exclaims, nibbling her sandwich. When she leaves, I notice she left me a tip—two dimes that I sweep into my apron pocket.

Grandma retreats to her bedroom to freshen her make-up and grab her purse. She hollers out, "I need a few things from the store. Wanna go?" That's code for "I'll buy you a treat." I'm at the door before she finishes the sentence.

We pile into her car, hit the locks and cruise down the road with Elvis blaring.

At the store, Grandma buys me two books, *Black Beauty* and *Heidi*. She knows how I bury my nose in a book every chance I get. Back at the apartment, I curl up on her sofa. My world fades into another, and I am now Heidi visiting her grandfather in the Swiss Alps.

Grandma interrupts my frolic through the mountains only to hand me a bowl with five scoops of our favorite—vanilla ice cream. She takes a seat beside me. I drift back to the Alps while Grandma gently strokes my back, soothing me to sleep....

It's Friday night, fifteen years later. I drive past Grandma's old apartment and pull into her new driveway for my weekly visit. Grandma remarried—a man she met while out dancing with her girlfriends. She now lives in a two-bedroom house in one of the city's older neighborhoods, only five minutes from where I bowl in a league.

I plop down on her couch and ramble about my week. I feel nine years old again. Grandma sits beside me and gently strokes my back, soothing away my day's pressures.

"You need a bite before you go," she insists.

"I'm not that hungry, Grandma."

"Okay, I'll fix you just a bite." I hear the clanging of dishes and remember my waitress days in her apartment. The refrigerator door opens and shuts four or five times.

"Only a bite, Grandma," I remind her from the living room.

"Yes, just a bite. It's ready."

I enter the kitchen to find the gray, Formica-topped table hidden beneath a banquet of dishes. There's meatloaf, leftover fried chicken, and slices of Wednesday's roast beef surrounded by bowls of snap peas, new potatoes, corn on the cob, green salad, sliced tomatoes, and diced pineapple. She sees me roll my eyes. "It's just a bite," she objects. "Sit and eat."

I do as I'm told and build a sampler plate of the feast laid before me. Stuffed to the gills, Grandma polishes me off with a bowl of our favorite—vanilla ice cream.

I help her clear the table and toss scraps into the trash under the sink. That's when I discover something new about Grandma. Tucked in a corner and partially hidden from view is a bottle of Jack Daniel's Black Label. The surprise must register on my face, because before I can ask, she answers, "Hush up. It's for medicinal purposes. Just one jigger a week helps my arthritis."

It's Saturday, another twenty years later. I roll up the nursing home's driveway for my weekly visit with Grandma. She came here under protest. Her frail body, weak with advancing dementia and depression from losing her husband, betrays her independence. Last week I took her out for our favorite—vanilla ice cream. Today I bring her something different.

She sits in her wheelchair, staring at the television in her room. I slip into a chair beside her and stroke her back, soothing away her anxieties.

"Grandma, I have a surprise for you."

Her tired eyes turn toward me, "What is it?"

I pull a glass and a can of Coke from my tote. Then I slide out a bottle of Jack Daniel's Black Label. "For your arthritis," I wink at her, mix a jigger-full with Coke and hand her the glass.

Grandma's face brightens with memories. She raises the glass for a toast, drains it, and smiles at me. "You're my favorite, you know, because you're my first grandchild. You're special."

I return her smile. "And you're my favorite too, Grandma. You're more special than you know."

~Gloria Ashby

Grandmothers

From the Mouths of Babes

73

Generation Gasps

Becoming a grandmother is wonderful. One moment you're just a mother.
The next you are all-wise and prehistoric.
~Pam Brown

As grandmother-in-residence I melt into the family stew. My activities are seldom noticed because I just "am." My four grandchildren pass me regularly but I have become like the wallpaper, a fixture, seldom noticed, always there. That is why I was quite surprised when one April morning eight-year-old Angus asked if he could join Bailey, my canine companion, and me on our regular morning walk down our country lane.

"Well, yes, we'd love to have you. Hurry up then, get a move on. Bailey is doing her pee pee dance," I replied with a delighted smile.

Soon we were out the door. Bailey raced ahead, her tail feathers dancing, to run forward, then back to make sure we were following her lead. Urging Angus to "get a move on'" as this was my main daily exercise, we set a good pace down the back lane. The spring air dug deep into our lungs and filled them with greening odours.

Just past the first field, Angus bent to secure his sneaker laces and burped loudly. "Angus," said I with a grandmotherly tone of disapproval, "excuse yourself and do try to contain that noise in a gentlemanly manner." I hail from a time when manners matter, regardless of where you are.

"Grandma, containing gas is not a wise idea. Did you know that the expulsion force behind a burp or fart equals the force behind a projectile traveling at the rate of thirty miles per hour? Imagine if that force was not allowed to escape the body! Don't you think you might damage something or blow out your innards?" offered Angus authoritatively.

I chose a silent reply, lips pursed as I rummaged in my pocket for a tissue to give my nose a good blow.

"Grandma, did you know that the human body produces enough snot every day to slime half the length of a bowling lane? What you expel into your handkerchief is only a small amount of what you produce. Mucus really acts as lubricant for most of your body parts."

"Angus, look, there's a chickadee," I uttered in an over-enthusiastic tone, trying to divert his attention.

"Grandma, did you know that most birds poop on the average of once every seven minutes? It is a known fact that this has become a huge problem where large birds gather. The Canada geese in Stanley Park poop so much that it has become a walking hazard. The city had to employ a whole crew just to keep ahead of the bird poop."

"Mind your step, Angus," I clipped as I stepped around a cow flap.

"Grandma, did you know that cow flatulence has become an international concern? Cows fart so much that there is a study underway to see what affect methane from their farts has on greenhouse warming."

"Angus, this conversation is disgusting. Can't we talk about something else? How was your hockey practice last night?"

"Okay. Coach says I am really improving. I am stick handling a whole lot better. Just as coach was giving us his usual pep talk, Peter Riley let one rip! Broke us all up. We laughed until we near peed our pants. Then when we were in the change room, Clayton Ball couldn't get his zipper up and we teased him that his weenie was going to freeze on the way home. Yep, it was a good practice."

At this point Angus raced off with Bailey and I raised my eyebrows and breathed deep as if to cleanse with country air. The high sun of spring was calling forth small shoots of new life. I bent to examine something peeking out from under dried grasses: a rare delicate hepatica. Angus and Bailey came roaring back.

"What's that?" Angus asked.

"Well, my dear, there are two harbingers of spring in this area, one is the trillium and the other is the hepatica. Hepatica are very shy and not easy to find but I just spotted this one. Look at how beautiful it is, pale pink with tiny dark veins running through each petal."

"Grandma, did you know that veins carry blood to the heart? If you cut a vein you don't bleed nearly as bad as if it is an artery. Boy, that's when the blood just spurts out, the heart is such a strong pump it can splatter blood everywhere! You just have to put pressure where the blood is gushing out real quick and press hard or you might bleed to death in no time."

Shrugging my shoulders and shaking my lost-generation head, we wound our way home. Angus approached me with a concerned look on his face.

"Grandma, do you think that every burp and every fart is polluting the world?"

"Well, now, that is a heady question," I replied. "Perhaps more important is the source of that issue, overpopulation. The daily needs of people, cars, heat, air conditioning, all cause more pollution than natural human expulsions."

"Good! Because I really have to let one rip."

"Angus," I screamed, then noticed the glint in his dark eyes.

"Grandma, you are so easy to gross out," he laughed as he kicked a stone to Bailey.

When we arrived back at the house, my daughter greeted us, ruffled Angus's thick mat of hair and asked if he had enjoyed his walk.

"Mom, did you know that the hepatica is one of the first flowers of spring? They are very rare and Grandma found one tucked under some dead grass. It has the most beautiful little flower. I never would have found it. Grandma's so cool!"

~Molly O'Connor

74

Ready to Go

For fast-acting relief, try slowing down.
~Lily Tomlin

When my grandson was two years old, I started a weekly ritual: driving to his family's apartment in Manhattan and taking him out for a day on the town. As soon as I walked through the door, Nathan would climb into his stroller. "Ready to go," he'd sing, over and over again, waiting for his parents and me to finish chatting.

When Nathan outgrew the stroller, he'd bounce into the elevator, wearing his New York Yankees cap and jacket, declaring, "I've got a lot of energy," and we'd take off—to a museum exhibit, horticultural display, magic performance, or puppet show. We'd gawk at the Statue of Liberty from the Staten Island Ferry and stomp to percussion groups at Damrosch Park. Sometimes I'd take him to my home in Queens, to look at the boats anchored in Little Neck Bay and the fishermen along the wharf. We'd drive out to Jones Beach, run along the surf, walk the length of the boardwalk, go to the playground, and play miniature golf. What great times we had.

But as my grandson got older, it became more and more difficult to schedule a get-together. Some weeks I didn't see him at all. After school he was enrolled in gymnastics, soccer, and hockey programs. He was signed up for music lessons, chorus, ice-skating, and swimming instruction. Evenings he did homework and practiced the piano. Weekends he participated in Little League games and activity-centered birthday parties.

One day, when Nathan was six, after not seeing him for two weeks, I arrived late, ready to rush out to a museum concert for children.

"Nathan doesn't want to go out today," his mom informed me, pointing to a crying, growling child, clutching his baseball cap.

"What's wrong?" I asked. "Are you feeling sick?" He shook his head.

"Do you want me to go home?" He shook his head again, and shouted, "I don't want to go to a concert. I don't want to go anywhere. I have too many activities. I want to stay home and play with my toys." Nathan was definitely not "ready to go."

"I understand, Nathan, I really do," I whispered, hugging him tightly and tousling his hair.

"Look," I said. "Let's make a deal. From now on, before I buy tickets, I'll check with you. If you have another idea, or if you want to do nothing at all, that's okay with me. How's that?" Nathan nodded his head in agreement, and off we went to the concert, crowded with hand-clapping kids and their toe-tapping grandparents. On a scale of one to ten, he rated the program a five. That was our last afternoon together on the town.

I truly did understand how Nathan felt: grandma and grandson were in the same place. When I first retired from my fifth grade classroom, I envisioned myself sleeping late, taking a mid-morning walk, or working at my computer. I was free—free to choose how I'd spend each day. As time went by, I found myself registering for courses, attending art lectures, world affairs seminars, and women's wellness sessions. I learned to square dance, played duplicate bridge, and joined a gym. There I was again, racing the clock, filling up all the spaces in my calendar.

I'm with you, Nathan, I thought. I too want to stay home: return telephone messages, read the Sunday papers, watch my favorite television program. But hadn't my energetic grandson omitted something when he blurted out his reasons for turning down the concert? He couldn't verbalize it, probably didn't know it himself, but leaving his new baby brother, Simon, home alone with Mommy and Daddy must have been a contributing factor.

So instead of his tour guide, I became Nathan's play date companion. We'd stretch out on his living room rug, pull out *Scrabble*, checkers, or a deck of cards; we'd play Casino or *Monopoly*, and watch his favorite baseball video, *Little Big League*. Innings, not outings! Having spent my morning in a yoga class, followed by a book discussion, Nathan was not the only one happy to be there, stretched out on the carpet and relaxed—at home plate.

The nature of my time with Nathan is ever-changing. In fifth grade he'd give me a hug and a kiss, perform his latest piano piece, and politely answer my questions about school. He might even say "No" to playing Casino or *Monopoly*. I'd watch as he'd shuffle in place, twist and turn. It was obvious he couldn't wait to get back to Game Boy, *Carmen Sandiego Math Detective*, or *Harry Potter*. Sometimes his brother would jump on his back, and I'd watch the two of them frolic on the floor.

"Grandma, will you play with me?" my younger grandson asks, spilling his Tinkertoy or Thomas train set onto the carpet when I come to visit. Simon has never been "ready to go." I've taken him for sleepovers; we've gone to the playground, thrown a ball around. But we've never gone out on the town. I recall my wonderful outings with Nathan, and think perhaps I'm shortchanging this youngster. Then I see him playing, engrossed, and so content. A child's work, after all, is to play. I wonder now, were the days I spent running around with Nathan for his benefit, or for mine?

~Ruth Lehrer

75

It's Family

*You do not really understand something unless you can explain it
to your grandmother.*
~Proverb

When I met my husband, forty-three years ago, he had recently moved back into his mother's house with his three beautiful little girls. A divorce from his wife was in progress, and we dated for nine months before we married in 1965. Over the years, we added three more children to our family.

When my husband was diagnosed with prostate cancer in 1997, we were uncertain about the future. His daughter Sharon lived in northern, middle Tennessee, and she suggested we sell our house in southern Tennessee to move closer to her so that she could help out when the going got tough. With the news that she was expecting a baby in May of 1999, we decided to make the move to be near our new grandchild. I would be the baby's childcare provider when Sharon returned to work after her maternity leave, and in May of 1999, a beautiful, blond-headed baby boy named Hunter entered our lives.

Happiness reigned for two months, until July 17 when we got the call that our twenty-eight-year-old son Donnie was killed when he fell asleep at the wheel. The bottom dropped out of our world. I cannot begin to describe the pain a mother feels over the loss of a child, and I did not know if my life would ever know happiness again.

Our children were all there to support us in spite of their own grief. Sharon was there right from the beginning to help in any way that she could. The youngest, Charlene, came from North Carolina to be with us and stay at the house to answer phones and greet people as we took care of funeral arrangements. Our son Steven was a tremendous help, and our youngest daughter Julie went about making photo collages for the visitation and funeral service.

The shock and numbness of his death slowly wore away for me, and the sadness settled in. I spent many a day holding my precious grandson in a rocking chair and crying tears onto his beautiful, blond head. I wondered if he, in any way, would absorb my sorrow or remember how heavy his grandmother's heart was at this time. He was a happy, smiling baby who reminded me of my own Donnie at that age! I truly believe that having him there helped me more than anything else in those first few months of my deepest sorrow.

When Hunter was seven years old, and still so very precious to me, my husband and I took him with us on a shopping excursion. We climbed in the car and headed for the mall.

"Where are we going?" he asked.

My husband replied, "Well, Grandma wants to go to the fabric store first, so that's where we'll head. We're going on a 'family adventure.'"

We stopped at my favorite "buy everything" store, and Hunter took my hand. As we passed the toy section, he looked up at me and said sweetly, "Grandma, I just love you so much!" I grinned and thought to myself, "I hope you will love me as much in the fabric department as you do in the toy department!"

Back in the car, as we were buckling up, Hunter enthusiastically asked his "Pop" where we were going next.

"I think we'll go to the electronics store…. what do you think, Hunter?" Pop replied.

"Oh no," I piped in. "NOT the electronics store! I might just wait in the car for you guys."

From the back seat I heard, "Grandma, you have to come with us. It's FAMILY."

I couldn't help but chuckle out loud! Then I heard Hunter seriously inquire, "Why are you laughing?"

I turned around and faced him in a matter-of-fact manner and said that Pop would probably be in the electronics store for a long time, and that electronics stores were not my cup of tea!

Hunter looked at me with the most crucially intense expression on his face, looked me straight in the eyes, and said, "It's FAMILY. It's FAMILY, Grandma... and one died!"

I wanted to laugh and cry and hug him all at the same time! This little guy who never knew my son, his Uncle Donnie, knew about him from his Pop and me and from his mother and aunts and uncles. And he was not going to forget him or the significance and impact it had on all of us—on his FAMILY.

I marveled at how exceptional it was for a seven-year-old to know the importance of family and these small heartfelt moments in our lives! Hunter has very special parents who are making sure he learns these valuable lessons. Perhaps I, myself, had a little to do with him having such a caring and loving heart. He just may have absorbed more than my tears. Perhaps he actually absorbed my sorrow.

All I could think of when I saw the earnest expression on Hunter's face that day with the tears welling up in his eyes was, "What a beautiful little soul you have, my grandson. And what a blessing you are to me!"

~Beverly F. Walker

How Big Was Your Computer?

My granddaughter came to spend a few weeks with me, and I decided to teach her to sew. After I had gone through a lengthy explanation of how to thread the machine, she stepped back, put her hands on her hips, and said in disbelief, "You mean you can do all that, but you can't play my Game Boy?"
~Author Unknown

My thirteen-year-old grandson has never lived in a world without computers in most every home and certainly never without one in his classroom. He has never lived in a world that did not have cell phones or one where people did not walk on the moon or where people could not fly around the world in a matter of hours. He has no conception of such a world.

We were talking recently and he said, "MeMe, I know that it was different when you were young, but exactly how big was your computer?"

I said, "Keith, we did not have computers when I was young."

To which he replied, "I understand, I know that they were really different, but just what did it look like?"

I said, "Keith, we did not have computers."

"It was probably really different and probably a great deal larger than ours, wasn't it?"

For the third time, I said, "Keith, listen to me. We did not have computers when I was young. We just barely had typewriters."

"No way!" was his quick reply. "You must be older than dirt! And what was that thing that you barely had?"

"A typewriter," I said.

"What's that?" was his reply.

And then I felt very old.

Keith thought for a moment and said, "You didn't have any computer games? What did you do, just watch TV?"

"Keith," I replied once again. "We didn't have a TV."

"No TV?" He was astounded but quickly rebounded with, "What did you do with your time?"

This answer I loved. "We played outside and rode bikes and visited with our neighbors in the evening while we caught fireflies. We went on picnics and skated and spent hours just talking with our friends—in person. We read books and drew pictures and pressed leaves because they were pretty. We helped our mom in the kitchen and then went to the yard to help Dad with the flowers and vegetable garden. We had a really good life.

"I'm sorry you missed it Keith, but your life will someday be just as old-fashioned to your children as mine is to you and you'll smile and then you will understand."

It is such fun to be a grandmother.

~Donna S. Watson

"When I'm your age, grandma, I'll probably tell my grandkids, 'When I was young, we had to get our music by downloading it on a computer.'"

77

More

When you look at your life, the greatest happinesses are family happinesses.
~Joyce Brothers

er tiny, delicate features drew me closer for another look. With my very first glance I thought her to be perfectly angelic. A halo of soft auburn hair framed the pretty little face that ever-so-shyly curved in a smile. Her tongue was reaching for something it couldn't find... a taste, a touch... just reaching, reaching.

"She's beautiful," I said to my son's girlfriend Amanda. Lilly was her daughter from a previous marriage. She and Jim had been dating for a few months, and this was the first time I had met them.

Jim had told me that Lilly had Down syndrome. I really had no idea what to expect. I'd known very few people with disabilities, and honestly was uncertain about what having Down syndrome entailed.

"Would it be okay to hold her?" I asked.

Amanda took Lilly out of her car seat and handed her to me. Her little head leaned softly on my shoulder as though she had known me forever. She smelled of baby shampoo and milk, the way my own babies smelled so many years ago. It broke my heart to think of her father and how he couldn't accept the fact that his daughter had a disability. The marriage ended in part because of his intolerance.

I spent the next few weeks getting to know Amanda and Lilly, and in those weeks came to understand the passion this mother had for her child.

"Lilly was born with a heart condition," Amanda explained. Apparently most Downs children are born with heart defects. "Lilly was one of the lucky ones. Hers was able to be fixed." This meant Lilly wouldn't endure the subsequent surgeries so many Downs children face during their childhoods.

Amanda's days were packed with work, doctor's appointments, and therapies for Lilly. While Lilly's heart was strong, her immune system was weak, and she had developed skin conditions and allergies to some foods. Still Amanda persevered with a smile and strong determination, never allowing her life's circumstances to get her down. She astonished our family with her amazingly upbeat attitude. The more we got to know Lilly, the more we understood how and why Amanda's outlook stayed so positive.

We started seeing Amanda mirrored in Lilly's eyes, Lilly's attitude, and Lilly's ever-changing and developing personality. We had initially met a small, rather shy peanut of a girl, and within months knew an active, happy little girl with the ability to melt hearts wherever she went.

In time we watched Lilly learn a few words, crawl in her offbeat way, and show favoritism for toys, foods, and people. Lilly's therapist was teaching her American Sign Language so we all tried to learn. Lilly and Amanda of course outshined us all, but we tried hard to keep up with the basics and signed to Lilly things like "fish," "all done," "I love you," and Lilly's favorite word—"more."

"More" is the word Lilly uses now to indicate she'd like another cookie. It means she likes her dinner and will eat a few more bites. It means she wants to play "this little piggy went to market…" for the umpteenth time, or sing "Twinkle Twinkle Little Star" yet again.

"More" took on a brand new meaning for all of us, too. It meant we could spend more time singing, laughing, tickling and teaching Lilly the things she seemed so eager to learn; and while she may not learn them as quickly as "normal" children, we all delight in the little steps of progress—the little things in life.

"More" means we sit a while longer at the dinner table and chat with one another about the day's events, while Lilly has another dish of fruit or another ginger snap, or while she tries drinking water from a sippy cup like the big kids do.

Above all else, "more" signifies the way Lilly and Amanda have enriched our lives since meeting them three years ago. By not judging and freely accepting this little wonder and her beautiful mom, we've learned love doesn't come in perfect packages. We've learned there's a lot to do to improve upon life's little bumps in the road, but that such improvements make us all better people in the end.

We've learned to love more freely. We've learned to hug more often. We've learned that wet and sloppy kisses on our cheek or on our eyebrow are sometimes the very best ones we can receive.

We've learned that life doesn't come with guarantees, but gives us incredible gifts we'd never expected. And we've learned just how precious those gifts can be when wrapped in the package of a sweet little girl with Down syndrome.

Jim, Amanda, and Lilly will soon be a family. A wedding is in the very near future, and that will make me Lilly's "Nana." In the meantime we're blessed to see them several times each week. When I hear my front door open, followed by the pitter-patter of uneven—sometimes clumsy—little steps coming down the hallway toward my home office, I smile. Joy seeps in and fills me up, as a little girl named Lilly walks through the doorway and smiles a big crooked smile, with arms outstretched, and calls me "Nana."

I look at Amanda, trailing swiftly behind, and my heart fills with love and gratitude for the precious gift she's nurtured and shared with us here. And it is then that I truly know I've been offered, as has my son Jim—and we've all freely accepted so very, very much "more!"

~Kimberly Ripley

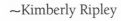

78

Just Checking In

A child is a curly dimpled lunatic.
~Ralph Waldo Emerson

When our three-year-old grandson began calling our house, my husband and I thought it adorable. In no time, he'd memorized both our cell phone and work numbers. If we didn't answer one, he'd dial the other.

Before long, our phones rang nonstop, but we considered the calls special.

"Clayton James here," he'd giggle.

"Why, hello Clayton James. What are you up to?" It was hard to get aggravated at that little spunky laugh of his.

"I just checkin' in."

One morning, he called my office three times before noon.

"Honey, Grandma can't talk to you now. She has to get back to work. Put Mommy on the phone."

"I not done yet, Grandma."

"Let me talk to Mommy."

Heaving a big sigh he repeated, "I not done yet."

Another five minutes of pleading and begging passed before he put my daughter on the line. "Sorry Mom. He's supposed to ask permission to use the phone."

When he began calling after we'd crawled into bed, it was no longer amusing. I'd scold him and tell him to hang up so Grandma and Papa could go to sleep. After his mom found out he'd phoned, she had another talk with him.

The calls stopped for a few days, but started up again relentlessly. Even though I hated to do it, I called his mother and complained. That prompted an angry call from Clayton.

"I no talk to you ever again." Clunk!

His threats didn't last long. A few hours later the phone rang. Surprise—it was Clayton. "Does your mommy know you're using the phone?" I asked.

In a hushed voice, he whispered, "No. I be in the closet."

I could almost smell his cookie breath through the receiver. A big smile spread across my face, and I decided not to rat him out.

All was well until the phone rang in the middle of the night. Worried the kids had been in a car accident, I picked up on the first ring. Relief flooded over me when it was only Clayton James checking in, but I scolded him just the same. "Don't call back. Grandma has to get up early for work."

The next day, when I reported the incident to his mom, she said, "I'm really sorry. I hid our cell phones before bedtime, but Clayton must've climbed on the counter and used the house phone. I'll have another talk with him."

Just as we sat down for dinner, the phone rang.

A tiny voice threatened, "Now you listen to me and you listen to me good. I no call you anymore!"

Before I could reply, the receiver banged down.

"Guess Clayton James got in big trouble for that late night phone call," I chuckled.

By the end of the week, he must have forgiven me because he called and said, "I just checkin' in from under the covers."

Just as I had suspected—an undercover phone call.

That night the alarm clock glowed 2:20 a.m. in neon red as I reached for the annoying phone.

"Clayton?"

"Clayton is that you?"

My questions were met with silence. "Hang up the phone and

go to bed," I barked. Finally I heard a squeaky "Hee, Hee, Hee," followed by the slamming of the phone.

My husband rolled over and mumbled, "He keeps it up and he won't see his fourth birthday."

As I tried to drift back to sleep I wondered, "Would I be a bad Grandma if I changed my number?"

The next day, I phoned his mother and ratted on him for calling in the wee hours of the morning. She apologized once again and said she'd moved the phones out of Clayton's reach. A thorough investigation revealed that he'd snuck his brother's cell out of his school bag.

Her reprimand prompted another call.

"I no like you any more, Grandma." Thump!

Papa and I placed bets on how long it would be before he called back. We didn't have to wait long. He called back within ten minutes.

Clayton's calls gradually tapered off as he got busy with kindergarten and sports. Soon we were calling him more often than he called us.

"Grandma, I'm playing with my friend. I'll talk to you later."

I hung up the phone and wondered how I'd ever thought of his calls as annoying. Now when the phone rings and it's Clayton just checking in, it's all the more special.

Unless of course, it's after midnight.

~Alice Muschany

"That was little Emma. She called to say that not only can she dial the phone herself, but now she can do it while she's on the potty."

Don't Bruise the Petals

What children need most are the essentials that grandparents provide in abundance. They give unconditional love, kindness, patience, humor, comfort, lessons in life. And, most importantly, cookies.
~Rudolph Giuliani

Flowers are one of God's most extravagant gifts. He created millions of beautiful flowers and scattered them over the earth for us to enjoy. I love flowers and have a large flower garden inside the stone foundation of an old house that tumbled down a hundred years ago.

One of my favorite times is when my four-year-old grandson, Peter, comes to visit. His eyes are as blue as Bachelor Buttons and his hair is as yellow as the petals on a sunflower. He often helps me plant seeds or pull weeds and sometimes when he "hugs" the flowers I tell him to be gentle because flowers are tender and we shouldn't bruise the petals or they can't grow and be beautiful.

One day I used the hoe to make a long trench in the garden and I crawled along on my hands and knees dropping the seeds two inches apart in the soft, damp soil. When I got to the end of the row, Peter was standing there waiting for me. His hands were filled with all the seeds I'd just planted.

"Look Grandma, you dropped all of your seeds! Aren't you lucky I was there to pick them up for you?" he asked proudly.

"I'm very lucky, indeed!" I said and put the seeds back into the envelope. I'd plant them tomorrow when he wasn't there to "help" me.

My Dahlias are my favorite flowers and for the past nine years they've taken the blue ribbon for the Best of Show at the Flower Club Competition. This year the rain and temperature had been perfect and my Dahlias were more beautiful than ever and larger than dinner plates. I had no doubt they were going to win the Best of Show for the tenth year in a row. I'd get a silver plaque and my picture in the paper and most likely would be elected the next president of the garden club.

One evening I noticed my flowers were looking a little droopy and wilted and thought it might be the heat so I gave them a little extra water. By morning they looked even worse. I couldn't imagine what I'd done wrong but it was obvious they'd be dead before the flower show.

I examined the leaves and stems looking for bugs that might have killed the flowers and I discovered their stems had been broken and then taped back together with bandages. "Peter," I called. "Do you know what happened to Grandma's flowers?"

"I was walking on the stone wall and I fell on them," was his answer, "but I know when I skin my knee, you put a sticky bandage on it and then I get better so I bandaged the flowers so they'd get better."

"Flowers don't get better," I said.

"I'm sorry, Grandma, I know how much you love your flowers." His blue eyes filled with tears.

"Don't cry. I do love my flowers," I said and hugged him, "but I love you a thousand times more than all the flowers in the world."

"I love you too, Grandma," he smiled.

"I think it's time for some milk and cookies," I said and led him to the house.

It didn't bother me one bit that someone else's flowers would win the Best of Show this year and that I wouldn't get the silver plaque or that I might not be president of the garden club.

I have a grandson who loves me and my most important job is helping him grow and bloom without bruising his petals.

~April Knight

Grandparents' Day

A grandparent is old on the outside but young on the inside.
~Author Unknown

I enter the elementary school cafetorium crowded with grand-parents. We're invited here to be honored at Grandparents' Day. This is a rare role reversal, since we're usually focusing on our adored grandchildren, who exist because we raised their parents.

Soon, the stage fills with awkward kindergartners preparing to sing. The audience chuckles at the little girl in the front row who pulls up her dress with one hand and waves with the other.

After several grade levels perform, the fifth grade chorus takes the stage and bursts into a lively rendition of "Rockin' Robin." Grandparents come alive and sing the familiar lyrics from the fifties, transporting us back to the sock hops and proms we attended decades ago. Bulging waistlines rock and happy heads roll to the rhythm, while hands dotted with age spots clap and wrinkled faces beam.

When the performances end, my seven-year-old grandson, Kyle, appears and escorts me to his classroom. I sit next to him and he hands me the papers he prepared for my visit. On one sheet he's writ-ten things he likes to do with me: bike riding, going places, fishing, and making pancakes.

On another sheet he writes my answers while he interviews me.
"Where were you born?"
"Michigan."
"What were your favorite toys as a child?"

"Dolls."

"What did your family like to do for entertainment?"

"Raise a garden."

"What is your favorite grade-school memory?"

"Riding horses."

"What do you enjoy doing now?"

"Being with my grandchildren."

"What is your favorite place in the whole world?"

"My home."

"What inventions have changed the way you live?"

"Television and computers."

"What one thing do you wish had not changed over the years?"

"My age."

Before I leave the school, Kyle and I sit at a picnic table outside and eat the lunches my daughter has packed for us. I share my appreciation for the wonderful Grandparents' Day and mention several observations.

"I noticed something too," he says.

"What?" I ask.

"I can tell when a lady is a grandmother."

"How?"

"Her hair turns blond."

~Miriam Hill

81

When Everything Changes

I ask not for a lighter burden, but for broader shoulders.
~Jewish Proverb

ife can change profoundly when the phone rings. In a few seconds, nothing is as it was. In my case, it was an ordinary Tuesday night when there was a call from our daughter Nancy. I remember my seditious thought as I reached for the kitchen phone: I was betting that Nancy, always a bit scattered, had lost the recipe for the dish she was supposed to be making for a family party.

Not quite...

Nancy was calling from a hospital where Danny—our red-haired, freckle-faced little bandit grandson—had been admitted with all the symptoms of type 1 diabetes.

Of course my husband and I started out in classic denial, positive it was all a mistake. Hadn't we just seen him days before when he was a bit diminished from a lousy cold, but basically still rambunctious Danny? Hadn't he triumphantly mastered his two-wheeler bike? Sure, he'd looked a bit piqued—and skinnier than in other times—but that nasty cold, we assumed, was the reason.

Let me cut to the chase: the diagnosis was absolutely accurate. Six-year-old Danny would remain in the hospital for the next few days, until his blood glucose level had stabilized, and his parents had mastered what it would take to keep this little boy alive: the delivery of insulin.

Nancy's scattered days were over.

It was a lot to absorb. And for the next few weeks, I felt the way I did after a bad case of the flu: a bit dazed, weakened, wobbly and drained. And sleepless.

I have six other grandchildren, but all I could think of was one.

I was starting a kind of grieving process, although I didn't know it then. And as a friend with a profoundly autistic grandchild later explained to me, I was grieving three times: once for Danny, of course, once for my daughter and her husband, and yes, once for Danny's grandfather and me.

At first, I found it hard to tell people about Danny's diagnosis. And when I did start talking about it, reactions were often uninformed. "Tell his parents to cut back on the sugar," several people suggested. It infuriated me once I became a quick study on type 1, which has nothing to do with too many sweets. Others were dismissive. "Oh, they have medicine for that...."

The more enlightened understood that there would be a long, tough road ahead and that Danny will depend on insulin—literally—for his life.

As the weeks, and now months, have gone by, I am keenly aware of the losses.

No more carefree, indulgent overnights with our little grandson. Not yet. No more carefree trips to museums and circuses for now. Not without one of his parents present, and surely not until we have full mastery of the insulin pump that this little guy wears on his body for insulin control. So these familiar pleasures, formerly so routine, are on hold.

I now understand that time alone with Danny will require careful planning and training, equipment and emergency supplies. Spontaneity is gone.

And there's one even mightier challenge: how do I balance love—and overprotection? How do I distribute the same attention that my other grandchildren have had from me now that Danny is my emotional focus in this profound new way?

I'm working on it.

The wonderful news: Danny himself is astonishing his grandfather and me.

This little boy who had complete and joyous freedom until now is keenly aware of all the cautions in his life. His play dates are orchestrated, he spends more time than he'd like with the school nurse, and he is tethered to the insulin pump that is a constant reminder that life is different now. Every few days, his parents have to go through a procedure to relocate its entry site into his body, which is uncomfortable at best, painful at worst.

And as many as six to ten times a day, Danny has to have his blood glucose checked. It involves a small finger prick, but little fingers start to get calloused and painful, too.

Through it all, Danny has been resilient and largely cheerful. Blessed with a glass-half-full outlook, even at six, he is gamely shedding his brief past for a far more complicated future.

Now and then, Danny will express anger. I take it as a good thing. "I hate diabetes," he said recently when it was time again for that blood sugar check. I wanted to weep—and cheer. My grandson was venting, and he surely deserved to.

On another visit, Danny and I began going over the basics of his pump. What a weird role reversal as this grandchild led me through the maze of steps he is mastering. I could only humbly follow, lost and confused.

"You'll catch on, Grandma," Danny reassured me. It was such a generous and sweet gift.

Recently, I experienced another first. Danny and I shared our first fundraising diabetes walk on a day when the rain came down in sheets and being outdoors was an act of faith.

I looked around that day at the hundreds of walkers stretching as far as I could see, umbrellas raised high, spirits even higher.

And I looked at my grandson. His little round face was flushed, his freckles stood out, and he was ready.

I wondered what Danny Levi Friedman Zinn would remember of this day years from now. I wondered whether we'd still be walking for the cure, or whether one would have been found and celebrated.

And then I began walking in the rain, holding Danny's hand. If we were going on this journey, in real and symbolic terms, it was going to be... together.

~Sally Schwartz Friedman

82

What Lurks Behind the Trees

Tell me a fact and I'll learn. Tell me a truth and I'll believe.
But tell me a story and it will live in my heart forever.
~Indian Proverb

A large oil landscape, featuring a mountainside covered with spruce and pine trees, hung above the sofa in our living room for several years. It is a decent enough painting, one of my earlier ones, and I enjoyed looking at it, but never without seeing what I could have done to make it better.

One day, Nicholas, my three-year-old grandson, climbed onto my lap and burrowed his head into my shoulder. It was nearing his naptime, and we both liked cuddling before he went to sleep.

"What's behind the trees, Grandma?" he asked me, drowsiness in his voice.

"What trees, sweetie?"

"In that picture." He pointed to the painting. Quickly, my imagination kicked into third gear.

"Oh, I think there's a small, spotted fawn, a baby deer, frolicking along a path that's shaded by the tall trees," I told him. "He's chasing a butterfly! There he goes, running and skipping up the mountain, around bushes, through the trees, having a wonderful time. Uh, oh!" I gasped.

"What?" Nick looked up at me.

"The baby deer ran right into a baby elk! They stood and looked at each other, and then the little elk started to chase the baby deer back down the mountainside! They ran and ran and then... Uh, oh! They ran right into the Daddy Deer! He's really big! Baby deer hides behind his Daddy, and the little elk stops so fast, his hooves skid."

"Then what?" Nick was no longer drowsy. He sat up, staring at the painting.

"Well, there they go, Daddy and Baby Deer, chasing Baby Elk! They run right back up the mountain. Uh, oh! Standing in the path, glaring down at Daddy Deer, is Daddy Elk! He is huge! Much, much bigger than Daddy Deer! Baby Elk runs behind his daddy and peeks around his legs. He sticks his tongue out at the deer family, and then the elk begin to chase the deer. Back down the mountain they go, faster and faster!"

I continued with the story, building it animal by animal, until there was a parade of imaginary creatures, each bigger than the last one, chasing each other up and down the mountain. The elk is vanquished by a larger moose and calf, who, in turn are dispatched by a ferocious grizzly bear and cub. I ended the story with a moral: Never bully or tease someone who is smaller or weaker, for there will always be someone bigger and stronger to bring down the bully.

The telephone rang, and Nicholas slipped from my lap. I went into the kitchen to take the call, leaving the little boy happily playing with some toys on the floor. He was no longer sleepy. My conversation took only a few minutes; and when I quietly returned to the living room, I had to completely stop in my tracks at the sight of my grandson.

He had climbed onto the back of the sofa. Cautiously, he was pulling the painting away from the wall. I watched as he slowly peeked around the edge of the frame, his little body trembling with suspense and a hint of fear at what he might discover "behind the trees." He pulled the painting away from the wall just a bit more, until he could get a clear view. Then he carefully allowed it to resettle to its original position.

I slipped quietly back into the kitchen, but stood where I could watch him. Nick sat on the sofa, his eyes glued to the painting, and watched it for several seconds before he went back to his toys. I resumed my position in the rocker-recliner, and it wasn't long before my little grandson was back in my lap.

He looked up at my face, his big brown eyes filled with wonder. "Tell me again, Grandma. Tell me about what's behind the trees."

It became his favorite "Grandma" story, and I repeated it, with embellishments, over and over to him and a few years later to his little sister, Jessica, and to their younger cousins, Scott and Stephanie, all of whom were born during the next five years. But it was Nick who first told his sister and his cousins "what lurked behind the trees" in Grandma's painting.

I remain in awe of the power in a child's imagination. Imagination. That's what really resides behind the trees, behind creativity, and, eventually, behind invention and production.

~Barbara Elliott Carpenter

Grandmothers

Oh My Aching...

83

Thank Heaven for Little Boys

My grandkids believe I'm the oldest thing in the world.
And after two or three hours with them, I believe it, too.
~Gene Perret

I called my friend Diana during my break from a weekend visit with two grandsons. Grandpa had taken them to see his old law office, which meant at least an hour of liberation from boy-exhaustion.

Diana had raised two boys, has three grandsons, and seems to have the boy thing knocked. So it was reassuring when she clucked sympathetically at the bone-weariness I described, and suggested that I take a nap before the boys got back. It was excellent advice.

Boy-energy is still new to me, even though I'd gotten my basic orientation fourteen years ago when Sam was born. Until the arrival of Sam, the first boy in our family in generations, I was totally conversant with girl stuff. I am one, I have a sister, three daughters, two close aunts and a close girl cousin.

Sam taught me a few lessons during our first overnight with him when he was about nine months old. I learned, for example, that he could crawl faster than I could run — that he could go on search and destroy missions with anything in his reach, and that he had a kind of raw energy that I'd never experienced before.

There have been three more boys born into our family, four reminders in all that boys are different.

On our recent weekend with Jonah, eight, and his little brother Danny, six, there was careful planning: we would take the boys to a science museum, to a play they'd both enjoy, and to a reasonably nice restaurant. We'd spend quality time with them watching the nature videos we'd rented. Maybe we'd even get a chance to talk about important things—values, goals, ideas.

So—let me tell you how it really went.

On the ride to our house from theirs, there was some pummeling going on in the back seat, and some taunting on both sides that turned physical rather quickly.

There were earnest conversations between grandparents and grandchildren about how we needed better behavior in that back seat, and how brothers shouldn't be mean to each other.

It was a very long car ride.

Danny discovered, seconds after getting into our house, that he could "pretend-skate" down our long hallway by taking off his shoes and skidding along in his socks. Jonah discovered that chasing Danny down that same hallway could add the thrill of competition.

"Be careful!" I begged as Jonah and Danny did what seemed to come naturally to boys. They raced, came perilously close to colliding on the return trips, piled on top of one another several times and then were hungry enough to down huge quantities of macaroni and cheese for lunch.

We never got to the science museum or the play. Instead, we refereed several altercations between these brothers, threatened to withhold dessert, and wondered when these fiercely energetic boys would wear down.

Not before we did, you can be sure.

Their mother, our daughter, has grown used to the noise, the movement, the tussles, the chases, the leaping from any and all inviting surfaces. She somehow takes it on faith that they won't injure themselves with their high jinks, to say nothing of their high jumps.

She understands that they take up a disproportionate amount of space, that they have seemingly limitless energy, perpetually dirty hands and faces and that underneath all the physical assaults, there is truly brotherly love.

We're still learning.

The nature videos were a hit. The deep, long talks were not.

Jonah loved the chicken I made for dinner; Danny proclaimed it "Yucky!" and settled for the unique menu choice of French fries, applesauce, jelly on a banana and cookies snitched from the pantry shelf.

We never got to a restaurant because it was pouring, and Danny refused to wear shoes.

We also built an impressive fort out of Tinkertoys, ate chocolate popsicles at the kitchen table, and played some silly games with abandon.

I told our grandsons stories about their mom as a little girl. I loved reading Danny stories and watching Jonah read a book with such intensity that I'd swear he was in an altered state.

Most of all, I adored kissing these guys goodnight after their baths, when their hair was wet and they had that luminous look that little ones get when they're shined up.

I learned more than I'd ever known about rockets, and was stunned to find out that even restless little boys love to hear the story of how their grandparents met. Who would have guessed?

And I adored greeting these two little guys in the morning, when there was just a hint of sleepy dreaminess left that rendered Jonah mellow and Danny willing to be cuddled. The fact that it was before 6 a.m.—well, no matter.

Okay it was definitely a relief to deliver our two grandsons back into the hands of their parents. It was wonderful to get order restored in a house that had lost any semblance of it.

"Piece of cake," we lied to our daughter, who wasn't fooled, before we collapsed into bed and slept for a week.

~Sally Schwartz Friedman

84

Shhhhhh

An hour with your grandchildren can make you feel young again.
Anything longer than that, and you start to age quickly.
~Gene Perret

I was babysitting my two-year-old grandson while my daughter and son-in-law went off for a needed weekend away. I had been in charge at other times, but only during the day and not over an extended period. Three decades have passed since I had full charge of a child. I hoped I remembered my mothering skills.

Everything was fine during the day. I changed diapers as necessary and had no problem keeping him entertained. We went to the playground, where he toddled up the steps and flung himself down the slide. We rode the elevator up and down in the store as we shopped in the local market. He had a two-hour nap after lunch and woke up happy. We took a walk in the afternoon and watched the trucks rattle along the road, a highlight of his day.

Easy, I thought.

Even dinner was a breeze. My daughter said he wouldn't eat cheese but he gobbled up a whole finger of string cheese. He ate two meatballs dipped in gobs of ketchup, a double helping of applesauce with cinnamon, and tasted a green bean, which he didn't eat but he didn't throw on the floor either—a definite plus. After his bath, my sweet grandson snuggled into my lap for a story. We read the book the traditional multiple times and then it was bedtime.

I put him in his crib, shut off the light, and was ready to leave when I heard the plaintive call.

"Up," he said.

"It's time to sleep," I answered in a whisper.

"No, up," he repeated.

"Goodnight," I crooned.

I gently patted his back until he settled down. When I heard his breathing get deeper, I thought it was safe to tiptoe out of the room, as I had done so many years ago with my tiny toddlers. I didn't reckon on my joints. My toes cracked with my first step. How could anything so little sound so loud? It was loud enough to wake him.

So I patted and shhhed until, once again, he was asleep. I wiggled my toes to warm them before starting my retreat. Then I moved very slowly, keeping each step balanced and light. I almost made it to the door when my knee exploded. CRACK. There was no way my grandson would sleep through that! Sure enough, I heard him call me.

I remained quiet, hoping he would turn around and go back to sleep, but he got agitated instead, crying to come out. So, back I went, shhhing and patting and silently reprimanding my body for its lack of cooperation. Once more I heard the deep, even breathing. I stopped patting but remained in place a little longer.

Threatening my body with dire consequences, like extra time at the gym or wearing shoes in the house, something my feet and I don't particularly like to do, if it should so much as creak, I gingerly headed toward the door. Each step seemed to take a day. I got to the threshold and slowly eased my way through. As I carefully pulled the door closed, I heard a stirring, a little whine, and a questioning whisper. I held my breath. Then all was quiet.

As I made my way down the hall, I ruminated on the difference between being a mother and a grandmother. It wasn't so much a shift in philosophy or a greater tolerance or even a more expansive understanding of bringing up a child; it was arthritis!

I hope I am getting wiser as I age but one thing is obvious—I sure am getting noisier.

~Ferida Wolff

"Grandma, you make funny noises when you walk.
Daddy uses this stuff to fix squeaky things."

Reprinted by permission of
Marc Tyler Nobleman ©2010

I wish I had the energy that my grandchildren have—
if only for self-defense.
~Gene Perret

Marnie's pulling Phoebe's hair.
Noah's climbing on a chair.
Phoebe's stamping Noah's toes.
Marnie's picking at her nose.
Noah's screaming, "My turn now!"
Phoebe yells, "Ka-pow, kap-ow,"
While poking Marnie with her gun,
And shouting, "Gramma, this is fun!"

Noah whines, "I hate these peas."
Marnie cries, "I skinned my knees."
Noah jumps into the pool,
Where Phoebe's broken every rule.
Marnie squirts a water gun.
Phoebe squirts another one.
Noah spills the bubble mix.
Phoebe shouts, "I'm almost six!"

"Gramma, Gramma, read this book!"
"Gramma, Gramma, won't you look?"
"Gramma, Gramma, where's my dinner?"

"Gramma, she says she's the winner."
Noah wants another bite.
Marnie thinks she's always right.
Phoebe whines and Noah cries.
Marnie spills her bag of fries.

"Gramma, how come you're so old?"
"Gramma, Noah says he's cold."
"Gramma, can we play with blocks?"
"Gramma, I can't find my socks."
"Gramma, is it time to go?"
Noah's screaming, "No! No! No!"
Marnie wants another chance.
Noah's pulling down his pants.

Gramma's tearing out her hair.
Grampa's sleeping in his chair.
Our sanity is on the skids.
"Daughter, come and get your kids!"

~Toni Somers

Cheerio Parties

Few things are more delightful than grandchildren fighting over your lap.
~Doug Larson

Our tiny house often rang with the laughter and occasional cries of our many grandchildren. They knew where Grandma kept the toys, books and their favourite snacks. The ones old enough to talk proclaimed the big old rocking chair as "Grandma's chair." They loved to curl up on my lap, often two or three at a time, for hugs and stories.

One day my daughter and her family stopped by. "Mom, will you keep the kids when I go to the hospital for this next baby?"

Without hesitation I replied, "Of course I will. No problem. That's what grandmas are for."

Several days later, my son and his family came for a visit. He asked, "Mom when it's time for our next baby's birth will you keep the other kids please?"

I looked at the calendar. The due dates were about three weeks apart, so without much hesitation I said, "Of course I will. Shouldn't be a problem. That's what grandmas are for."

I don't know what the odds are, but a few weeks later, within hours of each other, both my daughter and daughter-in-law were admitted to the hospital. Seven grandchildren aged one to six arrived at Grandma's for the promised sleepover, accompanied by what seemed to be a truckload of necessities. Piles of winter clothing littered the floor close to the front door. Bottles and sippy cups competed for room in the fridge. Diapers and clothes were stashed in the spare room while special blankets dragged behind children as they emptied the toy box and bookshelf looking for their favourite things at Grandma's house.

My youngest daughter surveyed the busy atmosphere and clutter of the house when she arrived home from school. Her face betrayed a mixture of excitement and being overwhelmed. I phoned Grandpa and warned him of the hopefully imminent birth of not one but two new grandbabies and he arrived home from work with supper in hand.

The evening passed in a blur of activity. Bedtime routines were anything but routine when I needed to change a one-year-old, two two-year-olds and make sure the two three-year-olds went potty before going to bed. There were bottles and sippy cups to fill and lots of little ones all anxious to be cuddled by Grandma in that big old rocking chair. Finally quiet reigned.

After sleeping lightly, while listening all night for any grandchildren who might need me, I felt less than ready to face the new day when the alarm's incessant ringing filled my ears. But seven little ones in a tiny house do not sleep through an alarm. Our day began with a rush of activities. Grandpa needed to go to work. Auntie needed to be ready to get on the school bus at 8:00 and the five- and six-year-olds would be picked up by Great-Grandpa who had been enlisted as taxi driver for their ride to school. Hungry children demanded breakfast. I grabbed the Cheerio box from the cupboard knowing they could feed themselves this finger food. Sippy cups of milk were spill-proof—well almost anyway. I started making school lunches while urging the older ones to hurry.

Auntie grabbed the last couple of bites of breakfast and shoved them in her mouth to hunt for her parka and boots. She grabbed her stuff and rushed out the front door to the waiting school bus. Great-Grandpa arrived early. I left the five littlest ones in various stages of sogginess and mess to help the older ones sort through the pile of mittens, hats, scarves and parkas to find the matching sets I knew they had arrived with yesterday. Quickly running a comb through their hair and doing a cursory check of backpacks, I helped them bundle up to face the frigid winter weather. By the time they left for school the clock only read 8:30. I felt like a whirlwind had gone through the house. As I glanced around I noticed it looked that way as well.

I took time to put away the milk and stack the dishes into the sink for later. Five little ones needed changing, clothes on, and their hair brushed. While changing the diapers and Pull-Ups I noticed that something—a diaper, sippy cup or bottle—had leaked during the night. I pulled the sheet from bed to throw in the wash and quickly grabbed a clean sheet from the cupboard. Might as well get it ready for naptime, as if anyone would want a nap other than Grandma. Finally I threaded my way through grandchildren, scattered toys and diaper bags to sit down for a moment or two. I smiled as I watched these precious little ones play contentedly side-by-side on the living room floor. I grabbed the ever-present camera and captured this priceless moment to share with their parents. Peace and quiet, at least for a moment or two, filled the house. I took advantage of it for a quick bathroom break of my own.

I shut the door. Within seconds silence greeted me with the intensity that could only spell trouble. No one called for me or demanded their turn for the bathroom. No sounds of fighting, crying or even playing noises sounded from the other side of the door. I quickly washed my hands and dried them as I opened the door, wondering what disaster would greet me. Abandoned toys littered the floor of the living room but not one of the five grandchildren could be seen.

In the spare room I saw my three-year-old grandson squeezed into the now empty little toy box. With his cousin's little Mickey Mouse hat perched on top of his head like a crown, he surveyed the kingdom of toys spread before him. When he looked up at me a grin lit up his entire face. Being a dutiful grandma I smiled, grabbed my camera and snapped a few photos before searching for my granddaughters.

Camera still in hand, I headed to the only other place they could be—the kitchen. The three-year-old and two two-year-old girls sat nicely on chairs at the kitchen table. The one-year-old, with mischief glinting in her eyes, stood in the middle of the table. She reached into the Cheerio box that I had forgotten to put away and placed handfuls of cereal in front of the others before feeding herself. She looked up and a huge smile wreathed her face. Being a dutiful grandma I smiled and snapped a few photos prior to rescuing her off the table. None of them were too impressed when Grandma spoilt their Cheerio party by putting the box of cereal away.

The grandchildren stayed for a couple more days before those new babies arrived and were ready to go home. My house rang with laughter and an occasional tired cry. Looking after the grandchildren's practical needs was interspersed with lots of cuddles and story times in the big old rocking chair. We even had time for more Cheerio parties, Grandma's way. It all added to making memories together the way grandmas and grandchildren do.

~Carol Harrison

Bring on the Rain

There are only two tragedies in life:
One is not getting what one wants. And the other is getting it.
~Oscar Wilde

We never took our kids to Disney World. Afraid this bordered on child abuse, I decided on a little preventive therapy in case they felt the urge to write a Mommy Dearest book. My husband and I announced we were installing an honest-to-goodness in-ground pool complete with a deep end and a diving board.

The grandkids squealed with delight, and the grownups high-fived. Visions of sprawling on a chaise lounge, a good book in one hand and a cold drink in the other, swam through my head.

We broke ground and my four-year-old granddaughter arrived wearing her swimsuit.

"Where's your pool, Grandma?"

"Sweetie, do you see any water?" I smiled and pictured her gazing at me on her wedding day, remembering the summers we'd spent in the pool.

The next few weeks, anxious swimmers hung over the deck watching the progress. Then the skies opened up and the rains poured down, delaying the project. Disappointed children marched in and out. The two-year-old showed up wearing his life jacket and chomping at the bit. Finally the weather cleared, and the liner was installed.

Day One—The first of twelve truckloads of water arrived amidst swimsuit donning and fits of frenzy. Moments after the last drop dribbled into the pool, we jumped in and swam our hearts out, smiling through chattering teeth. Surrounded by loved ones, I was overcome with bliss.

Day Two—The heat pump ran all night, and the water temperature rose to 80 degrees. We spent the entire afternoon in the water and hopped out only long enough to grill burgers. That's when I discovered a one-hour casserole cannot survive three hours in the oven. As the day wore on, the grandchildren grew bolder. Even the toddler flew off the diving board wearing his Coast Guard-approved suit.

Day Three—Our swimming days were numbered since we opened the pool late in the season, but was one night alone asking too much?

Two children whizzed by. "Slow down," I yelled and dashed inside for Papa's referee whistle, initiating five-minute penalties for running and pushing.

At last, the exhausted swimmers left. My husband suggested we spend next summer in Canada. We collapsed on the couch and listened to the forecast. Blue skies and sunshine the remainder of the week.

I considered doing a rain dance.

Day Four—My grandchildren spun out of control. The youngest performed a double flip off the diving board, and the four-year-old dove in without water wings. The kindergartner refused to wear a life jacket. The eight-year-old almost hit her head jumping backward off the board. The nine-year-old wouldn't quit splashing, and the teenager wanted her own space. Thanks to the shrill referee whistle, by the end of the day I couldn't hear a thing.

Day Five—My house was filthy. I waited for the "Merry Maid" fairies to arrive. What was I thinking when I gave each grandchild a large, fluffy monogrammed towel and insisted the towels stay at Grandma's? And when would I find time to replenish the pantry? The only thing left in the icebox was mold.

Day Six—They're baaaack! Grandchildren arrived hourly. My

sister dropped in for a swim. Another sister arrived with her crew. A few neighbors joined the party. "No running," I repeated and wondered when I'd become a mynah bird. The whistle was a lifesaver.

Shhh! Was that thunder? I glanced upward. Not a cloud in sight—only an airplane. Forget cleaning. Forget relaxing. Forget sanity. The perfect hostess, I spent the day in the water socializing.

That night I closed my eyes, thankful I'd survived a full workweek and swimming every night until the stars twinkled.

Whose idea was it to put in pool lights anyway?

My husband nudged me awake. "You've been crying out in your sleep."

"What did I say?"

"No running."

Day Seven—I thought I heard the pitter-patter of little feet. Not already! I peeked outside and grinned as big, fat, glorious raindrops plopped on the concrete.

Alleluia. Sunday was going to be a day of rest after all.

"Lord, I don't know what I did to deserve this, but I thank you from the bottom of my heart. Oh, and can we please have an early fall?"

~Alice Muschany

Grandma Goes Crazy

On the seventh day God rested.
His grandchildren must have been out of town.
~Gene Perret

My dear friend, Jane, just returned from a week at her children's home in Washington, D.C. Her job was to babysit her three grandchildren—Samantha, age eleven, Susan, eight and Wendy, three—while her son and daughter-in-law took a much-needed vacation in an area so remote they could not be reached by telephone. Jane arrived on Saturday and was handed a list of instructions to be carefully followed. She hasn't been herself since she returned.

School Lunches: Samantha and Susan will need lunches for school. These can be prepared the night before. The girls enjoy being part of food preparation. Or, they can buy lunch up to two times a week. Samantha will also need a snack in her backpack every school day as she has a late lunch. Wendy eats lunch at home after school. Snacks include: something healthy, not sweets. They like tortillas with cheese, apples and peanut butter, yogurt, and fruit. Susan likes cereal sometimes, but only Captain Crunch and Cheerios. Wendy is hungry and thirsty after her nap, so if you are going somewhere with her, plan on bringing snacks along like cheese, fruit, milk or juice box, carrots and a few chips. Even though she is potty trained, accidents can happen. Bring along Pull-Ups just in case. Do not leave dry cat food out in bowls. Wendy tends to eat this and is particularly fond of Kibble 'n Bits. The cats' dishes are kept on their own table in the kitchen, which Wendy can't reach.

Dinners: I have left meal suggestions as well as places to call for takeout if you absolutely don't want to cook. On school nights, the girls should eat at home. Please note that if you must resort to takeout, delivery can take up to an hour. The day-by-day schedule I have included suggests specific places according to the girls' food preferences. Desserts: sweet desserts, be they ice cream, a few chocolate chips and cookies are fine for weekend nights, but Sunday through Thursday are always fruit dessert nights or the girls get too wired.

Naps and bedtime: Wendy can be a challenge. You need to set clear limits on what will and won't happen or she may continually ask for more. She should use the bathroom before naps and bedtime. She wears Pull-Ups in bed when most "accidents" tend to occur. The routine is as follows both for naps and bedtime:

1) Air purifier must be turned to quiet setting, shades and curtains closed.

2) She will expect two stories and a song, which you must sing in a low, comforting voice.

3) Water must be left on night table.

4) Lights out.

5) Say: have a good nap or "nightie-night" in a firm but upbeat tone. Check for monsters under the bed. Exit the room quietly and close the door, leaving it open exactly two inches. After Wendy is quiet for twenty minutes, check on her. If she is still awake or playing in her room, tell her she needs to go sleep or she won't derive the desired benefit. She must not sleep on the floor. If she doesn't nap in the afternoon, she will be harder to handle and should go to bed earlier, 8 p.m. the latest. If she has napped, then bedtime is 8:30. Never resort to baby talk. We treat our children as small adults.

6) Baths—for all girls every night before bedtime. Rubber ducky mandatory.

7) Homework: Samantha has a challenging math class this year and needs help with homework. I trust you understand the new math. If not, you may call a parent who can be of help. I will leave numbers of our math-proficient friends. Tuesdays, Susan has a "Mad Math Minute" which will be a timed test on subtraction skills, fifty problems in two minutes. I have clipped a few of these to her wire cubby in kitchen. She must do one "Mad Math Minute" on Sunday and again on Monday. Tuesday morning before school is helpful but optional. She also has a math quiz on Fridays. She should study for this on Wednesday and Thursday after school.

Piano Practice: The big girls should be encouraged to practice every day after homework is done. Please check their piano notebooks for notes from previous lesson and sit with them while they practice. Susan practices twenty minutes a day, Samantha thirty minutes, but only if Wendy isn't sleeping. The target time for piano practice is on the white board in the kitchen. Ms. Underhill arrives every Thursday promptly at 5:00 for Samantha and Susan's lessons. She should be offered hot tea and cranberry scones from The Sweet Tooth bakery, which must be warmed up. Ms. Underhill is not a patient woman but she gets the job done.

Groceries: We will leave enough food for the week, for school lunches, several dinners and snacks. If you need to add to this, go to Safeway, which is nearest to home, Giant near Wendy's school (after drop-off or before pick-up is convenient), or Whole Foods which has the best produce and gourmet foods (for you, not the kids). We will of course reimburse you for all out-of-pocket expenses.

TV/Computer Use: On weekend, Samantha and Susan may watch maximum two hours TV a day or two hours TV plus computer time. Wendy should do no more than an hour of either. An exception would be watching a special movie, but nothing *with violence of course. We have selected a few choice films. Do not deviate from this list. Weekdays, Samantha has no time for morning TV. If Susan and Wendy are up early, they may watch one or two shows or do a half hour on the computer. In the afternoon, Samantha and Susan may not watch TV unless their homework is completed. Encourage them to read.*

Extracurricular Activities: Gymnastics, Irish dance class, soccer, ballet, drama class, ballroom dancing and etiquette, religious school, Brownies, play dates, piano lessons, French lessons, swimming practice, diving, field hockey and arts and crafts. All dates and hours are listed below for each child. Play dates will be at our home this week under your watchful eye. Employ time-outs as needed.

Emergency Contact Numbers: Destinations for which we will provide a map are in red. Contact names are on a separate sheet marked in green. These include: hospital, pediatrician, veterinarian, carpool names for Mondays and Thursdays, plumber, handyman and electrician, takeout restaurants, play date friends, cleaning lady, and my mother in California (she's very neurotic and doesn't like hearing bad news). Don't hesitate to call 911 should an emergency arise like a sudden fire or if anyone chokes, including the cats. We trust you are able to perform CPR and the Heimlich maneuver.

Wear comfortable clothes.

When Jane arrived home, she immediately took to bed. When questioned about the week, she relayed the following: the dishwasher broke and flooded the bathroom below. This blew out the light sockets when water got in, which in turn kept everyone up all night as light sockets were smoking. There was no hot water the rest of the week. The plumber, electrician and handyman were called, but didn't consider this a dire emergency and showed up three days later. All three children became ill with a variety of ailments, and Wendy, who was "absolutely potty trained," wasn't. Jane also said she got lost three times when trying to find the pediatrician's building. Both cats threw up on Jane's bed and have bubble gum in their fur. The cleaning lady never showed up.

Jane doesn't look good. As of yesterday, she was still in bed, requiring as much sleep as possible. The good news: her son called to tell her that the children are now well and thriving. Jane, however, has developed strep throat, two aching knees, back spasms, tension headaches, and is considering going back to see her shrink. She has fulfilled her grandma duties for at least the next six months or until her son and his wife decide to take their next vacation.

~Judith Marks-White

Living Life Soaking Wet

Grandmothers are just antique little girls.
~Author Unknown

Soaking wet, water dripping down my jeans and sweater, floor splattered and hair wet. That was me about twenty minutes ago. I was giving my almost one-year-old granddaughter a bath.

How can such a tiny little thing cause so much, well, wetness? Not to mention the whole, hear the water and it makes you want to "go," thing definitely also applies to little babies… and of course it happened the minute after I took off her diaper. The bathmat is the next thing to get a bath.

I wish you could have been there. Rubber ducky and baby girl had so much fun that it made me want to jump in. I heard belly laughs and tiny, adorable giggles that I hadn't heard before. She was cracking herself up, mindless that she had an audience. This laughter wasn't for me, or anyone else that could have been watching. She wasn't showing off. She was totally having a blast.

Every time I reached down to get her out, I got a mouthful of water. She did not want this bath to end! So engrossed was she in entertaining herself that she forgot to get bored. The water was getting cold, her little fingers and toes were turning to prunes, and still she did not want to get out. I finally had to fight her when I noticed the goose bumps on her compact little body. She wasn't ready for her adventure to end, but since I am the older and supposedly wiser one, I realized I had to take her out of the tub.

It made me think back to the last time I had so much fun that I laughed belly laughs and didn't want to stop what I was doing, regardless of a little discomfort. Sadly, I couldn't. Probably because I can't remember being a toddler. But that made me realize that somewhere in our long lost "baby years" we lose our sense of unselfconscious fun. We lose the knack of entertaining ourselves to the point of laughing and giggling regardless of who is watching.

In my self-righteous "grandmotherdom," I just assumed I would be the one teaching, and helping her grow along the way. I figured I'd be the role model and, along with her parents, help show her the ropes. I thought that I would be the one who helped her learn to be a self-confident member of the human race. Boy was I wrong. Instead, from my almost one-year-old, sweet, adorable granddaughter, I have learned the secret of a stress-free life. I have learned how not to be self-conscious, while either naked or laughing to myself.

I have learned to just enjoy the exact moment I am in—and if I'm having a blast, not to worry if I'm a little cold—because the fun will outweigh the discomfort every, single time. Thank you dear, sweet granddaughter for showing me what I had forgotten so long ago. To laugh and smile and giggle and have a blast, even when my jeans are soaked and my newly blown dry hair is dripping wet. Thank you for reminding me that right here, right now, is where I want to be and what I want to be doing—living this minute—because this is where I am supposed to be, even if it's a little bit soggy.

~Karen Kelly

"No, I didn't bathe her yet. This is
just from brushing her teeth."

90

Granny Tries the Jacuzzi

Humor is a reminder that no matter how high the throne one sits on,
one sits on one's bottom.
~Taki

Ah sweet solitude! I was finally alone in our summer rental since the family had left the night before. It was the perfect time for this grandma to try the Jacuzzi bathtub without fear of interruption. I had been looking forward to this moment for two weeks and I was well prepared. My box of Tropical Waterfalls water softener that guaranteed to transport me to a tropical isle now beckoned me.

I must admit I did have some trepidation about bathing in a tub that had an electrical switch. I thought back many years to when our then five-year-old son experimented with taking a bath with his own lighthouse. I could remember my horror when I opened the bathroom door and there he was splashing away with a lit lamp bobbing in the water. I was hysterical as I pulled him from the tub. His guardian angel had protected him and I counted it as a miracle that he was not electrocuted.

In light of that event a few precautions seemed to be in order. I took off my robe and placed it where I could reach it, I got my cell phone and placed it on top of my robe. I ran my bath, poured in the Tropical Waterfalls, and flipped the switch. Voila! How inviting those turquoise bubbles appeared. I slowly entered the tub, big toe first in case there were some electrical currents gone awry. I figured I could quickly retreat. So far so good. I eased the rest of my body into the bubbling water and it was wonderfully decadent. I relaxed and totally enjoyed the experience.

After about a half hour I decided to leave my tropical lagoon and return to reality. I released the drain and attempted to get out of the tub. I could not! The construction of the tub was such that it was wide on top and narrow on the bottom. To get out seemed easy, just bend my knees and stand up. Easy enough, right? Wrong! I had two knee replacements and lacked the knee flexibility to bend them enough. No matter what I tried, the narrowness at the bottom of the tub held my seventy-five-year-old bottom securely and prevented my maneuvering into a standing position.

After several foiled attempts at twisting and turning I realized I needed to think seriously about what I was going to do. The first thing I did was pray. The next thing I did was reach for my robe, so at least if my fate was to die of starvation and dehydration in an empty Jacuzzi tub/tomb I would not be indecently exposed. I had forgotten about my cell phone, which I had placed on top of the robe. When I pulled my robe from the top of the commode the phone clattered to the floor and skittered out of reach. My excursion to a tropical isle had turned into being stranded on a tropical isle.

I tried with no success to capture my phone with a towel and pull it towards me as I sat in the tub. They say necessity is the mother of invention. I found it to be true. It occurred to me that if I wet the towel it would have more weight and if I could land it on top of the phone I could pull it towards me. It worked! I dialed 911 and explained to the officer on the other end that I was stuck in a tub and couldn't get out. From the sound of his voice I could tell this was not an everyday kind of emergency call, but he said he would dispatch help right away. Thank goodness I had left the door to the apartment unlocked. Before I knew it, two very strong and good looking police-men knocked on the bathroom door asking me if I was decent. Of course I was decent! I was a deaconess in my church for goodness sakes! "Yes," I shouted back, "decent and stuck." In they came, not knowing what to expect, but they quickly assessed the situation and with the help of their strong arms I was able to hoist myself up and out and I was free at last.

I believe every story has a take-away lesson in it. What would this one be?

An obvious one would be, don't enter a tub unless you are sure you can get out. Another one might be just stick to showers. Or a more interesting one, if you are young and single, which I am neither, it might be a great way to meet a handsome young policeman.

~Phyllis Tomberg Giglio

91

Camp Grandma

I have a warm feeling after playing with my grandchildren.
It's the liniment working.
~Author Unknown

"We found this great deal on plane tickets to Saint Lucia, and since we haven't had a vacation in years, we thought it would be nice to get away. Would you and Dad watch the kids for us?"

My daughter's words ran together in an excited muddle. Caught up in the moment, I blurted, "We'd love to," without giving a thought to what my husband might say.

I reconsidered. "That is, if your dad's okay with it. How long's your trip?"

"Five days," she replied.

Five days. With two toddlers. How bad could it be? Only one of them was in diapers. I had visions of them glued to the TV watching Disney videos and eating raisins. I'd raised three children. They'd been close in age, and at one time three toddlers were running around our house. We'd all survived the experience. I assured myself, child raising was like riding a bike. Once you learned how to do it, you never forgot.

"Five days?" My husband's eyebrows furrowed over his glasses. "That's a long time."

"I don't think it'll be too bad," I said. "I'll keep them busy."

"Okay," he said. "But I think both of us will be under a doctor's care by the time they leave."

When my daughter and son-in-law appeared on the morning of their departure, I was stunned to see the amount of paraphernalia two small children needed to spend five days with their grandparents. A double-occupant stroller, along with a Radio Flyer two-passenger red wagon, was parked on the porch. A Pack 'n Play, which would serve as my granddaughter's bed, dominated the guest bedroom. An oversized suitcase filled with clothes, pajamas, underwear and shoes stood by the front door. Next to it were two duffle bags. One was filled with toys, while the other held a multitude of stuffed animals and blankets, all of which were essential to helping the children go to sleep. Teetering on top was an economy-sized box of diapers.

"If you run out, just buy some more and we'll pay you back." My daughter handed me a list with cell phone numbers, as well as the number of the hotel, the pediatrician, and the pet hotel where they'd lodged their dog. We also were given a copy of their flight schedule and daily itinerary.

"That ought to do it," my son-in-law said with a grin.

"Thanks so much," my daughter said. A flurry of hugs and kisses followed. The next minute they were gone.

The front door no sooner closed when my grandson said, "Let's cook." He ran to one of the bags where he pulled out a crumpled chef's hat he'd gotten at a birthday party.

"Cook," said my granddaughter and raced to the pantry with her brother.

"Wait," I cried, but it was too late.

"Sorry, Grandma," our grandson said in a mournful voice as he and his sister watched our dog lap up the spilled sugar and flour.

"Sowee," piped our granddaughter.

Four dozen sugar cookies and baths followed. It was almost time for dinner, but both kids begged to go to the playground. My husband and I wrestled two car seats into the back of the car, and armed with a bag full of juice boxes, water, and a diaper change, buckled the kids inside.

Chasing two small children down slides, pushing them on swings, and squirming through tunnels could only be compared to boot camp training. After an hour, my husband panted, "I think it's time for dinner."

As he was unlocking the car, he whispered, "Do we have any Bengay? Better yet, a heating pad?"

From the beginning, our grandson was homesick, and asked non-stop for his parents. "Where are they? When are they coming home? I want my mommy." He only wanted me, cuddling close, and wailed whenever I tried to pass him off to my husband.

I was doing double duty. From infancy, our granddaughter and my husband had been best pals. Now, she wanted nothing to do with him. She might have been attached to my side with Krazy Glue as I made beds, and did laundry, dragging her behind like a tiny, rag doll.

"She's a great sleeper," my daughter assured me. "Count on her to sleep until at least eight o'clock in the morning."

The first morning at 5:45, I felt little fingers tugging at my arm.

"Gwandma," I heard a soft voice. Looking down, there was my granddaughter, her curly locks standing around her head like a halo.

"Pancakes," she chirped.

"It's too early to get up," I said. I ignored her vehement head shaking, and said. "Listen, do you hear the birds? No? Well, that's because the birds aren't awake yet. Everyone's still sleeping. You need to go back to bed, Come on, I'll take you."

Her curls bounced with another shake of her head.

"Pancakes, Gwandma," she said.

"How about if we sit in my bed and watch TV?" I reached across my slumbering husband for the remote.

"Look, sweetheart," I said, "It's Curious George. You like Curious George."

"Pancakes," she said in a firm voice, stomping towards the kitchen.

Every morning she came to get me at 5:45, and the two of us, with me trying to focus through sleep-glazed eyes, walked hand in hand to the kitchen and made pancakes.

My biggest worry was losing the night-nights. Five worn receiving blankets were the constant companions of my grandson. They made the climb up the big hill behind our house, and went on nature walks through the woods. Before we went to the goat farm, a night-night count was taken. I could only wash them when my grandson was asleep since he never let them out of his sight. One day he asked me to throw them in the dryer even though they weren't wet. After I took them out, he burrowed into them like a lonely rabbit. It was clear the night-nights offered more comfort than I could.

On our last evening together, I took the kids for a ride in their wagon. On the way home, I trudged past my neighbor. Recently widowed, he stepped off his porch and asked, "Are these your grandchildren?"

"Yes," I replied. "We're just coming back from a walk."

"You know what you're doing, don't you?" He stared at me with clear blue eyes. "You're making memories. They may forget the material stuff you buy them, but they'll always remember spending time with Grandma."

Later, after going through the usual routine of baths, snacks and a story, I tucked the children into their beds and said, "Sleep well. Remember, tomorrow your mommy and daddy are coming home."

"I love you, Grandma," my grandson said in a tired voice.

"I wuff you too," my granddaughter grinned.

Every muscle in my body hurt. My house was overrun with the scent of diaper cream and peanut butter. Play dough covered the carpet. After their departure, I'd probably spend the rest of the day in bed.

I didn't entertain a single doubt about doing it again.

I looked into their sleepy faces, and smiled. "And I love you too," I said. "More than you'll ever know."

~Ellen Fink

Chapter 10

Grandmothers

Grand Adventures

Free-Falling Grandma

Anything I've ever done that ultimately was worthwhile...
initially scared me to death.
~Betty Bender

W hy would a reasonably sane person leap out of a perfectly good airborne airplane? I'm still asking myself this question. Perhaps my mistake began when we caved in to demands of family who thought we should give up life on the Oregon coast and move back to Southern California in order to "bond" with the grandkids.

We had retired to a quiet life in Oregon and saw no reason to leave our paradise on the Pacific Ocean. But guilt is a powerful thing—and, after all, grandkids do grow up and maybe we did need to do the "bonding thing" while we still had the energy.

We relocated exactly five minutes from one particular granddaughter who had put on the most pressure. That would be Autumn, a taller-than-me, typical teenage Valley Girl. Looking back, it seems she has never stopped talking or asking questions. She refused to call me "Grandma" from the get-go, insisting on "Beverly Jo," the name that appears only on my legal documents. Autumn marches to her own drummer.

Once we got resettled in Los Angeles, she followed me everywhere. Picture Autumn trailing me even into a bathroom. I'm not kidding. She never ran out of questions. "Now listen, Beverly Jo," she said, perched on the bathtub while I brushed my teeth. "I need to know so many things about when you were a teenager."

"For instance?" I asked.

"Well, like, PMS?" she asked. "And what about boyfriends? Did you ever get grounded? Did you smoke? What about drugs? Did you ever wreck the car? Did you ever want to get a tattoo? Do you have a tattoo?" And so it went. I never knew what the next question or subject might be, and kept my so-called guard up until one day when I forgot.

The telephone rang. It was Autumn.

"Hi," I said.

"Hi," she said. Then, in rapid-fire teenage talk, she continued.

"Listen, Beverly Jo," she said, "you know my birthday is coming up. My eighteenth!"

"So?" I said.

"So," she said, "I've decided we need to do something extra special together, to celebrate. You've never ever said no to me, so you have to say yes. Right now!"

I remember trying to think fast about what she had in mind. My first thought was probably some spendy, high-end Beverly Hills restaurant. I was up for that. Autumn had recently discovered there were places to eat other than Burger King and Dairy Queen.

"Okay, Autumn," I said, saying yes. "Now tell me what you want to do to celebrate this epic birthday."

"Okay," she said, sucking in her breath. "I went on the Internet and made the arrangements. It's all set and remember, you said 'Yes' and now you can't say 'No.'"

"So tell me," I said, my guard completely down.

"We're going skydiving. You and me. We're going to jump out of an airplane together."

I nearly choked. "Excuse me? You want me to do what?"

"Skydive, Beverly Jo. It will be such fun. Totally cool. And just think, we will always have the memory."

If I live through it, I thought. Breaking this latest harebrained Autumn idea to my husband was not easy. He has a way of looking stricken every time one of these wild adventures crops up in our marriage. I reminded him that I had said "yes" and that I am a woman of my word.

As the big day drew closer, I grew more and more nervous. By this time, my daughter Rocki (Autumn's Mom) knew what the birthday plan was. Her attitude about life and adventure and taking risks is "Bring it on!" Rocki said, "You are not doing this without me!"

On the day of our reservations, we all drove out to the skydiving school, which was a hotbed of airplane activity. Planes in the sky, people floating to ground attached to colorful parachutes, everyone seemingly thrilled and excited. I was a nervous wreck, but my poor husband even more so.

We checked in. Autumn had to prove she was of legal age to skydive. I was hoping they had an "old age limit," but no such luck. There was a weight restriction, however—no one over 250 pounds. We were herded into a room, and the "Skydiving Lectures" began. Now, looking back, I think the scariest part was having to watch a lengthy video of a lawyer, dressed in suit and tie, sitting behind an important-looking desk and explaining all the legal papers we each had to sign. As in "signing your life away in the event something goes terribly wrong." How comforting, I thought.

Here's the scoop in case you don't know. There are two ways to skydive. By yourself, which means hours and hours and hours of training and tests, or you can do a tandem skydive where you are attached to a professional skydiver who knows the ropes—you hope—especially the rope also known as The Ripcord.

After about five hours of lectures and paper signing we were finally led to an area, given a "flight suit," and assigned to a "professional dive master." I got Eddie, a kid with pimples who looked about twelve.

By now I was feeling very nervous but trying to look cool. My husband was picturing himself a widower and made no attempt to look "cool." He did, however, manage to take photos of the three of us in our blue flight suits.

Now it was time to head for The Airplane. Rocki, Autumn, and several other enthusiastic people ran happily ahead to board the plane while I shuffled along bringing up the rear. This meant I was the last to board, along with Eddie. There were no regular seats in the plane, just a row of benches along each side. I sat down, and only then noticed there was no door on the "door" we had just climbed through. The plane looked like a vintage 1945 warplane. It even had tiger teeth painted on its nose, to add to the drama.

The plane taxied down a short runway and we were soon airborne. I kept staring at that open door in front of me, oblivious to all the merriment taking place back in the plane with everyone singing "Happy Birthday" to Autumn. Between the roar of the engines, the open door, and my pounding heart, I couldn't hear much anyway.

We ascended to approximately 13,000 feet. During the flight up, my dive partner fastened about a thousand buckles between his flight suit and mine. I vaguely remember the lawyer saying you can change your mind if you are really, really frightened. But I was right there by the open door. How would all the others go out that door without pulling me along, anyway?

Suddenly, just as I was thinking of ways to kill Autumn, Eddie tapped me on the shoulder, shoved me to my feet, hollered "One-Two-Three" and out the door we went. I did not notice the professional photographer guy who dived out first to get everything on camera. I vaguely remember the world down below looking terribly small.

You free fall for about 7,000 feet. This consists of spinning, spinning, spinning and forgetting every single thing you were told during all those pre-flight instructions. We were told to listen for a ringing sound at 5,000 feet, which meant it was time to do something, like pull the ripcord. Since I forgot to pull the ripcord when a bell—or something rang—Eddie tapped me on the shoulder, and then he pulled the cord. A parachute flapped open and suddenly Eddie and I were abruptly and rudely jerked upwards into the sky before slowly descending towards Planet Earth. The whole experience seemed as if it lasted hours, when in fact the trip down was more like five or six minutes.

So, you're wondering, was it fun to skydive? Would I do it again? Three words come to mind. Never! Never!! Never!!!

~Bobbie Jensen Lippman

"She's a typical grandma--she knits, does crosswords, reads large print books..."

Time-Traveling Grandmother

*The real voyage of discovery consists not in seeking new landscapes
but in having new eyes.*
~Marcel Proust

The band of earnest eighth graders decked out in royal blue cap and gowns gathered in the vestibule at St. Mary's Church. The pews quickly filled to capacity as the organist played and church officials took their places. It was graduation day for our grandson, Joey.

Although engulfed in a sea of blue, I immediately spotted him looking impossibly grown up at fifteen. A grandparent's vision may get fuzzy with age, but somehow we always manage to scope out that one special child at a group event. Through misty eyes, I tugged on my husband Chris's arm and said, "Look at him. He's so handsome."

Our eldest grandchild seemed to be moving through each new life passage at warp speed. I've always suspected that we unconsciously measure time against our age. The older we become, the faster the wings of time beat.

Chris smiled in agreement, and then said, "Now, don't forget. You promised to behave."

I knew exactly what he was talking about and it wasn't our grandson.

Chris was worried about Bobby Rydell. More precisely, he was worried about my reaction to Bobby Rydell. The very same heart-throb from the late 1950s was parked on the pew directly in front me. I'd heard through the grapevine that his grandchild was also graduating that day. Be still my heart, I thought.

"I'll try. I really will," I answered. "But it's a tall order, you know."

He knew. Chris and I grew up together in a small town in southern New Jersey. As Bobby Rydell's career moved skyward, he made appearances at local venues in our area. I was fifteen when I saw him in person. I remember standing by the small stage with a throng of overzealous girlfriends screaming Bobby's name as he snapped his fingers, wiggled his hips, and belted out "Kissin' Time." We were all deeply, madly in love with the skinny South Philly kid with a massive pompadour and wide smile. It was a mob scene at the edge of the stage. I hadn't a prayer of capturing his attention.

So, there I sat many years later, within shoulder-tapping distance, staring at the back of Bobby Rydell's head. Sure, he looked older. The pompadour was gone. But I saw that mischievous trademark smile as he turned sideways. What to do? I was dying to talk to him. How many times in life does the opportunity for a do-over come along? He was literally a captive audience.

Chris, a quiet, reserved man in public, glared at me. He didn't have to say a word. After many years of marriage, I could read his mind. I didn't like what it was saying.

The processional began. A reverent hush fell over the gathered families. Everyone stood to honor the class of graduating students. They made their way down the center aisle to a lightshow of camera flashes. I saw my Joey walking sure and proud. I instantly turned back into a woman of a certain age in awe of her grandchild. But every time I looked at Bobby, I traveled backward through a time tunnel.

As I sat through the formalities, intently listening for my grandson's name to be honored, I had an epiphany. I suppose I will forever think of my grandchildren as just that—children. But the rush of teenage angst that overwhelmed me at the sight of my teen idol took me back to fifteen. I suddenly remembered with great clarity how intense each emotion feels at that age. And here before me stood my fifteen-year-old grandson, the one I stubbornly still viewed as a sweet, blue-eyed baby boy.

I silently made a promise to myself that day. I would remember to respect the feelings of my grandchildren as they made their way to adulthood through the rough passage of the teen years.

If we're lucky, the crazy mix of part child and part grown-up defining those years remains in us, giving us permission to act silly now and again. Hmmm… After all the pomp and circumstance had ended, Bobby Rydell was still sitting in front of me.

Chris looked at me. "You're not?" he asked.

Seize the moment, resounded in my head. "Yeah… I am."

I caught the eye of Bobby's daughter-in-law, who was seated next to him, and whispered, "Is it okay?"

She smiled and nodded, obviously having been through this situation before. That's all I needed. She whispered something in Bobby's ear and he turned around, looking me right in the eye. Zap—fifteen again! I said something inane about seeing him forever ago at a dance hall in South Jersey. He smiled knowingly and wistfully said, "Oh yes, that was a very long time ago, wasn't it."

I wonder if he was having his own epiphany that day.

~Judy Harch

The New Refrigerator

The best babysitters, of course, are the baby's grandparents.
You feel completely comfortable entrusting your baby to them for long
periods, which is why most grandparents flee to Florida.
~Dave Barry

S ince I am the grandmother of seven, blessed with vast experience and lots of free time, I'm used to being called to help out in a variety of different situations, ranging from picking up a sick child at school, taking one to a doctor's appointment, or providing a place to hang out when there is a school holiday. So when my daughter called to ask if I would stay with her twenty-year-old son, Geoff, who had just had four wisdom teeth pulled, I quickly agreed.

Since my daughter had taken the day off to be with Geoff, she also arranged for delivery of a new refrigerator in the afternoon. However, she had just been called into work for an emergency meeting. All I had to do was keep an eye on Geoff, change his dressings and get a glass of water down him every two hours. Nothing sounded easier.

Arriving at my post, I showed the proper sympathy to my six-foot, five-inch grandson, who was curled up on the couch, his mouth stuffed with cotton and drool running from his slack lips.

The counter that separated the kitchen from the living room was covered with food items that are normally housed in the refrigerator and I assumed that the old appliance was ready to be replaced.

I settled myself down with a good book. At the appointed time, I woke up the patient, who insisted that he didn't want to have the packing replaced nor did he want a drink of water. I won, the cotton was changed and the soggy slimy packing discarded.

When the phone rang, I was surprised to hear my oldest granddaughter's voice. She had just been called in to interview for her dream job and she needed a sitter for her thirteen-month-old daughter.

"It will just be for an hour or maybe a little more. You're my only hope," she pleaded. I quickly weighed my options and realized I had none—I was needed.

Before long I had a grandson drooling and sleeping on the couch, a baby balanced on my hip and a dog scratching at the door to get in.

Thirty minutes after the baby's mother left with a wave and a smile, the refrigerator deliveryman made his appearance, early. He refused to make the delivery through the back door because there was a dog in the yard.

So I plopped the baby in the large overstuffed chair with a bottle and opened the sliding door to get the dog. The dog, thrilled to be included in the fun, bounded into the house and jumped on the baby, who started screaming. Geoff flopped over on the couch, mumbling. I grabbed the dog and dragged him into the master bedroom just as two men appeared with the dolly. They asked me if the old refrigerator was empty, and to my dismay I found the freezer crammed full. The men waited patiently while I unloaded the food. The baby was leaning over the back of the chair watching with fascination and the patient appeared to have returned to his peaceful slumber.

As the old kitchen appliance was being hauled off, things began to fall apart. I was faced with an empty space behind the old fridge that was littered with stray dog and cat food, dried peas, pet hair, milk bottle lids, bread wrapper clips, a broken pencil and dust.

Trying to keep one eye on the baby, I got busy with the broom, finishing up just as the shiny new refrigerator was wheeled in and positioned at the end of the counter—blocking my exit. The deliverymen returned to their truck to get some tools.

So, here's the situation: Geoff was on the couch, the dog was in the bedroom, the baby was in the chair, I was stuck behind the new fridge in the kitchen and the sliding door was open.

The baby spotted the open door and off the chair she went. My calls of, "No, no, Makayla. Don't go out!" were unheeded as she headed for the wide world beyond. I couldn't squeeze between the refrigerator and the cabinet so I had to force my ancient knees and legs up and over the counter, being careful not to kick any food onto the floor. I reached the baby just as she got the first handful of dog food into her mouth.

The deliverymen finished their job, I put the dripping items back in their new home and the dog was put back outside. All was well in the world.

Geoff stirred, peeked his tousled head over the back of the couch, and through soggy cotton and drooling lips, he muttered an indistinguishable sentence ending in "dog."

Dog! I forgot the dog. With the baby clinging to my neck, I threw open the sliding door and tore around the corner of the house to confirm my worst fear—an open gate and no dog. I closed the gate, as my mind sorted through excuses, hoping to find one my daughter's family would accept for the loss of the family pet.

Back in the house, I changed a now fragrant diaper, replaced Geoff's packing and forced water down his throat. I dug around in the closet until I found the dog leash and headed out for what was expected to be a fruitless search. To my delight, when I opened the front door, there sat a silly brown dog with her tongue hanging out, panting after a good run.

The baby's mother returned to find a sleeping baby. My daughter came home to a new fully stocked refrigerator, a tired dog in the backyard and a son sleeping peacefully on the couch.

Smiling, I said, "A good time was had by all."

I stopped by the store on the way home to get a good bottle of wine.

~Ruth Smith

95

Pyramids and Pillowcases

Age is an issue of mind over matter. If you don't mind, it doesn't matter.
~Mark Twain

My grandmother arranged the pillowcase to cover her face, peered through the holes, and headed out into the blazing Egyptian sun. She was literally cruising around the world on a three-month journey alone. It was the trip of a lifetime, with a meaning beyond sightseeing. And nothing would stop her from seeing the pyramids. Nothing. Not even her pride, which would possibly suffer a bit under the pillowcase.

She journeyed in honor of her late husband's promise. Married just after the Depression, they knew there would be no honeymoon. In fact, she returned to work at a doctor's office the very next day. But Grandpa promised that one day he would make up for it. He would take her to see the world. As two children and the responsibilities of life came, the promise remained on the back burner. Then, at only fifty years old—far too young—he passed away, the promise unfulfilled.

But my grandmother would not forget that dream. While she enjoyed smaller trips, she carefully planned for the journey of a lifetime: a cruise around the world. Finally, after many years of preparation and patience, she boarded the ship.

Her tour took her to South America, Asia and Europe. Of all the sights along the way, going to Egypt to see the pyramids topped her list. But sadly, she suffered a severe sunburn in India just before the ship arrived in Egypt. The ship's doctor, who treated her blistered skin, forbade her from going out in daylight until it healed. Undaunted, my grandmother convinced him to allow her to go... if she would completely cover her badly burned face with a pillowcase. So she did. And she rode the busses out into the Egyptian desert determined to see history.

This verve, this determination to grab life, defines my grandmother for me. She continued travelling after that trip. In fact, there is no continent she hasn't visited and a relatively short list of countries she hasn't seen. At age seventy-two she took an African safari. At eighty she travelled to the Antarctic where she stepped out onto the icy continent. (The penguins called to her... so strongly that she returned more than once.) And at ninety-one? That's when she travelled to Churchill, Canada to see the polar bears and ride on a dog sled.

This year, she turned ninety-five. Remaining strong in mind and spirit, if her strength would keep up she'd still be travelling. And whenever I visit her, I want what she has. I long for the willingness, courage, and determination to grab life and make my dreams come true. I want to grow into a woman who chases the joy and beauty life offers, even if it means sacrifice and, perhaps, a little humility.

It's a secret my grandmother knows. And, it struck home when I heard what happened that day at the pyramids. She stepped out of the bus, covered in protective white literally from head to toe, and walked in the midst of the tour group, ready for the sights. She determined she would ignore the stares at her questionable pillowcase head covering. But as she entered the pyramid grounds, she noticed that the Egyptian workers preserving the ruins were turning and bowing. As she walked, she looked to see what they might be honoring. Suddenly, she realized they bowed to her. Apparently, they thought a priestess hid behind the white pillowcase veil. What could she do but accept the honoring gestures? She cracks up about it today. But to me, those Egyptians were pretty close to right. My grandmother does have a few sacred secrets to share, especially about living fully. I hope I'll keep listening for them... and learning.

~Diane Gardner

96

A Child Is Born

If becoming a grandmother was only a matter of choice,
I should advise every one of you straight away to become one.
There is no fun for old people like it!
~Hannah Whithall Smith

I love all twelve of my wonderful grandchildren, but number eleven has a special place in my heart because of the unusual circumstances surrounding her arrival into the world. November 11th, eight years ago, was a stormy Georgia day. It was two o'clock in the morning when the expected phone call came. I scrambled into my jeans and shirt from the day before, grabbed my already-packed bag, scribbled a note for my husband, and hurried out the door. I backed out of the garage into the thunderous night. Turning my windshield wipers on high, I said a quick prayer as I made my way around the lake, across the covered bridge and onto GA Highway 53.

I can usually get to my daughter's house in about ten minutes, but it seemed more like thirty by the time I finally turned into her wooded subdivision. Even in good weather, the drive through her neighborhood is one that requires concentration and an eye out for the deer who live in this beautiful area, reminding the inhabitants that they were there first.

As I passed the first of the fine houses, nestled well back from the road on large tree-studded lots, I said another prayer—a longer one this time. The winding road, which is difficult to drive even under normal conditions, was wet and thus even more hazardous.

I spotted the mother deer as I came over the first hill. She was eyeing me too. The baby, hovering behind his mother, waited for her to give the signal and start across the road, then followed at her heels. My first thought was, "Why does that mother have her baby out in this weather?"

I slowed and let the deer pass, then drove the short distance to my daughter's house. Going slowly down their steep driveway, I parked in the circle as close to the front door as possible. Opening the door against the wind, I made a dash through the cold rain and reached the porch without slipping. All the outside lights were on, as well as several within the house, so I had no trouble letting myself in with my key.

All was quiet inside the house so I presumed that my daughter and her husband had left for the hospital. I checked on the three children asleep upstairs. Liz, a beautiful eight-year-old, was sound asleep. Five-year-old Rob was asleep with a smile on his handsome face. Grace, a precocious two-year-old, had fallen asleep with a book open on her small chest. Satisfied that they were secure, I tiptoed back downstairs to settle myself on the sofa. Just as I stretched out, book in hand, I heard a cry, and I realized that it was not from the two-year-old.

Through the partly opened back door, I heard the soft cry again, followed by my son-in-law's calm voice. "Noni, I need a little help here." For an old lady, I can move fast when I need to. I was out in the garage in a flash and surprised to see him holding—like a football—the tiny baby that I had heard crying. My daughter was sitting up in the front seat of their Tahoe, talking to someone on her cell phone. "We need to keep the baby warm," she instructed, so I wrapped the tiny bundle in the blanket that was on the seat and held the swaddled baby to my chest. I was filled with love instantly. My heart pounded and my chest throbbed when I looked down at the tiny blessing in my arms. Boy or girl—it didn't matter. This baby, just minutes into the world, was already so much a part of my life.

My daughter then instructed her husband to go upstairs and get the new shoelaces for his running shoes and the scissors from the kitchen drawer. Before she could remind him to sterilize the scissors, we both realized what had to be done. He looked at me, and I said quickly, "I'm not tying the cord and cutting it off!"

All this time I was amazed by the two of them, who were as calm as if they did this every day. My daughter continued to communicate on the phone with EMS, who were on their way, while the cool as a cucumber father, who had just delivered his own fourth child, went inside to get scissors and shoelaces so he could reluctantly take care of the umbilical cord.

The baby was breathing smoothly and sleeping in my arms, but I handed the sweet child to her mother and started to clean up the mess—just like a grandmother! In the midst of all this, I looked down the driveway and saw my husband, the grandfather, arriving on the scene and from the "deer in the headlights" look on his face, I knew that he was thinking the worst. I hurried over and to tell him that everything was fine.

The three children slept through the whole thing—the people coming and going, the bright lights, and the sirens. Oh, to be able to sleep that well.

So who cut the cord? Well, the medic from the EMS crew got there in time to do the deed. My daughter and the baby were taken to the hospital, where both were declared to be "just fine," according to the proud father. "It's a girl," he added.

Every year, as we celebrate Mary's birthday, I recall this exciting and memorable event and marvel once again at the miracle of a child's birth.

~Frances R. Ruffin

97

Emily and the Flying Fish

Keep your fears to yourself but share your courage with others.
~Robert Louis Stevenson

*H*er little hand was locked in mine. When I tried to shift it just to relieve the pressure on my fingers, Emily would have none of it. She just clutched harder.

We were standing together in line under a blazing sun at a gigantic theme park, Emily's first visit, my—well, I've frankly lost count. When you have multiple grandchildren, these places become inevitable destinations, and Emily, then five, was due for her visit.

In another line, my husband was shepherding Emily's older cousin Danny, a fierce little daredevil who insisted that he was absolutely, positively sure he could handle the Vapor Trail, a semi-tame child's version of a heart-stopping roller coaster.

Emily herself had just as absolutely, positively declined the Vapor Trail, and had risked her reputation for serious bravery in the process. She was more than a little embarrassed by her surrender to fear, and quite determined to prove her mettle. Not an enviable spot.

So Emily had insisted that I lead her to a ride that at least looked scary, even if it clearly wasn't of the fright-magnitude of the Vapor Trail. And there we stood, hands locked, as this five-year-old tried to figure out whether she truly could conquer the Flying Fish.

Mind you, these marine critters that "flew' had adorably friendly faces and fish bodies, but the ride itself involved being carefully strapped into a small seat, then swooping up and down inside these fish.

Emily wanted desperately to climb aboard and prove to herself, and to her cousin, that she, too, was brave. Self-image at five not only exists; it can be tricky.

I knew I had to leave it to this granddaughter to make the final decision. But as the line snaked its way to the gate, I could see that she was panicking. The closer we got to the step-off point, leaving terra firma behind for at least three or four minutes, the harder she pressed my hand.

Grandmothers are supposed to be wise, maybe even all-knowing. This grandmother was hardly that.

My well-meaning mistake was to tell Emily that it was fine to change her mind. "I'm not changing my mind!" Emily fumed. "I'm not scared!"

So what that this poor little child was speaking in opposites? So what that we both knew it? My blue-eyed, pink-cheeked grand-daughter didn't want that acknowledged, let alone spoken.

So much for wisdom.

The moment of truth came before either of us was ready. "She goes in first," said the young guy whose sole job was to make that order of entry clear to the "guardians" with small children.

Now Emily really panicked. Her faulty assumption was that she would get strapped into that little fish alone—without me by her side. Not a pretty image for a child who was losing whatever vestiges of courage she had.

The next seconds became a blur. Emily struggled like a champion to fight back tears, but down her cheeks they rolled. She was truly speechless with fear.

"I'm coming too, right after you," I told her. I repeated it three times. And that third time, she believed me, and allowed herself to be lowered into the seat. I climbed in beside her.

In a flash, the motor started, the fish began to fly, and we were off. A stiff breeze cooled us, the ground got farther away and sud-denly, a little girl and her grandmother were going up, up and away.

The panorama below us became a blur of people, flowers, strollers. Above us, just clouds and sky...

The next sound I heard was Emily's wonderful laugh—a chortle of delight, of joy, of excitement and yes, of pride.

She'd done it. She'd proven to the most important person of all—herself—that she could.

And for perhaps two golden minutes, a five-year-old and her grandmother left everything else behind them and just basked in the sweet, sweet pleasure of Emily's bravery.

Of course, when our fish slowly descended, Emily hated to disembark. But there was one more thrill ahead.

A triumphant little adventurer could tell her big cousin that she, too, had been brave. That she had ridden the Flying Fish. "I rided," Emily shouted to Danny when we reunited. "I rided!"

There will surely be many more triumphs in Emily's life, triumphs of presumably far more consequence.

But on one golden afternoon at a theme park, a very grateful grandmother was happy to have shared Emily's bold, giant leap.

~Sally Schwartz Friedman

98

Adventures in Etiquette

Grandchildren: the only people who can get more out of you than the IRS.
~Gene Perret

Life is a circle. First I taught my children, and then my grandchildren, all the major skills they'd need for life. How to speak. How to eat. Even how to use the toilet. Little did I know, at sixty years of age, suddenly I would need everything re-taught to me. Maybe not so much as re-taught, more like, translated.

In April 2009, I accompanied my grandchildren, Katie (then ten) and Andy (then eight), along with their parents, to visit their other set of grandparents in Gifu, Japan. I had pored over travel guides before my visit and asked my daughter millions of questions. I was prepared. Or so I thought.

"Granny, you're bowing like a man." Katie moved my hands to the front of my thighs instead of beside them.

"And you say 'domo arigato.'" Andy corrected my blundering attempt at a polite thank you.

My tongue struggled getting around these unusual sounds, and now they wanted me to put a graceful dip on top of it? But I did it. Every day while I was in Japan. To my son-in-law's parents. To the affable shopkeeper. To random villagers on the street. Soon it became easy.

The act of eating didn't come naturally either. I had been rather pleased with my dexterity with chopsticks, finding Japanese rice much stickier and easier to manage than the Uncle Ben's at my house. As my grandchildren grabbed furikake—which looked suspiciously like what their mother used to feed her pet goldfish "Fred" as a child—to put on their rice, I grabbed the bottle of soy sauce.

Andy put his hand on top of mine. "Granny, you can't put soy sauce on your rice. It's rude."

"That, too." Katie took my chopsticks, which were sticking out of my bowl of rice, and laid them across the bowl instead.

Though Toshi's parents politely ignored my social gaffes, I was determined to make it through the rest of dinner without embarrassing myself. Having been brought up in Britain, I had become proficient with a knife at an early age. Now I was knifeless in Japan, trying to get a long sliver of very tender, very expensive beef from my bowl to my mouth without either choking or dropping it in my lap. I managed to conquer the beef, but the noodles had me flummoxed. Again, I looked to my grandchildren.

"More slurping, Granny," Katie advised as she suctioned up a pile of thick, creamy white udon noodles. My Inner Brit was horrified.

"Really, it's okay, Granny. You're supposed to slurp," Andy said as he pulled a tangle of noodles from his bowl with his chopsticks.

Taking hold of the slippery noodles was hard enough. Getting them into my mouth without them dribbling sauce down my chin was quite a feat. But I did it. I just had to excuse myself after supper to wash my face and a few spots off my shirt.

Eating became easier every day. After my manners were up to par, then I could concentrate on the names of the foods I was eating: ringo (apples), nori (seaweed), and ebi (shrimp). I parroted my grandchildren over and over just like they had once done around my dinner table.

Finally, I've been potty-trained for quite a while now, so I never realized that my grandchildren would even have to teach me how to use a toilet! But sure enough, they did.

"Granny, shoes." Andy pointed down.

I had read my travel book thoroughly. I knew that you never wore shoes into a Japanese person's home. I had even brought my own slippers to use indoors. The travel book hadn't mentioned, however, that you are not supposed to wear your slippers into the bathroom.

"You have to wear the special ones." Andy pointed to the pair of plastic slippers at the edge of the tile floor.

I deposited my enormous size-8 slippers at the edge and crammed my foot into the tiny slippers, my heels hanging off the back by a few inches. Surely the rest of the task I could figure out by myself. Wrong. The toilet had more buttons than my DVD player!

"Katie, could you come in here?" I yelled out the door a few minutes later.

After a tutorial on gadget-y toilet usage, I felt more comfortable using the facilities while out in public. That is, after another lesson on which kanji symbol means "woman" so I could go in the correct door.

Later, back at home in Virginia, my friends marveled about my exotic adventure abroad.

"You had to sleep on the floor?" they asked.

"Yes. I'd come back after my ofuro, my bath, each night to see that Katie and Andy had laid several layers of futon out for me to snuggle into right next to theirs."

Of course I had to further shock my friends with the tale of how my grandchildren had dared me to eat uni (sea urchin) sushi. Granny is not a wimp!

Though going to Japan purely as a tourist would have been exciting, I know that I received such a gift—not to mention an edu-cation—by going with my grandchildren. Now that I can speak (a little), eat, and use the bathroom solo, I look forward to going back to Japan with them in the future. Besides, I have to go back. I have a reputation to uphold. Andy has dared me again.

"We have to go back to the kaiten-zushi restaurant." Andy reminded me of one of our favorite places, a shop where little plates of sushi ride on a conveyor belt around the room and patrons pick which plate they want. "You still have to eat the giant shrimp, head and tail and all! Even the eyeballs!"

You're on.

~Rosemary Francis with Sara Francis-Fujimura

99

Sliver of Bed

Do you know why grandchildren are always so full of energy?
They suck it out of their grandparents.
~Gene Perret

As I clung to the edge of the bed, hoping for sleep, a small foot snuck over and poked my leg. Long ago I learned that placing a body pillow between me and a granddaughter makes sleeping a possibility. Yes, it creates just a sliver of bed, but it is all mine.

Sleeping with a child is near impossible. I didn't do it much with my children, and when I have both granddaughters, I cannot snooze with both of them at the same time. Two beds, one me. However, this night I only had one girl. Although I knew that I would not sleep, with little toes jabbing at my legs and arms whopping me at unexpected times, this did not deter me from my promise to sleep next to my granddaughter Gabby.

Set for battle against flailing limbs, I walked into the chamber of "no sleep" and prayed that some would find me in spite of the challenges. As I moved the toasty child from my side of the bed, she mumbled words I could not understand and wiggled from the chill outside of her warm cocoon as I unwrapped the bedding twisted around her small body. I moved her over, tackling the logistics of sleeping. Arms spread wide and two legs that seem more like six, she mumbled. The spare room called to me with its inner peace and quiet, but I had promised a small girl that I would sleep with her.

The sleeping part of sleepovers always seems to elude me when my granddaughters visit. Obviously, a time will come when they no longer want to share Grammy's bed or when even coming over to see Grammy will be less thrilling, perhaps even a bother. So when they ask that I snuggle, I'd better do it. Plus, crawling into a cold bed and finding warm feet is always a bonus.

"Well, how long have you been awake?" I asked in the morning, rolling over from my sliver of mattress, with the sun sneaking through the blinds.

"A long time. I said 'hello' to your back, but you didn't answer," Gabby said.

Smiling, wide awake, and smelling of sleep, she was happy to see that I had not escaped my sliver of bed for refuge in the spare room. Later a nap was required… for me. That night I crawled under the covers alone. I would find sleep but miss those precious warm feet.

A sliver of bed, a snuggly child: Life is good when you are a grandma.

~Pamela Loxley Drake

"If it was just me and my two granddaughters in the bed,
I would've slept fine. It was the 21 stuffed animals
that foiled that plan."

MTN

100

Land of the Rising Sun

Grandmother-grandchild relationships are simple.
Grandmas are short on criticism and long on love.
~Author Unknown

"I'll take you to Europe when you graduate." I believed my granddaughter needed a bribe to stay in high school. "Choose three European cities and we'll visit them."

But Mariel wasn't interested in Europe. "Can't we go to Japan?" Her fantasy life sprang from the cartoon dramas of Japanese anime and manga. Her social life revolved around the anime club at school. Outfitted in goth mode of black and metal, accessorized with black hair, lipstick, and nails, she belonged to the international culture of alienated teens.

Japan wasn't high on my list of travel destinations in retirement—it wasn't on my list at all. But if it nudged Mariel closer to a high school diploma? "Sure, let's go to Japan."

Nearly six feet tall, overweight and depressed, my granddaughter's moods flowed from sullen to charming to hostile and back in a flash. Ridiculed and bullied at school—"Grandma, not a day goes by that someone doesn't call me retard or fat pig"—she put little faith in others.

When Mariel began disappearing from home or school for short but alarming periods, my daughter enrolled her in a boarding school for overweight teens where she lost sixty pounds and earned a high school diploma. At her graduation I sealed our bargain with a copy of Lonely Planet's guidebook to Japan.

Mariel found a steady job, took some courses at the local community college, and claimed to be teaching herself Japanese. We signed up with an Australian company whose Land of the Rising Sun tour and philosophy of responsible travel appealed to both of us. We would move around the country in a small, loosely organized group, use public transportation, and stay in locally owned inns. Because our itinerary called for only one night in Tokyo, we arranged for three more there on our own before joining the group.

As soon as our plans were firm my worrying started. Was I up to the task of escorting my unpredictable granddaughter to Japan? With departure a few days away, my therapist neighbor spoke up. "You seem uneasy about this trip. What's the worst that can happen over there?"

Jane's calm, therapeutic tone helped me find words for my fears. "Mariel will disappear and no one will find her." I told Jane I was dreading the trip. Japan, especially Tokyo, had become a labyrinth of blocked passageways through which I searched in vain for my granddaughter. Perhaps I'd feel better about things if I'd learned some Japanese. But it was too late now.

Jane suggested meditation might help restore calm — both before leaving and on the trip. I was skeptical but willing to try. When my yoga breathing became slow and relaxed she introduced a technique for letting go of stress. "Find the place in your body that harbors the emotion… visualize it in a bubble… let the bubble rise and evaporate into the universe."

Like spectators welcoming royalty, cherry trees in full bloom lined the tracks as our train sped from the airport into Tokyo. Fearing our timing made us too late for the show, Mariel slapped my hand in a high-five to celebrate our good fortune.

"Grandma, you know I'm not just interested in anime and manga, don't you?" But I didn't know. We roamed the grounds of the Imperial Palace, attended a Classic Noh Theatre performance, and scouted out "the best ramen restaurant in Tokyo." With practice and a few missteps, we built confidence in Tokyo's subway system, pronouncing it superior to New York's in every way. And when we joined the crush of costumed young people in Harajuku, the weekend gathering place of Tokyo's disaffected youth, I noticed that Mariel absorbed the flavors of the scene as an observer, rather than a cult follower.

Throughout our days alone in Tokyo my granddaughter cupped her Japanese phrasebook in the palm of her hand. After rehearsing a question or greeting under her breath, she scanned the surroundings for likely recipients. Shy around adults at home, she didn't hesitate approaching them here, where courteous replies and deferential bows rewarded her efforts. When we lost our way in search of the ramen restaurant in Tokyo, her language dexterity, not my map skills, rescued us. "Thanks for bringing me to Japan," I said.

It was Mariel's birthday the night we met our traveling companions: six Brits, four Aussies, and our group leader from Romania. When Kata asked what brought each of us to Japan, Mariel replied, "I've been interested in Japan for as long as I can remember. I like its history and culture and how everybody respects you here."

That night, from the tower of an office building, we looked over the lights of the city spread for miles in all directions. "Your Japanese is very good. Where did you study?" Kata asked Mariel. Learning she taught herself from books and computer programs without ever having a conversation with a Japanese speaker impressed Kata even more. "Most Japanese don't understand beginners, especially Americans. But your pronunciation is perfect."

My granddaughter had a gift for the Japanese language. No one deserved it more. The pride and joy I felt at her triumph was tinged with regret at not having believed such a moment possible.

Later that night, some of us dropped into an English pub to get better acquainted and to help Mariel celebrate her birthday. Gifts of alcohol soon filled the table in front of her. A tankard of beer and a Grey Goose martini competed for attention with plum wine and shots of shochu. When slurred speech and spasms of laughter aroused my protective instincts, I snapped, "Slow down!" Poised to deliver a lecture on the perils of mixing drinks, I was interrupted by

Andrew, a father from England. "It's not your job to tell Mariel what to do. Leave that to us. Your job is Grandma. And you don't want to spoil the relationship."

Inhaling a deep yoga breath, I found the place in my body where fears still lingered... visualized them in a bubble... and let the bubble rise until it evaporated into the night sky over Tokyo.

~Ann Barnett

Jordan and Mandi Spend the Night

When grandparents enter the door, discipline flies out the window.
~Ogden Nash

After weeks of promising my eight-year-old granddaughter, Jordan, that she and her friend, Mandi, could spend the night, I finally found two days in my busy schedule that were free. I e-mailed Jordan (that's how grandparents do it these days) to invite her to come on a Wednesday night and stay until Thursday. I told her I had some fun plans and to make sure and invite Mandi.

I picked them up at 3:00 Wednesday afternoon. Our first stop was the market to pick up hot dogs, buns, chips, marshmallows, and pop for dinner over the campfire. When I was a parent, my children did not eat hot dogs and very rarely ate any kind of sugary item—especially something as blatantly nutritionless as marshmallows! Pop was also on the banned list of allowed beverages in Jordan's mom's growing-up years.

Following our trip to the market, we stopped at Blockbuster Video where I let the girls loose to pick out a movie to watch that evening. An hour later they had finally settled on *Nim's Island*—about the only movie neither of them had seen or were willing to watch one more time. Good! It looked like we had a fun evening planned and so we headed home.

My husband and I live on twelve acres of pastureland and I am always hopeful that my suburban grandchildren will find pleasure in exploring the outdoors while visiting. I decided to mow the lawn and let the girls explore the property. They wandered down to the creek to view the salmon making their way back upstream to lay their eggs. They twirled and cartwheeled in the way of eight-year-old girls until they were dizzy and fell giggling on the ground. They lay in the hammock on the porch and swung themselves so high that they literally ejected themselves from the hammock, off the porch and onto the lawn. I was enchanted by how, when given a world of farmland, children can lay down their cell phones, computer games and iPods and enjoy life's simplicities.

As the golden light of the autumn afternoon seeped into dusk, we moved inside where Barbies, puzzles and books were brought out of the toy room, the piano was played loudly and harshly, and pictures were drawn on large sheets of butcher paper.

My husband's arrival from work was greeted with shouts and squeals of "Hi Papa! Did you know we were spending the night? Will you throw the Frisbee for us? Can we roast hot dogs on the fire pit?" A rousing game of pony rides commenced on the living room floor and then it was time for dinner.

As my husband built the wood fire that would be our cook stove for the evening, the girls cartwheeled on the lawn and sang camp songs. The hot dogs were roasted in that perfectly burned way and the marshmallows oozed off the roasting sticks and dripped into the fire. It didn't matter if dessert was eaten before dinner or vice versa. When grandchildren are involved, all rules of childrearing vaporize. I even ate several sticky black marshmallows myself!

After dinner the movie was put on upstairs in the TV room and the girls seemed to be winding down. At 10:30 p.m. I finally got the girls to bed. (Bedtimes for grandchildren are also quite negotiable!) My husband had an early day so we retired also. At 10:45, as we are just falling asleep, there is a knock on our bedroom door.

"Grammy? Mandi is homesick and we can't sleep."

"Okay girls, it's time to settle down. Mandi honey, if you go to sleep you won't be homesick anymore." (Quite proud of myself for such a clever solution).

We all traipse back to bed... all quiet... just falling asleep... knock on the door.

"Grammy, Mandi is really homesick." By this time Jordan is teary-eyed.

I get up, tuck them in with lots of calming words and hugs. "Goodnight girls."

It's now 11:00 and my husband is getting a tiny bit (well maybe I'm downplaying this a little) irritated because he is just falling asleep each time before the inevitable knock. Mandi is now in the living room calling her mom to please come and get her!! I go out and sit with her and can hear both her mom and dad on the other end of the line saying, "She lives in Wilkeson—I don't even know where that is!" They convince Mandi to stay. I send the girls back to bed with a terse "Now girls this can't continue. Papa has to get up early in the morning and needs to go to sleep." Everyone is once again tucked in for the night.

11:10—Tap tap on the door. Jordan has a headache. Of course I only have adult aspirin and it's obvious nothing short of a major dose of drugs will calm her down. Oh hey, here's some children's Benadryl that I gave to our dog once... for allergies... yup, must be an allergy headache from being by the creek... this should do the trick... here ya go, Jordan... now back to bed... last time, okay?

11:30—Knock knock. "My tummy hurts." That's what I get for feeding my granddaughter a bag of marshmallows before she goes to bed.

At this point I kick my grouchy husband out of his own bed to sleep on the couch where he can get some uninterrupted shuteye. "Girls, come into my nice poofy cozy bed.... Oh Toby [our silky terrier] you might as well join the party also. Everyone comfy??? Good!"

They were both asleep instantly and I spent some quiet moments enjoying hugging my sweet granddaughter as she slept, softly snoring. I stayed awake for an hour... finally fell asleep... and got up at 1:30 to go to the bathroom. When I came back, Jordan had claimed my side of the bed as her own. Okay enough... Toby, let's go sleep in the granddaughter's room.

I slept until 8:00 when I was awoken by two sweet, tousled, tired-looking girls who were hungry for breakfast. By this time my husband had already left for work but I found out later that day that as we all lay sleeping soundly, he was kept awake on the couch by a horrendous thunder and lightning storm and torrential rain.

Now I remember why life is so peaceful since the children left home and why being a grandparent is one of life's greatest blessings.

~Margie Pasero

Meet Our Contributors

Linda Williams Aber is a writer, editor and packager of more than one hundred and fifty novels, activity books, and humor books from clients including Scholastic Inc., Random House, Reader's Digest Children's Publishing and many others. Her latest book, *500 Things to Do with Your Kids Before They Grow Up* was co-authored with her son Corey Mackenzie Aber.

Gloria Ashby is a writer, speaker, and teacher. She is published in a local church newspaper (circulation 8,000) and is writing inspirational stories about God encounters. Living in Texas with her husband, Jim, Gloria enjoys reading and digging in her butterfly garden. E-mail her at gloria.ashby7@gmail.com or read her blog at http://gloriaashby.wordpress.com.

William Mark Baldwin is earning his PhD in Earth and Atmospheric Science at Mississippi State University. Mark is from Crossville, TN, and is a graduate of Tennessee Technological University (B.S.) and Western Kentucky University (M.S.). Mark enjoys running, storm chasing, and traveling. E-mail him at wmb3@msstate.edu.

Ann Barnett grew up in a factory town in Pennsylvania. Moving to New York she raised two daughters, taught school, and lived on the Hudson River in an old wooden boat. Now retired, she surrounds herself with good books, sharp pencils, and an up-to-date passport.

Marcia Berneger is an educational specialist in San Diego. She is married and has two wonderful sons. She enjoys crocheting tiny "fidgit bears" to help her very active students focus in class. Marcia writes children's books and hopes to find a publisher for them. E-mail her at meberneger@cox.net.

Elizabeth Bostock is British. She studied Modern Languages at Cambridge University and now teaches English in Brussels, where she lives with her husband and a small black cat. She is also a columnist for *Brussels Weekly* and spends her spare time writing stories. E-mail her at liz.bostock@btinternet.com.

Barbara Brady is a retired RN. She and husband, Merris, have three children and eight grandchildren. She and her husband enjoy family, friends, and travel. Barbara is an active member of Kansas Authors Club. Reading and writing are her favorite pastimes.

Donna Brothers received her B.A. in Communications from California Polytechnic University. She worked for CBS Television before receiving a teaching credential in Language Arts from California State University, Fullerton. She recently published a short story in *Women's World* magazine and enjoys photography, scrapbooking, and hiking. E-mail her at djeanbrothers@gmail.com.

Sallie Wagner Brown writes stories inspired by her kids, who think they are grown up, by her dogs, who think they are her kids, and by old Douglas firs surrounding her home. Retired from teaching English at fifty, she bought a used, red Corvette. She knows she isn't grown up.

Talia Carner's novels, *Puppet Child* and *China Doll*, were hailed for exposing society's ills. Her next novel, *Jerusalem Maiden*, depicting a woman's struggle for self-expression against her society's religious dictates will be published in June 2011. Carner's award-winning short stories and essays have appeared in numerous anthologies and literary publications. Learn more at www.TaliaCarner.com.

Barbara Carpenter has many creative interests, but is most passionate about writing. Her work has appeared in national magazines, and she has three novels in print, as well as memoirs for a physician and for the founder of radio WJBD. E-mail her at bjlogger2@aol.com or www.becblog.com.

Emily Parke Chase, named after the poet Emily Dickinson, is now a grandmother herself. She speaks at conferences and retreats and is the author of six books, including *Help! My Family's Messed Up*. Learn more at www.emilychase.com.

Jane McBride Choate loves being a grandmother. Though she doesn't knit, make cookies, or wear her hair in a bun, she delights in spending time with her four grandchildren (two of whom are adopted). She plays silly games with them, squirts whipped cream from a can in their mouths, and gives them the roots that every child needs.

Courtney Conover believes everyday life provides the perfect inspiration for her stories. A graduate of the University of Michigan and an avid yoga practitioner, she resides in Michigan with her husband, Scott. She still thinks her Grandma Tucker is the coolest woman she's ever met. Learn more at www.courtneyconover.com.

Linda C. Defew and her husband, Eddie, live in Salem, KY, where she is a freelance writer. Articles on everything from her love of nature to living with a disabling disease have appeared in *The Writer*, *Grit*, *Christian Woman*, *Antiques & Collecting Magazine*, and online at *Good Dog!*, *The Writer's Eye* and *Women Bloom*.

Pam Drake began her writing career as a playwright writing social dramas for teens. Along with writing for magazines she writes two blogs: one about growing up on a farm (www.neffroad.com) and another about a woman who is still learning (www.agrandparentsvoice.com). She resides in Beaverton, OR. E-mail her at pamldrake@gmail.com.

P.S. Durham began writing stories in 2007 as a way to express her memories and love of family. She previously worked in human resources for various employers until 2005. She is the published author of the book *Cliffie's Life Lessons* and is the grandmother of three.

Jane Ebihara is a retired middle school teacher who enjoys reading and dabbling in poetry. She lives in rural Warren County, NJ. Her grandson lost his beautiful mother to breast cancer, but flourishes in the loving care of his father and a village of devoted friends and family.

Although blind, **Janet Perez Eckles** thrives as a Spanish interpreter, international speaker, writer and author of, *Trials of Today, Treasures for Tomorrow—Overcoming Adversities in Life*. From her home in Florida, she enjoys working on church ministries and taking Caribbean cruises with husband Gene. She imparts inspirations at www.janetperezeckles.com.

Terri Elders, LCSW, lives near Colville, WA. Her stories have appeared in dozens of anthologies, including multiple editions of *Chicken Soup for the Soul*. She is a public member of the Washington State Medical Commission. In 2006, she received the UCLA Alumni Association Community Service Award. She blogs at http://atouchoftarragon.blogspot.com.

Melissa Face lives, teaches, and writes in Virginia. She has contributed stories to several *Chicken Soup for the Soul* titles and writes regularly for *Sasee* magazine. E-mail Melissa at writermsface@yahoo.com.

Elizabeth Reardon Farella is a graduate of Molloy College where she received her teaching degree. She went on to earn her masters degree in Literacy. Elizabeth currently teaches reading and literature at St. Edward the Confessor School in Syosset, NY. She enjoys reading, writing stories and traveling with her husband and daughters. E-mail her at Jeeec@aol.com.

With four active kids, a husband and a crazy dog, **Danica Favorite** is never short on inspiration for her latest story, whether entertaining a live audience or crafting her latest novel. She and her family make their home in Denver. You can connect with her at www.danicafavorite.com.

Ellen Fink and her husband live in Georgia, and are the proud parents of three exceptional children, and the grandparents of two beautiful, intelligent and talented grandchildren. Ellen's work has appeared in several publications, including *Chicken Soup for the Soul: Thanks Mom*. E-mail her at Elfinxx@aol.com.

Pat Fish is a dedicated blogger. She blogs about gardens, politics, reality TV shows, books, cooking and, of course, grandchildren. Her blog is http://patfish.blogspot.com or you can e-mail her at patfish1@aol.com.

Rosemary Francis lives in the Northern Neck of Virginia. She enjoys visiting and traveling with her two grandchildren. This is her second essay for Chicken Soup for the Soul, and she has also been published in the British children's magazine, *Aquila*.

A grandmother of seven, **Sally Friedman** taps into that rich source of inspiration in many of her essays. She contributes to *The New York Times*, *The Philadelphia Inquirer*, *AARP Magazine* and numerous other regional and national publications. She is a frequent contributor to the *Chicken Soup for the Soul* series. E-mail her at pinegander@aol.com.

Valerie J. Frost is a freelance writer and an office administrator at Horizon Christian Fellowship in San Diego. She and her husband Terry are the parents of three grown children. They have nine energetic grandchildren, and two turbo-charged Jack Russell Terriers named Rocket and Daphne.

Diane Gardner is a freelance writer and editor with a master's degree in journalism. Her writing has appeared in the books *Love Is a Flame*, *Chicken Soup for the Soul: Thanks Mom*, *True Stories of Extraordinary Answers to Prayer: Praying Together*, and in *EnCompass Magazine*. She lives in Colorado with her husband, John.

Phyllis Tomberg Giglio is an inspirational author, speaker and counselor. In her published autobiography, *When You Come To The*

End of Your Rope, There is Hope, she describes her life as the mother of six sons, six daughters and thirty grandchildren—she doesn't lack material to write about. She enjoys walking, reading and writing. Her motto is, "The best is yet to come."

Arlene Rains Graber is a freelance writer in Wichita, KS. Her writing career spans more than twenty-five years with articles, essays, and devotionals published in numerous newspapers, magazines and periodicals. In addition, her first devotional book, *Devoted to Traveling*, was released February 16, 2010, by AWOC Publishers. Visit her at www.arlenerainsgraber.com.

Judy Harch is a freelance writer and author. Her work has appeared in *The Philadelphia Inquirer*, *PrimeTime*, the magazine of the *Cape Cod Times*; and online at Grandparents.com. She is the co-author of the book *Alzheimer Solutions: A Personal Guide for Caregivers*. Judy is the grandmother of four. E-mail her at judyharch@verizon.net.

Robin Rylee Harderson enjoys reading, writing, painting and her beautiful granddaughter. She has been married for twenty-eight years to her husband, Marty. Robin has been previously published in *Women's World* and *Sewing Memories*.

Carol Harrison earned her Bachelor of Education from the University of Saskatchewan and is a Distinguished Toastmaster. She is a motivational speaker and author of *Amee's Story* and has two stories in *Chicken Soup for the Soul* books. She enjoys time with family, reading, scrapbooking and speaking. E-mail her at carol@carolscorner.ca or visit her website www.carolscorner.ca.

Nancy Hatten received her Bachelor of Science with highest honors from the University of Houston in 2002. She coordinates legal education courses at the State Bar of Texas. Nancy enjoys music, walking, yoga, reading and is a die hard Chicago Cubs, Chicago Bears and University of Texas Longhorns fan.

Hilary Heskett graduated with a Bachelor's degree in Business from San Jose State University. When not creating corporate communications, she writes young adult, paranormal romance and science fiction. You can learn more about her work at www.hilaryheskett.com.

Miriam Hill is a frequent contributor to *Chicken Soup for the Soul* books and has been published in *Writer's Digest, The Christian Science Monitor, Grit, St. Petersburg Times, The Sacramento Bee* and Poynter Online. Miriam's manuscript received Honorable Mention for Inspirational Writing in a Writer's Digest Writing Competition.

Cathy Howard lives in Grand Island, NE, with her husband John. This is her thirty-fourth year at Central Catholic High School/Middle School where she teaches middle school and high school English. She and John have two sons, Kenny and Tommy, and two cats, Willy and Blackie. E-mail her at cathyhoward428@hotmail.com.

Karen M. Jameson is a writer and editor with a B.A. in Business from Vanderbilt University. She is delighted that her son, daughter, and three nephews now sneak candy from the same drawer that she did (and still does)! E-mail her at kmjameson17@comcast.net.

Jewell Johnson lives in Arizona with her husband, LeRoy. They are parents to six adult children, and grandparents to nine. Besides writing, Jewell enjoys walking, reading, and quilting. E-mail Jewell at tykeJ@juno.com.

Kara Johnson was a collegiate gymnast for Boise State University, and currently lives in Boise, ID, with her husband Jim, and dog Barkley. She enjoys traveling, scuba diving, camping, rafting, hiking, writing, and is a mentor for college girls. She feels blessed and incredibly indebted for the love Joan has shown her. E-mail her at karagym777@hotmail.com.

Karen Kelly is a former radio personality in Dayton, OH. She has a weekly column in several newspapers, and also does freelance writing, radio and TV voice-overs and motivational speaking. She lives with her husband and an occasional boomerang child. E-mail Karen at karenkellybrown@aol.com.

Karen R. Kilby is a Certified Personality Trainer with CLASServices, Inc. and a speaker for Stonecroft Ministries. Karen has had several stories published in *Chicken Soup for the Soul* books as well as other publications and has published *Becoming A Woman of Purpose, A 31 Day Devotional*. E-mail her at krkilby@kingwoodcable.net.

Laudizen King was born in Manchester, CT, and lives in Los Angeles. His stories have appeared in the *Tonopah Review*, *Word Catalyst Magazine*, the *MilSpeak Memo*, the *Raving Dove* literary journal, and the *Wilderness House Literary Review*. Visit his website at http://laudizen.com.

April Knight loves spending time with her grandchildren. She's an artist and freelance author and just completed a Christian romance book titled *Stars in the Desert*.

Lisa Kulka grew up in Texas less than a mile from her grandparents. She "ran away from home" several times as a young girl, and headed straight to Mamaw's house. She's now an elementary school librarian in Colorado Springs, CO, where she lives with her husband, three sons and a couple of furry friends.

Sharon Landeen, a retired elementary teacher, enjoys working with youth. She's been a 4-H leader for over twenty years, volunteers as a reading mentor and art teacher at local schools, and makes blankets for Project Linus. But, her greatest joy is being Grandma.

Ruth Lehrer, a New York City elementary school teacher, published her first personal essay at age sixty-two, after she retired. Now, twenty years later, she's written over one hundred stories, and published her first book, *My Book of Ruth: Reflections of a Jewish Girl*. E-mail her at ruthartl@gmail.com or visit www.reflectionsofajewishgirl.com.

Gretchen Lendrum is a retired English teacher from Middletown, RI. She now has the free time to write, read, travel, tend to her many pets, and, thanks to her grandson, explore the world and celebrate the day. E-mail her at glendrum45@aol.com.

Bobbie Jensen Lippman is a prolific professional writer who lives in Seal Rock, OR. Bobbie's work has been published nationally and internationally. She writes a human interest column for the *Newport (Oregon) News-Times*, in addition to a radio program which is available as a podcast on www.knptam.com. E-mail her at bobbisbeat@aol.com.

Linda Lohman has a B.A. in English. She is a frequent contributor to the Chicken Soup for the Soul family. She has also been published in *Reader's Digest*, *The Sacramento Bee*, the *Sacramento News & Review*, and *Solidarity*. Retired, she enjoys Red Hat friends and beading. E-mail her at laborelations@yahoo.com.

Christine Long received her Bachelor of Arts in English in 2009. She teaches sophomore English in North Texas. She enjoys camping, sewing, writing, and spending time with her family. She plans to write a how-to guide for second-generation parents.

Donna Lowich works as an information specialist, providing information to people affected by paralysis. She enjoys writing about her family and personal experiences. Other hobbies include counted cross stitch and reading. She lives with her husband in New Jersey. E-mail her at DonnaLowich@aol.com.

Rita Lussier's "For the Moment" column has been a popular feature of *The Providence Journal* for over eleven years. She was a first place award winner of the Erma Bombeck Writing Contest in 2010 and 2006. Her essays have also been featured in NPR and in *The Boston Globe*. E-mail her at ReetsAl@aol.com.

Melinda Richarz Lyons earned a B.A. in Journalism from the

University of North Texas. Her freelance work has appeared in numerous publications, and she has authored several books, including *Murder at the Oaklands Mansion*. She is the proud grandmother of eight. Visit her at www.MelindaLyons.com.

Judith Marks-White is a *Westport News* (CT) award-winning columnist of "The Light Touch," which has appeared every Wednesday for the past twenty-six years. She is the author of two novels published by Random House/Ballantine: *Seducing Harry* and *Bachelor Degree*. Judith teaches humor writing and lectures widely.

Margaret M. Marty, a lifelong resident of Rock Creek in East Central Minnesota, is a wife, mother, grandmother and retired certified professional secretary. Her interests are flower gardening, writing, and scrapbooking. In retirement she established a personal historian business, Portraits in Prose. E-mail her at mmarty@northlc.com.

Cynthia Morningstar received her Bachelor of Music in Piano Performance. She works as an off-site Collection Development Librarian at Sandusky District Library, and as the Choir Director/Organist at the First Presbyterian Church of Shelbyville, where her husband, Mark, is pastor. Special family members are daughters, Amanda, Jill, Beth and Beth's new husband, Matt. E-mail her at cbmorn@hotmail.com.

Beth Morrissey is a freelance writer based in Dublin, Ireland. She loves to make new friends, so please visit her online at www.bethiswriting.com.

Lee Ann Sontheimer Murphy grew up in St. Joseph, MO, in the shadow of the short-lived Pony Express, but now lives in the Missouri Ozarks. She is a full-time writer, member of both Missouri Writers Guild and the Ozark Writers League. Her short fiction has been widely published and her novel, *Kinfolk*, debuts from Champagne Books in July, 2011.

Alice Muschany writes about everyday life with a touch of humor.

Her family, especially her eight grandchildren, make wonderful subjects. Her stories have been published in the *Chicken Soup for the Soul* series, *A Cup of Comfort* and *Sasee*. She is also an Opinion Shaper for the local *Suburban Journal*.

Marc Tyler Nobleman is the author of more than seventy books including *Boys of Steel: The Creators of Superman* and one due out in 2012 about the "secret" co-creator of Batman. His cartoons have appeared in more than 100 international publications. At noblemania. blogspot.com, he reveals the behind-the-scenes stories of his work.

Molly O'Connor lives near Ottawa. She walks every day accompanied by her dog and her camera. She attended York University in Toronto and Carleton University in Ottawa. Retired from the corporate world, she turned her talent from writing press releases to publishing a collection of short stories titled *Fourteen Cups* and a memoir titled *Wandering Backwards*.

This is **Margie Pasero's** second published Chicken Soup for the Soul story. Margie is retired from the Renton School District and now teaches African drumming and is a Health Rhythms facilitator, bringing wellness through rhythm to senior citizens in retirement homes and senior centers.

Kay Conner Pliszka is a retired high school teacher who enjoys writing, public speaking, golfing, bridge and singing. She is a frequent contributor to *Chicken Soup for the Soul* books and very much enjoys reading her stories to various groups in the community. E-mail her at kmpliszka@comcast.net.

Marsha Porter has co-authored a video and DVD guide and published numerous articles. She got her start in essay writing when the 500-word essay was the punishment du jour at her Catholic school. Currently she teaches high school English.

When **D.R. Ransdell** isn't busy playing Auntie, she's a composition instructor at The University of Arizona. Her first novel, *Amirosian Nights*, recounts the experiences of an American musician in Greece. Learn more at www.dr-ransdell.com.

Currently "Grammy" to eight, **Carol McAdoo Rehme** relishes her young grandchildren and believes they are life's natural sweeteners. A veteran freelance editor and writer, Carol publishes widely in anthologies and magazines. She is the co-author of several gift books and two books in the *Chicken Soup for the Soul* series.

Kimberly Ripley is a freelance writer and published author from New Hampshire. A wife, mother of five, and "Nana" to two, she loves spending time with her precious grandchildren, Lilly and Aiden.

Sallie A. Rodman has contributed to many *Chicken Soup for the Soul* anthologies, *A Cup of Comfort*, *The Orange County Register* and various magazines. She received her Certificate in Professional Writing from California State University, Long Beach. E-mail her at sa.rodman@verizon.net.

Pam Rogers and her husband, Jeff, have three children and two grandchildren. She teaches preschool programs in West Central Florida. Pam enjoys working with children, scrapbooking, reading, and family time. E-mail her at progers5213@yahoo.com.

Frances Ruffin, retired teacher and administrator, has co-authored three books for Blue Ridge China collectors and publishes *The Blue Ridge China Quarterly*. Frances is a member of the Oconee Cultural Arts Foundation Writing Group and Southeastern Writers Association. When not writing she enjoys activities with her twelve grandchildren.

Jessie Miyeko Santala finally feels comfortable saying that she is a writer. She would like to thank her husband for supporting her and for pushing her to pursue her passions. E-mail her at J.Santala@yahoo.com.

Joanne Wright Schulte holds a B.A. from California State University, Fullerton. She is a freelance speaker and writer who enjoys reading, writing, music and gardening. She is actively involved in her church, particularly with women's groups.

Margie Reins Smith worked as a middle school English teacher and a journalist. Now retired, she is a freelance journalist writing for local magazines, newspapers and websites. She has three children and five grandchildren and is currently writing her first novel. This essay was first published in the *Grosse Pointe News*. E-mail her at ms0006@comcast.net.

Ruth Smith was raised in Golden, CO. Ruth has been married to her husband, Ralph, for fifty-seven years. She is mother to three children, grandmother to seven and great-grandmother to six. She enjoys reading, traveling, family gatherings and recording her memories in stories. E-mail her at msgslbc@bak.rr.com.

LeAynne Snell discovered the joy of writing in fourth grade, then spent her career as a psychotherapist and thirteen years as a home-schooling mother. Now living in the Ozark Mountains with her husband of thirty-six years, and armed with a keen insight about people and relationships, her passion for writing ignited.

Aaron Solly is an aspiring author. He lives in Vancouver, B.C. with his wife Mandy and son Benjamin. You can contact him through his website www.BetweenYourEars.ca.

Toni Somers received a B.A. in Art from Columbia College in 1986. She is a retired photographer, guitar teacher and adult education teacher. She has five married children and nine grandchildren and currently lives with her husband, John, in Springfield, MO, where she enjoys drawing and writing.

Suzette Martinez Standring is syndicated with GateHouse News

Service, is the award-winning author of *The Art of Column Writing: Insider Secrets from Art Buchwald, Dave Barry, Arianna Huffington, Pete Hamill and Other Great Columnists*, and hosts the TV show, *It's All Write with Suzette*.

Joy Faire Stewart began her writing career upon retiring from a high school guidance department. She has worked with children and taught Sunday School for more than thirty years. Along with writing, she enjoys traveling to places she reads about, rose gardening, and she loves animals—especially Siamese cats.

Ann Summerville, author of *Storms & Secrets*, was born in England, and in search of a warmer climate, moved to California before settling in Texas. Ann is a member of Trinity Writers' Workshop and resides in Fort Worth, TX, with her son, two boisterous dogs and a somewhat elusive cat. Learn more at www.AnnSummerville.com.

B.J. Taylor loves talking to her grandsons via the Internet. An award-winning author, her stories have appeared in *Guideposts* and *Chicken Soup for the Soul* books. She and her husband have four children and those two adorable grandsons. Reach B.J. through her website at www.bjtayloronline.com. Sign up for her dog blog at www.bjtaylorblog.wordpress.com.

Terrie Todd and her husband Jon live in Portage la Prairie, Manitoba, Canada where she works as an administrative assistant at City Hall and writes a weekly column for a local paper. Her grandsons Keegan and Allistar make life so much fun! E-mail her at jltodd@mts.net.

Bettie Wailes owns Wise Owl Tutoring in Winter Park, FL. She is a marathoner, working toward completion of 100 marathons. She has two children, five grandchildren, and two great-grandchildren. She has written *The View From the Back of the Pack*, a memoir about her running life, to be published soon.

Davi Walders' poetry and prose have appeared in more than 200 publications. She developed and directed Vital Signs Poetry Project at the Children's Inn and NIH which was funded by The Witter Bynner Foundation for Poetry.

Beverly F. Walker lives in Tennessee and cares for her ailing husband. She enjoys writing and scrapbooking pictures of her grandchildren. She has stories in many *Chicken Soup for the Soul* books, and in *Angel Cats: Divine Messengers of Comfort*. Her cherished grandson Hunter is now almost twelve years old.

Henry Matthew Ward holds a B.S. from Middle Tennessee State University and a M.A. from Ohio State University, both in music. He enjoys writing, and has three published books and a fourth on the way. He resides in Murfreesboro, TN, with his wife Pat.

Luann Warner has had stories published in a variety of *Chicken Soup for the Soul* titles. She has over thirty years experience as a copywriter in the advertising and marketing field. Her life experiences and relationships are the inspirations for her short stories as well as the book she hopes to finish writing in the near future. E-mail Luann at lkwarner3@comcast.net.

Donna Watson is the author of several books, including *How To Get and Keep A Job* and *Tough Times Don't Last But Tough Women Do*. She is a wife, mother, grandmother and an international lecturer who has more interest and hobbies than time. E-mail her at dswphd8@cox.net.

Ferida Wolff is author of seventeen children's books and three essay books, her latest being the award-winning picture book *The Story Blanket* and *Missed Perceptions: Challenge Your Thoughts Change Your Thinking*. Her work appears in anthologies, newspapers, magazines, in www.seniorwomen.com and in her nature blog http://feridasbackyard.blogspot.com. Visit her at www.feridawolff.com.

Meet Our Authors

Jack Canfield is the co-creator of the *Chicken Soup for the Soul* series, which *Time* magazine has called "the publishing phenomenon of the decade." Jack is also the co-author of many other bestselling books.

Jack is the CEO of the Canfield Training Group in Santa Barbara, California, and founder of the Foundation for Self-Esteem in Culver City, California. He has conducted intensive personal and professional development seminars on the principles of success for more than a million people in twenty-three countries, has spoken to hundreds of thousands of people at more than 1,000 corporations, universities, professional conferences and conventions, and has been seen by millions more on national television shows.

Jack has received many awards and honors, including three honorary doctorates and a Guinness World Records Certificate for having seven books from the *Chicken Soup for the Soul* series appearing on the New York Times bestseller list on May 24, 1998.

You can reach Jack at www.jackcanfield.com.

Mark Victor Hansen is the co-founder of Chicken Soup for the Soul, along with Jack Canfield. He is a sought-after keynote speaker, bestselling author, and marketing maven. Mark's powerful messages of possibility, opportunity, and action have created powerful change in thousands of organizations and millions of individuals worldwide.

Mark is a prolific writer with many bestselling books in addition to the *Chicken Soup for the Soul* series. Mark has had a profound influence in the field of human potential through his library of audios, videos, and articles in the areas of big thinking, sales achievement, wealth building, publishing success, and personal and professional development. He is also the founder of the MEGA Seminar Series.

Mark has received numerous awards that honor his entrepreneurial spirit, philanthropic heart, and business acumen. He is a lifetime member of the Horatio Alger Association of Distinguished Americans.

You can reach Mark at www.markvictorhansen.com.

Amy Newmark is Chicken Soup for the Soul's publisher and editor-in-chief, after a thirty-year career as a writer, speaker, financial analyst, and business executive in the worlds of finance and telecommunications. Amy is a *magna cum laude* graduate of Harvard College, where she majored in Portuguese, minored in French, and traveled extensively. She and her husband have four grown children.

After a long career writing books on telecommunications, voluminous financial reports, business plans, and corporate press releases, Chicken Soup for the Soul is a breath of fresh air for Amy. She has fallen in love with Chicken Soup for the Soul and its life-changing books, and really enjoys putting these books together for Chicken Soup's wonderful readers. She has co-authored more than three dozen *Chicken Soup for the Soul* books and has edited another two dozen.

You can reach Amy through the webmaster@chickensoupforthesoul.com.

Chicken Soup for the Soul

Thank You

We owe huge thanks to all of our contributors. We know that you poured your hearts and souls into the thousands of stories and poems that you shared with us, and ultimately with each other. We appreciate your willingness to open up your lives to other Chicken Soup for the Soul readers and share your own experiences as grandmothers and grandchildren, or as astute observers of same.

We could only publish a small percentage of the stories that were submitted, but we read every single one and even the ones that do not appear in the book had an influence on us and on the final manuscript. Reading these stories was great fun, as we shared in your joy at becoming a grandmother, your adventures in babysitting, your pride in your grown-up children and your grandchildren, your reconciliation of your own aging process with the fountain-of-youth benefits of being a grandparent. We owe special thanks to our editor Barbara LoMonaco, who read every submission to this book and narrowed the list down to two hundred finalists. Our assistant publisher, D'ette Corona, worked with all the contributors as kindly and competently as always, obtaining their approvals for our edits and the quotations we carefully chose to begin each story. And editors Kristiana Glavin and Madeline Clapps performed their normal masterful proofreading.

We also owe a very special thanks to our creative director and book producer, Brian Taylor at Pneuma Books, for his brilliant vision for our covers and interiors. Finally, none of this would be possible without the business and creative leadership of our CEO, Bill Rouhana, and our president, Bob Jacobs.

Improving Your Life Every Day

Real people sharing real stories — for seventeen years. Now, Chicken Soup for the Soul has gone beyond the bookstore to become a world leader in life improvement. Through books, movies, DVDs, online resources and other partnerships, we bring hope, courage, inspiration and love to hundreds of millions of people around the world. Chicken Soup for the Soul's writers and readers belong to a one-of-a-kind global community, sharing advice, support, guidance, comfort, and knowledge.

Chicken Soup for the Soul stories have been translated into more than forty languages and can be found in more than one hundred countries. Every day, millions of people experience a Chicken Soup for the Soul story in a book, magazine, newspaper or online. As we share our life experiences through these stories, we offer hope, comfort and inspiration to one another. The stories travel from person to person, and from country to country, helping to improve lives everywhere.

Share with Us

We all have had Chicken Soup for the Soul moments in our lives. If you would like to share your story or poem with millions of people around the world, go to chickensoup.com and click on "Submit Your Story." You may be able to help another reader, and become a published author at the same time. Some of our past contributors have launched writing and speaking careers from the publication of their stories in our books!

Our submission volume has been increasing steadily—the quality and quantity of your submissions has been fabulous. We only accept story submissions via our website. They are no longer accepted via mail or fax.

To contact us regarding other matters, please send us an e-mail through webmaster@chickensoupforthesoul.com, or fax or write us at:

Chicken Soup for the Soul
P.O. Box 700
Cos Cob, CT 06807-0700
Fax: 203-861-7194

One more note from your friends at Chicken Soup for the Soul: Occasionally, we receive an unsolicited book manuscript from one of our readers, and we would like to respectfully inform you that we do not accept unsolicited manuscripts and we must discard the ones that appear.